DATE DUE

"I met Linda in her early twenties and have watched her determination and commitment to find personal growth in the physical, spiritual and pyschological aspects of her life. Her tenacity and her search for truth have moved me to profound respect for her research in all areas."

Kathleen Santucci, M.A. in M.F.C.C.
Counselor, Cancer Patients and Families
Brotman Medical Center, Culver City, Calif.

"Linda Wright has shared her experience with sickness honestly. It will be eminently profitable for those who are not satisfied with less than a comprehensive view. In a time in which many are struggling to see beyond one-sided cliches about healing, this book makes a vital contribution."

Walter Bodine, Ph.D.
Director, Near Eastern Research

"As a registered nurse, a mother of five, and a woman deeply involved in others' lives, I encourage all to read Linda Wright's book, *Hope for the Sick and Hurting.* The well will learn how they might understand and encourage the chronically ill, and the sick will learn how to move from hope to hope."

Gwen Martin, R.N.

"The author has done an excellent job in presenting the many aspects of dealing with sickness. Her insight, delicate and gentle handling of each topic, if met with an open mind, will promote understanding and prepare for helping others and/or dealing with your own sickness and steps of healing. As you read Linda's story, you will see how peace came to her even though at the time she was not yet well."

Richard A. Chase, D.C., N.D.

"This is a needed statement in a universally painful area both to the sick and those who stand by in concern. A helpful treatise!"

Reverend Jack Taylor, Pastor
Anchor Church, Fort Worth, Texas

"Friends, able and disabled, professionals and lay persons, don't miss reading *Hope for the Sick and Hurting.* It is written with wisdom, sensitivity, and insight. Linda's experience is practical, encouraging, helpful, and provides a challenge for her readers. This book makes a much-needed contribution in the area of health and personal disability."

Dorothy Clark
Founder and Director,
Congregational Awareness

"Linda Raney Wright's unique book *Hope for the Sick and Hurting* is a comprehensive look at illness, its causes and cures. The book is assessed from the viewpoint of the ill. Linda's fresh experience and insight provide much hope and investigates perspectives and treatments which merit the reader's attention."

Ralph V. Ford, M.D., P.A.

HOPE
FOR·THE
SICK·AND
HURTING

HOPE FOR·THE SICK·AND HURTING

Linda Raney Wright

THOMAS NELSON PUBLISHERS
NASHVILLE

Published in Nashville, Tennessee, by Thomas Nelson, Inc., and distributed in Canada by
Lawson Falle, Ltd., Cambridge, Ontario.

Printed in the United States of America.

Unless otherwise indicated, Scripture quotations are from THE NEW AMERICAN
STANDARD BIBLE, Copyright © 1960, 1962, 1963, 1968, 1971, 1972, 1973, 1975,
1977 by The Lockman Foundation and are used by permission.

Scripture verses noted KJV are from THE KING JAMES VERSION OF THE BIBLE.

Scripture verses noted NKJV are from THE NEW KING JAMES VERSION. Copyright
© 1979, 1980, 1982, Thomas Nelson, Inc., Publishers.

Scripture verses noted RSV are from the REVISED STANDARD VERSION of the Bible.
Copyright © 1946, 1952, 1971, 1973 by the Division of Christian Education of the Na-
tional Council of the Churches of Christ in the U.S.A. Used by permission.

Scripture verses noted TLB are from *The Living Bible* (Wheaton, Illinois: Tyndale House
Publishers, 1971) and are used by permission.

Scripture verses noted NIV are from The Holy Bible: NEW INTERNATIONAL VER-
SION. Copyright © 1978 by the New York International Bible Society. Used by permission of Zondervan Bible Publishers.

To

CHALMERS CREE

"In sickness an example for us all"

*and to the many who helped me
on my journey to health.*

CONTENTS

11 *How to Help the Sick*

Consider the practical suggestions in this chapter for helping the sick. Friends and family can make a significant difference. A section on helping sick children is included.

ACKNOWLEDGMENTS

I wish to thank many who assisted with this book. Those willing to read the manuscript and give feedback include: Corinne Adams, Sandra Auer, Evelyn Bence, Jay Carson, Dorothy Clark, Judy Downs Douglass, Ron Dunn, Ginger Gabriel, Dian Ginter, Susan Heckmann, Anne Iverson, Gwen Martin, Diana Mason, Pat Palau, Kathleen Santucci, and Betty Tafflinger.

A special thanks to Dr. Earl Radmacher for his input on several matters.

I wish to thank Judy Downs Douglass, Sarah Chisholm, and Kathy Freeman for editorial help.

Ron and Carolyn Haynes, with Thomas Nelson Publishers, have been a tremendous help and encouragement. Jennifer Farrar has been an exceptional in-house editor.

For help in typing this manuscript hearty thanks is given to Betsy Rogers.

Rusty Wright has read through the manuscript many times, offered advice, edited, typed, and assisted me with other needs during the writing of this book.

Thank you heartily!

INTRODUCTION

I began the day driving through our warm, pine-scented mountains on my way to visit a friend. Later, I would work on a new book idea, play with my beloved cat, prepare a leg of lamb for a group of friends, enjoy my garden, and end the day expressing gratitude to God. All this I would accomplish with sufficient strength and stamina. I would smell not only the roses but the petunias, pansies, honeysuckle, chrysanthemums, and lilacs surrounding my cabin. I'm healthy. I'm enjoying a vital life.

This wasn't always the case!

This is a book I have lived!

My experience has not been as a doctor or nurse assessing the needs of the ill; nor as a social worker addressing the plight of the ill; nor as a minister, comforting the ill; nor as a philosopher, explaining the ill.

I have been sick for twenty years! Much of that time bedridden. Mostly in the hands of better-than-average physicians. Gratefully, a Christian throughout the ordeal.

Amidst trauma, panic, sleeplessness, pain, despair, confinement, emergencies, fever, collapse, fear, and desperation, it seemed reasonable to conclude that illness and all it entails may be the worst condition of the human race. And as I have received enormous amounts of counsel and advice—medical, spiritual, philosophical, and "know it all"—it has been a simple deduction to view the sick as one of society's greatest victims.

Sickness is no longer my state! And good health has been

only one of many rewards. Along the way to health it was necessary to ask questions, seek help, and find answers. Was illness a fluke of nature, unmonitored and unabated? Was it cradled in the plan of a diabolical character? Was mankind fostering many of its own illnesses through misuse of the earth's resources? Had nature, itself, provided cures to lingering maladies which much of the Western world ignored?

My years of sickness seemed like a waste of time and personal resources. Was that true? What did the Bible, one of humanity's oldest and most provocative guides to life, have to say about sickness, its causes and cures? Were New Age techniques appropriate to pursue in the course of healing? Was health totally in my hands, based solely upon the degree of my optimism, the extent of my efforts, or the amount of my faith? Or were there other factors to be figured into the equation? What kind of power might Jesus of Nazareth have over sickness in my life and the lives of others? Does anyone really care when I am sick? How does one best seek healing?

It is my hope that within the pages of this book some of these questions may be at least partly answered. Included are suggestions for how to deal with fears, frustrations, and how to help the sick, the sick child, and those who love the sick. Appendices A and B describe innovative treatments that helped me and give reasonable thought to alternative forms of healing. In addition, I hope many will be encouraged by observing the results of one who pursued health against many odds until it was finally obtained.

To write this book it was necessary to dip into difficult experiences many have suffered during illness. The accounts of these experiences are always a prelude to the reasons, hopes, and helps.

This book may be written from a perspective that is new to you—at least in some respects. You may not be convinced by my investigation. However, my struggle has been an honest one which has proved over and again a workable answer. As you read, don't reject my findings at the first foreign thought. The life you save may be your own or that of someone you love.

CHAPTER 1

THE WORLD
OF THE SICK

*S*ickness comes in many varieties. There are the little nags of sinus, backache, headache, nerves, constipation, head colds, and the like, which do not debilitate as much as annoy. However, the same symptoms, experienced frequently and severely, do more than pester. They may bring the best souls to despair of living.

I was given the name Linda Elizabeth Raney. Though Linda Elizabeth means "beautiful dwelling place of God," my "temple" at birth had already been damaged by weakened arteries, leaving some of its intended beauty marred. In addition, just prior to my mother's eighth month of pregnancy, my father sought a bit of adventure. Driving my mother high up Mt. Helix in San Diego, he perched aloft a cliff; I was literally and prematurely scared out of my mother's womb.

The terrible twos were not nearly as terrible as my third year of earth journey, when pneumonia thrust me to the brink of death, seriously damaging both kidneys. As puberty approached all seemed well. I was chosen president of my elementary school, achieved a straight E (for excellent) report card, and was easily popular with the boys. My future promised to be exceptional, yet my body and mind gave way to a breakdown. Doctors diagnosed me as overstressed by "too much activity." Unable to sleep by myself at night, I would lie awake in my parents' bedroom fearfully imagining the end of the world and my death. Years passed before any explanation could be given for this mental side of my sickness. Fortunately through rest and family support, the strain was short-lived, but it devastated my confidence.

With uncertainty I moved through junior high into the challenging high school arena. Hecklers—depression, fear, fatigue—played at my nerves, stamina, immune system, and motivation. Several years into college my body complained even louder. I had trouble concentrating. Mood swings, food cravings, fatigue, severe flus, and colds (which hung on and on) frequently disturbed me. These left my weakened body prey for other complications. A whirlwind of illness was about to explode.

At a winter conference for college students I was exposed to mononucleosis. The culprit took me under siege, but went undiagnosed for several months. It had a deadly effect on my cells and arteries. Repeatedly I fell asleep in classes only to be awakened by the stir of classmates leaving the room. Constantly drained, I would enter the women's lounge at the university, stretch out on the couch and awaken hours later—the chatter of women, the surge of faucets, and flush of toilets never fazing my deep solitude.

As my body failed once again, depression set in. My mind was not working for me but against me. I experienced erratic sleep patterns—deep drug-like sleep, then days of insomnia. Concentrating on studies became increasingly difficult. An unshakable gloom and heaviness fell over me.

Problems of the Ill

In the midst of this trauma I was inducted into the world of the sick. I began experiencing a long list of difficulties connected with ill health.

One frustration was finding good medical help. Society is having growing concerns about the medical profession. Though many fine doctors and nurses work with care and excellence, there have been enough mishaps in recent years to put a blight on the entire profession and concern in the minds of the ill.

Common sense, derived from taking time to listen to a patient's complaints, has in some instances been replaced by long waits in the doctor's office, quick consultations, a battery of expensive tests, poor diagnosis and treatment. As a result even the medical world suggests getting a second, or third, opinion.

Television talk shows and recent articles in respected magazines have cited an array of other troubles: unreliable lab reports, malpractice, fraud, doctors on drugs, molestation of patients, untrained medical dispatchers, inadequate emergency room procedures, insurance graft, even failure to properly sanitize hospital facilities, which has resulted in thousands dying each year of causes contracted in the hospital.

Nor is it unusual to find sick individuals caught between medical rivals. Without the benefit of understanding the merits or liabilities of different methods and remedies, one can feel helpless.

MEDICAL COSTS

The financial burden incurred by the sick is often staggering. In some states the cost of caring for the ill reaches as high as $2000–$3000 a day. Operations can easily exceed $20,000. Even doctors who love the sick and wish to accommodate them are compelled by expenses (insurance, equipment, fees) to charge more than they wish. Physicians are often helpless to contend with the expenses of the medical system.

Delays in insurance companies' claims may leave patients and their loved ones without cash to pay bills. Many insurance companies will not cover natural forms of treatment though this type of preventive measure has proven cost effective. Insurance premiums continue to rise. Whichever way the sick turn, the financial picture is dismal. On top of everything else, the sick persons and those providing for them must weather the enormous cost of getting well.

MISUNDERSTOOD

What else describes the world of the sick?

"I had never been seriously ill," Tina, a forty-year-old shared. "I had even been somewhat naive concerning the difficulties of the sick—maybe even unconsciously believing they got what they deserved."

She went on to say: "At a critical time of sickness I was experiencing pain, discomfort, confinement, loneliness, and assorted emotions; but perhaps nothing was as difficult to bear as judgments, indifference, and pity from people who had little understanding of my situation."

The quandary of being misunderstood affects many of the sick and those who love them. One teenage son would not cooperate in the home. Imploring, prodding, punishing, loving—nothing motivated him to participate positively in the family. When he ran away from home, professional help was finally sought. Upon his return he was diagnosed as having a condition which predisposed him to mood swings, hypertension, and mental dullness.

Another woman, who for many years was afflicted with PMS, a hormone imbalance, received undeserved criticism because she was often edgy and uptight.

"Did others think I wanted to act this way?" she asked. "I simply did not have the wherewithal to respond well in stressful situations. People constantly thought I was 'difficult,' when I was merely trying to survive. Why did others avoid me when I was desperate for help? Couldn't they have at least tried to understand?"

ISOLATION

Other frustrations? The segregation of confinement. In my situation there were a few who gave above and beyond the call of duty to my many needs. But for the most part I spent tens of thousands of hours alone without needed help.

I gave the subject of isolation little thought until many years into my illness. One evening I felt good enough to go to a baby shower for a friend. At this gathering, my friends discussed the need for everyone to chip in and fix a meal during the time the new mother was in the hospital. Suddenly, without warning, a feeling of anger and rejection swept through me. None of these women, knowing of my own serious illness, had ever offered to assist me in any way. They were willing to pitch in and help someone with a semi-serious need for two weeks, but someone who had a chronic need for years was conspicuously overlooked. How different twenty years of illness might have been, or how many fewer years I might have been ill, if I had received needed help and encouragement.

Many people do not like being with the sick, preferring the company of those less needful. Others become uncomfortable when confronted with illness, wishing to avoid an encounter with their *own* vulnerability and mortality. Hence, for the sick, the game of pretending you feel better than you really do can become *modus operandi*.

The frequent downs, discouragements, depression, pain,

fear, and hopelessness of the "long-term" ill would not be appreciated by many. In fact, many seriously ill individuals are sadly neglected in their time of greatest crisis.

We can't demand that people love us, help us, provide for us, come by and chat with us. The sick have nothing to give in return for the time and love bestowed upon them. The principle, "I'll scratch your back if you scratch mine" does not apply.

MONOTONY

What does a confined person do with time? In my own case, advanced circulation problems made it impossible to read or write for many years. Viewing television was possible only in limited segments as my mind was too weakened. Even listening to music was not entertaining. It tired me.

A friend once suggested that I do a simple art project—cut out pictures, glue them to a prepared board, and shellac. But severe allergic reactions made fumes intolerable. Painting was also out of the question. Chronic fatigue made any outdoor activity comparable to a "normal person's" scaling Mount Everest. Talk to the walls, talk to the cat, talk on the phone—most of my close friends were long distance and calling was too expensive for my budget. So what was I to do with myself?

Lack of activity fosters guilt. One questions self-worth and a reason for existence. Battles related to self-image raged within me the first years of my illness. Because of an unresponsive body and poor performance, self-loathing threatened to overwhelm me. I would push myself to breaking points so I would have something—anything—to show for myself.

UNSPOKEN LAW

There is an unspoken law in the minds of many. The ill, in spite of their sickness, should behave as the well. Should we force others to understand that one cannot perform normally when ill? This is a delicate proposition. Some, attempting to explain their illness and its effects, may be categorized as hypochondriacs, self-occupied, or "complainers."

However, if the illness is not understood, worse may be assumed. When unproductive, I was accused of being "lazy." When unenthusiastic (sickness creates this), I was dubbed "uncaring." Doubtful, ingrown, apathetic, irresponsible—in twenty years my list of unearned labels branded me as surely as a seared iron on my forehead. For one who longed to be poised and respected, who wished to reach out and make a difference in the world, how such judgments hurt!

Why are many sick individuals seen as negative? Keep in mind the mental state of the sick. They truly do not feel well. This occupation with pain and discomfort and the other trials of sickness dominate their thinking. This focus monopolizes their communication.

Well persons, thinking they would do better under the same circumstances, may prove naive. Remember the last time you had a bad cold or flu? Do you recall how miserable you felt, achy all over, feverish, listless, uncomfortable, grouchy, and irritable? Were you wonderful to live with during this time? But then you knew you'd soon get over it and you did. The chronically ill may feel even worse, yet they have no anticipation that it will all be over in a few days. For many it is a way of life. The old Indian saying rightly asserts, "Don't judge another man until you have walked a mile in his moccasins."

DEHUMANIZED

Sickness dehumanizes. A sick person, young or old, is viewed as just that—the sick one. Former adjectives describing the inner person—intelligent, generous, talented, kind, useful—are replaced by dour verbs and adverbs—complaining, fearing, uncertain, confused, useless. This is a great humiliation for the ill!

Hospitalization can agitate this process of dehumanization. When a patient enters a hospital, he or she may cease to feel like a person, only a malfunctioning body. Jewelry and other identification is removed. He or she wears the same dreary garb as everyone else. Sterilized rooms bring a peculiar and often offensive odor. Surroundings bear no resemblance to the friendliness of the patient's home.

Change of personnel does not permit close attachments. The critically ill see friends or family for only limited spans. Television, rather than personal communication, dominates hospital wards. Sedation leaves patients floating between reality and oblivion. (One of the greatest difficulties my mother experienced as a nurse was the doctors' practice of sedating whole floors of patients because the hospital where she worked did not hire enough personnel to care for them.)

Those confined to home often stay with relatives. Guilt casts a shadow as the ailing watch their care providers spend hours attending them. Feelings akin to hatred for their plight can attack an otherwise optimistic person.

"I feel I have lost any semblance of control over my life," one woman explained to me. "Decisions have been taken out of my hands. I feel helpless. How I despise it."

Often such was my own plight. I was at the mercy of others. How easy it was to waver between guilt (for being such a burden), contempt (because help was not forthcoming), fear (that no one would be there if I needed help), anxiety (that if I asked for help, I would be rejected), anger (at a body that refused to cooperate), self-pity (that I could not function normally), panic (from things I did not understand), dread (that I would get worse, not better), despair, hopelessness, worry, irritability, and frustration!

CARETAKERS

Sometimes those who bear the constant responsibility of caring for the sick experience the most difficulty. Day in and day out care drains their energies. One can easily resent such occupation of his or her life. Yet, if you are such a person, may your reward be great and your vitality rekindled!

Illness affected Beth and Wilbur Forseth early in their married life. Wilbur's health had deteriorated by the time children had entered the picture. He sought medical help but was told that there was nothing wrong. Yet, mental fatigue and poor stamina dogged him daily.

"Trying to get help for Wilbur was just one of our problems," reports Beth. "When we did finally succeed, after years of effort, in finding the right kind of help (outside of traditional medicine), we were told that our insurance wouldn't cover the costs." By this time Beth and Wilbur were barely holding on.

"Here I was," says Beth, "with three children under six and a sick husband to care for. On top of fixing special meals, assuming total care for the children, and juggling a critical financial situation, I had no time left to get any outside spiritual or mental help."

The trauma continued for many years. Wilbur improved slowly as he received various helps and treatments. Still he was unable to share in the family. Unable to cope he retreated to his room. "It was worse than being a single parent," continues Beth.

"I had the children and all the responsibilities plus a sick person to protect, feed, encourage, and many times put up with. One final assault came when a relative suggested I divorce Wilbur for the sake of the children. My life was 'hell' at the time. I had developed low blood sugar under the stress. To hear someone actually suggest divorce, to abandon Wilbur when he was so desperate, really was like pouring salt on an open wound."

How do children respond in such a situation? "Not too well," shares Beth. "They clung to me when Wilbur was having an especially difficult time. Wilbur, who normally was optimistic, kind, and forgiving, became progressively irritated and depressed. His behavior confused the children. His stability and well-being were crucial to their own sense of security. This weighed on both of us. Wilbur didn't want to be this way, and I, living under such extreme stress, could not always compensate for his deficiencies. Nor could I keep from getting angry with him."

STAYING ON TOP?

One of the greatest challenges for both the sick and those who love them is to "stay on top" of the illness.

I juggled everything at once!

The number of my diagnoses increased until I wondered how anything else could be wrong with me: hypothyroidism; low blood sugar; hypotension of the vascular system; Epstein-Barr virus; Premenstrual Syndrome; severe food, pollen, chemical, and dust allergies; low blood pressure; mercury poisoning; temporomandibular joint (TMJ); cranium and vertebra misalignment; damaged spleen; a twisted and sluggish colon; kidney infections and failure; candida albicans; poor digestion; gallstones; fibroid tumors; damaged kidney membrane filters; severe low potassium; mineral imbalance; nerve damage; cysts; hypopituitarism; and adrenal failure.

For many years I had to stay on top of each problem, not knowing what the problems were or how to correct them. No little assignment! However diligent I was at various treatments, few results were forthcoming—those problem areas that still had not been diagnosed and treated continued to resist healing like a riptide fighting against my body. When flus, shingles, infections, strep, parasites, fungus, and other invaders pounced on my already battered body, the experience was like falling off a steep cliff. I had been scaling the treacherous precipice dragging my debilitated body precariously up the tricky walls. Now at the bottom—fragmented and frightened—I was asked to get up and start climbing again.

I would think, *Maybe after this treatment, I will be stronger.* Then the well-worn cycle of diminishing returns would begin again. Like a farmer seeing his crop destroyed year after year, or a business person watching one deal after another topple in spite of his best efforts, I watched as one gain after another was lost. How could I survive?

Welcome to the World of the Sick

Welcome to the world of the sick—a land filled with frustration, fears, worry, stress, despair, and hopelessness.

Are there really any answers?

Fortunately for those willing to search them out . . . there are!

Points to Ponder

1. Have you done all the doctor told you and are still no better, maybe worse? Are there other avenues of healing? Have you sought a second opinion?

2. The cost of some health care is exorbitant. Do some, who have their health, need to help those who are sick find excellent sources of healing? Do our communities need to more closely examine the benefits of varied health care, the existence of qualified doctors, and alternative plans for financing health care?

3. As an individual caught in the throes of ill health, do you have a proper understanding of your own needs? Do you feel guilty or inadequate because your body will not cooperate? Do you feel rejected because few care about you? You need to accept yourself and understand your situation. Use your confinement and this time of seeming uselessness to reflect upon your life.

4. If you are helping the sick, may God grant you grace and patience as you seek to understand and assist.

CHAPTER 2

WHO WILL HEAL YOU?

F ollowing the onset of mononucleosis, illness continued to plague my body and mind. I finished school and began writing for various magazines with limited physical and emotional energy. My travels took me to the northeastern part of the United States.

During a period when my ability to write lessened due to decreased circulation, I was delighted to sell two stories to the *Ladies Home Journal*. One of the subjects was the wife of a university president. The *Journal* asked for more information. Plans for an interview, which included a trip to Tulsa, were set in motion. I had written ahead asking for accommodations at the university while in Tulsa. Two weeks later I received confirmation for the interview and room.

It was mid-December. I had been enjoying the crisp autumn days. As colder weather approached I looked forward to the drive across the United States to the Midwest. The trip provided rich memories of clear blue skies, red and gold leaves falling from oaks and maples, while stately firs and pines formed an emerald backdrop. As I moved westward peaked mountains were replaced by rolling hills and flat brown plains. The cold became biting.

Several days into this trip I stayed overnight with a relative who was coughing from bronchitis as she prepared dinner. I ate the meal gingerly. By the next evening I had flu symptoms. Arriving in Tulsa with a full-fledged case of the flu, I pushed to reach the university and a warm bed. My '72 Maverick, without snow tires, was difficult to maneuver on the icy and treacherous roads.

Pulling into the university around 10:00 P.M., I was escorted to the security office where I explained my situation. The security guard could see I was ill. He offered me the couch in the women's lounge while he sought to confirm my information. I hoped it would be a short time before a secure mattress materialized.

How rude the interruption seemed when I heard a sharp rap on the door after midnight. The guard informed me that he had been unable to locate any evidence of a room reservation. With less than $100 to my name I was in no position to rent a motel room for a week. I felt stranded.

"We've got it all arranged, Ma'am," he said. "One of our men will guide you downtown to the Salvation Army. You can stay there until we work this out."

The Salvation Army was twenty minutes away. By now my lungs had filled with congestion; a fever was steadily rising. As I drove over the slippery roads, I concentrated on two red lights on the back of the car ahead, praying for enough strength to drive. Tulsa looked horribly bleak.

I parked outside the Salvation Army building. The university security guard pulled away. I knocked on the door and waited for an answer. No one came. I knocked again—louder. Still no one came. It suddenly occurred to me that I was alone in the middle of downtown Tulsa at 1:30 in the morning in freezing weather, with one of the worst cases of bronchitis I had ever had. My sandals and light jacket were no more protection against the cold than my car, should I be forced to sleep in it.

Finally I noticed the door of the Salvation Army was not locked. Wandering in I found someone awake who assigned me to a bed. "Wake up call," I was told, "is 5:00 A.M."

"I'm sick," I explained.

"Those are the rules. No exceptions." She wasn't unkind. With so many transient strangers using the facilities, rules must be enforced. I should have protested further—making my desperate need heard. But I did as many sick do. I failed to voice my concern loudly enough. This ended up hurting—not helping—my chronic situation.

I sank into bed at 1:45 A.M. It was neither warm nor secure. The four bare walls and a mentally troubled woman in the bed next to me were not conducive to peaceful slumber. The next day, Sunday, I suffered through "required" church meetings on two hours of sleep.

Though no human could have foreseen it, this flu (with its complications) was a major blow to my system. As the weeks passed, my condition grew worse. I went to bed. I remained bed-ridden for many years.

What Is Our Focus?

Since illness devastates our bodies, and often our minds as well, who can help us?

Who in history has done more for the sick than all others? Many historians, doctors, and theologians may answer . . . Jesus of Nazareth. The life of Jesus is of prime importance to the subject of healing. How could that be? Who is he? Exactly what did he say concerning the sick? Why do so many turn to him today in their hour of need? Most importantly, can he do something for you?

Years of habitation on my sickbed allowed me to hear many ideas concerning Jesus. I wasn't sure what it all meant—not all of it made sense. But I was determined to find out. If Jesus had something to offer me I wanted to know about it. I offer you the following research.

Who Was Jesus?

Jesus of Nazareth was born almost two thousand years ago. More than three hundred prophecies were compiled and recorded by Old Testament writers, hundreds of years before Jesus was born, concerning the birth and life of Jesus. History documents that each extraordinary prophecy was fulfilled!

Jesus' life and teaching had such an effect on history that we date our calendar by his life: B.C. meaning "before Christ"; and A.D. *anno Domini,* the Latin words meaning, "in the year of our Lord."

JESUS CLAIMED TO BE GOD

What claims did Jesus make about himself? He claimed to be God—not a god—but the one true God.

Jesus said that he and the Father were one. He said he was God manifested in a human body so that we could see and understand what God in essence is truly like.[1]

Many accounts of the life of Jesus testify to his life and

words. Flavius Josephus, a Jewish historian who was born in A.D. 37, commanded the Jewish forces in Galilee in A.D. 66 and was captured by the Romans, wrote:

> Now there was about this time Jesus, a wise man, if it be lawful to call him a man, for he was a doer of wonderful works, a teacher of such men as receive the truth with pleasure. He drew over to him both many Jews, and many Gentiles. He was the Christ, and when Pilate, at the suggestion of the principal men among us had condemned him to the cross, those that loved him at the first had not forsaken him; for he appeared to them alive again on the third day; as the divine prophets had foretold these and ten thousand other wonderful things concerning him.[2]

Besides the eyewitness accounts of Jesus recorded in the New Testament, Eusebius, Polycarp, Irenaeus, Pliny the Younger, Origen, and many others wrote in the first centuries after Christ of the events surrounding Christ's life.

Jesus claimed he had the ability to forgive sins.[3] His death and resurrection, which are pivotal to his message, are two of the best attested facts of history. Many historians, using accepted methods of legal/historical inquiry, have documented the life, death, and resurrection of Jesus. Thomas Arnold, the famous headmaster of Rugby for fourteen years, author of *History of Rome,* appointed to the chair of Modern History at Oxford, wrote on the historic trustworthiness of the death and resurrection narrative recorded by first century writers:

> The evidence . . . is good according to the common rules for distinguishing good evidence from bad. Thousands and tens of thousands of persons have gone through it piece by piece, as carefully as every judge summoning up on a most important case . . . I know of no one fact in the history of mankind which is proved by better and fuller evidence of every sort, to the understanding of a fair inquirer.[4]

DID JESUS HEAL?

What was Jesus' experience with the sick?
Mark, a first-century writer, gives an eyewitness account:

> And when they had come out of the boat, immediately the *people* recognized Him [Jesus], and ran about that whole country

and began to carry about on their pallets those who were sick, to the place they heard He was. And wherever He entered villages, or cities, or countryside, they were laying the sick in the marketplaces, and entreated Him that they might just touch the fringe of His cloak; and as many as touched it were being cured.[5]

Picture the countryside of Judea in the first century A.D. This fertile landscape, coveted by many nations, is under the rule of Rome. Tiberius Caesar is the emperor of the Roman Empire, Herod Antipas the tetrarch of Galilee, and Pontius Pilate the governor of Judea. The *lingua-franca* of the empire is Greek; of the Jews, Aramaic. Peace reigns in Israel, but at a price. Taxes are high; exploitation abounds.

Thirty years prior, in the city of Bethlehem, the birth of a child stirred wise men to travel from eastern countries in search of him to worship. His birth also prompted an arrogant king, fearful of the Messiah's prophecies being fulfilled, to seek his death. Entertaining the blessing of the wise men while escaping the bloodshed of Herod the Great, this child and his parents fled to Egypt. They later returned to Nazareth where Jesus was raised. Here he excelled in carpentry until his self-proclaimed ministry began.

At age thirty Jesus was saying some astounding things—so astounding that people flocked to hear him speak. In the midst of speaking he touches a person and the person is healed. He speaks and one regains his eyesight, for another, her spine is straightened. The word spreads. The sick and those who love the sick make their way, however frightening the travel, at whatever cost it may take, for they sense that they too will be made well.

EYEWITNESS ACCOUNTS

What did eyewitness accounts record that Jesus did for the sick?

"Jesus went about . . . healing all manner of sickness".[6] He healed "every kind of disease and every kind of sickness,"[7] Matthew, a former tax collector and one of Jesus' followers, states.

In our modern world we are inclined to believe that some diseases can be healed and others are terminal. Yet on a hillside in Galilee Jesus did not divide diseases into categories. "All manner" and "every kind" of sickness is a broad and encompassing spectrum *without exception*.

When I met Diane Williams she had been told that nothing could be done for multiple sclerosis. She drew on the provision of Jesus through prayer and a specialist. Today, she is well—walking and functioning normally. George was told that his heart would bring about an early death. "Go walk on the treadmill and I will heal you," he sensed the Lord saying to him. The doctors marveled that an "irreversible" heart problem reversed itself. Dr. Carey Reams was instantly healed of paralysis when someone prayed over him in Jesus' name. Lou Gehrig's disease, Alzheimers, Parkinson's disease, cancer, diabetes, leukemia—contemporary people claim that they were cured in Jesus' name. Not one or two, but thousands worldwide make this boast. Can Jesus heal today?

Leo Meister, a respected man in my own community, tells his own story.

*F*or the past few years it's been almost impossible to read a newspaper or watch a newscast without having a story about the dreaded disease, AIDS. I thank God every day of my life that AIDS wasn't around the first fifty years of my life. Because if it had been I am quite certain that someplace along the line I would have come in contact with it. I'm not gay. I'm not a drug user. I'm a hemophiliac. At least I was.

I have been overdrawn at the blood bank since the day I was born. I have had a minimum of two hundred transfusions, probably a lot more than that. The day I was born I was circumsized and immediately started bleeding. Before the day was over I had my first transfusion. That I survived was a miracle because back in those days they didn't have the techniques and equipment to work on infants that they have now.

Two years later I had appendicitis which required surgery. Once again I started bleeding. This time I needed four transfusions. It was at this time my family was told I had hemophilia. It was then, and still is today, an incurable, hereditary blood disease which manifests itself by uncontrolled bleeding.

Shortly before my sixth birthday my oldest brother, Lou, had his tonsils removed. Two days later he was

dead—he bled to death. That was Lou's one and only bout
with hemophilia. But it was also the beginning of the end
for me. My parents, realizing how serious the disease
could be, got so scared that from that time on I was
watched like a hawk. My principals and teachers were
instructed that I was not allowed to play. At recess or
lunchtime I had to sit on a bench and watch other kids
play, or I could sit in the classroom and read a book.
When school was over I would go home, sit on the porch
and again watch the other kids play. You don't make many
friends sitting by yourself. After a while I was the butt of
every joke.

It took me eleven years to finish eight grades of
elementary school, primarily because I spent so much time
in hospitals. Consequently by the time I got ready to go to
high school I was almost as old as the kids who were
getting out of high school. The kids in the community
thought I was some sort of a klutz—here I am a big,
overgrown goof starting high school. I ditched school as
often as I went. It wasn't long before the authorities
started giving my parents static, threatening to put me in
juvenile hall.

World War II was going on at the time. I told my
parents I wanted to enlist. They laughed at first. But I
badgered them until they agreed to sign the approval
papers if I passed the physical. I tried to enlist in the
Marine Corps; they turned me down. I tried the Navy;
they turned me down. I tried the Coast Guard. But by now
I had learned a thing or two. They didn't ask me about
hemophilia. I didn't volunteer the information. I passed
the physical.

Three days later I was in boot camp—a rude
awakening. Here was a screwball kid who had never run a
step in his life, had never thrown a ball or taken any
physical education since he was two years old. I was last
at everything, but for the first time I was feeling good
about myself.

After boot camp the Coast Guard sent me to radar
school. Everything was fine until I came down with a heck
of a cold which I couldn't get rid of. After a few days I

went to sick bay. When I opened my mouth the doctor said, "Your tonsils have to come out immediately." I tried arguing but it didn't do any good. I knew I had an ace up my sleeve; I could have gotten out of surgery by telling my family history. But I also knew they would have kicked me out of the service. I kept my mouth shut. It was a long night thinking about it. Yet, I decided I would rather be dead than leave the Coast Guard and return to the life of a semi-invalid.

The following morning I checked into sick bay. My tonsils were taken out. Later that day the slow seepage of blood from the incision turned into a gush. They frantically pumped the blood back into me. The next morning they put me in St. Peter's room, where they took people they figured were going to drop dead. Six weeks and sixteen transfusions later, I pulled through.

Sometime later I had a tooth that was giving me a lot of trouble. It had to come out. Two hours after the dentist pulled it my parents rushed me to the emergency room of the hospital in Santa Monica. They pumped in a jug of blood and transferred me to the VA hospital in Los Angeles. Once again I was put in St. Peter's room. Sixteen weeks and thirty transfusions later I pulled through.

Over the next years I got married and started to raise a houseful of kids. Then I got a bleeding ulcer. They operated. I pulled through again with the help of yet another thirty-two pints of blood.

Then, through the influence of one of my sons, I started attending church. The people there believed that Jesus could heal. I heard stories about healings; I started seeing healings. I started believing in healings. But I didn't think to ask the Lord to heal me of hemophilia. For fifty years I had been told there was no cure for hemophilia. I believed that.

When my grandson was born a hemophiliac it tore me apart. I started asking God to heal him. I wasn't sure whether he would heal this boy but I thought, "Well, there is a possibility Jesus would do that for a kid."

Then one night my wife and I went to Santa Ana to Channel 40, a religious broadcasting station. Suddenly, while I was sitting in the audience I felt like my body was on fire. It startled me at first, but it didn't scare me. My blood started rushing through my body. It felt like a high-pressure hose racing the blood through. Then I heard the guest on the show say, "Right now there is somebody in your audience whom Jesus is curing of an incurable blood disease."

I said, "Thank you Lord. That's me. I accept it." Instantly my blood settled down and I cooled off. I guess that I made a funny noise because my wife looked at me and asked me what was wrong. I just laughed. She thought I was nuts. Later that evening, as we left the studio, I handed her my Med-Alert tag.

"What's this for?" she said.

"I don't need this any more, I got healed tonight."

The next day at work I got careless and slashed my thumb open. That day I had to squeeze and squeeze my thumb just to get some blood out of that cut in order to wash the dirt out. Several months later I walked into a dentist's office and had him pull seven teeth at one time. I had no problem with excessive bleeding. It bled what it would for any normal person.

We didn't know it at the time, but my grandson was healed that night as well. It was six or eight months after that special night that the doctor called my daughter and said, 'What did I do to make you mad? You don't bring David in to see me anymore.'

"Well," she said, "David's had no problems. He has been healed." This was the same doctor I had. He told my daughter, "Well, you are as nutty as your dad is."

That may well be, but David's had no problems since then, I have had no problems since then. It's been many years. I say Jesus healed me that night. And he healed my grandson. "Thank you, Jesus."

Many people *respond to stories* such as this with either skepticism or incredulity. At first I had misgivings that such healings really happened until I personally knew some of the people before and after. I have now watched healing in the name of Jesus happen or heard reliable reports of it happening so many times that it has become a natural occurrence to me. I am no longer skeptical.

IMPOSSIBLE HEALINGS

According to eyewitness accounts length of illness had no effect on Jesus' ability to heal. Consider the duration of illness in some of those Jesus healed:

- Thirty-eight years; man of Bethesda[8]
- Eighteen years; woman bound with an infirmity[9]
- Twelve years; woman with hemorrhage[10]
- Blind from birth[11]

At one point in my life I looked in vain for a contemporary model—someone who had been as ill as I for as long as I and who had subsequently been healed. If someone else *like* me were healed, maybe there was hope *for* me, I reasoned.

One day I was talking with a friend. We were lounging in a Spanish-styled home, exchanging experiences, and encouraging one another. In our conversation I explained what hopes I had of one day being well—well enough to travel, write, speak, lead, help others, and share with them those things that had helped me.

"I want to be free of being occupied with my body—always having to be overattentive to how it should or should not function. But," I continued, "I know others who have been as sick as myself and have killed themselves, are in mental institutions, exist on drugs, have died, or have become discouraged and embittered."

I mentioned people by name, telling grave tales. Finally my friend stopped me, "Linda, you've got your focus in the wrong place," she said emphatically. "God became like us. Jesus is God. We can see for ourselves how he loves and heals. Linda, Jesus can heal you!"

Why Did Jesus Heal?

History reveals that Jesus loved people. Over and over the followers of Jesus write about his compassion and concern, even his grief, as he confronted sickness in others. Individuals witnessed the following during the life of Jesus:

"They [the multitudes] followed Him on foot from the cities. And when He came out, He saw a great multitude, and felt *compassion* for them, and healed their sick"[12] (italics mine).

"And moved with *compassion,* Jesus touched their eyes; and

immediately they received their sight, and followed Him"[13] (italics mine).

"And moved with *compassion,* He stretched out His hand and touched him . . . and immediately the leprosy left him"[14] (italics mine).

And for those who love the sick:

"And when the Lord saw her, He felt *compassion* for her, and said to her, 'Do not weep.' And He came up and touched the coffin; and the bearers came to a halt. And He said, 'Young man, I say to you, arise!' . . . And Jesus gave him back to his mother"[15] (italics mine).

Is not this love and compassion sufficient reason for the sick and those who love them to call upon Jesus?

POWER

Why else did Jesus heal? Jesus said about himself, "All power is given unto Me in heaven and in earth."[16] Jesus not only made such a claim . . . he demonstrated it. During a brief three years when Jesus walked throughout Israel his fame grew so that multitudes of people came to hear him and be healed.[17] Leprosy, palsy, spinal disorders, deafness, mental illness, hemorrhaging, all were healed by Jesus and recorded by eyewitnesses.

Cathy Christiansen Taylor of Lake Arrowhead, California, shares her story of healing against hopeless odds.

*A*s a child, I lived on TV dinners and had normal allergies like kids do. When I became twenty years old, I seriously abused my body. It was the late sixties and early seventies when the drug culture thrived. I did marijuana, sleeping pills, downers, valium, and some psychedelic drugs.

Drugs appealed to me because the world seemed too harsh. I decided that I couldn't handle working in a world that was so cruel. Drugs would coat the world over and make everything seem loving, even though it wasn't.

I was modeling at the time. I did commercials and magazine ads. The modeling world is a meat market. Obviously you get hit on all the time by producers. If you sleep with a guy, maybe you can get more jobs. But I never did that sort of a thing. I didn't need to.

A photographer, Tony, helped me build up my portfolio. He had done a fabulous job for me. As a matter of fact, I was just signing a big contract with Max Factor, and was to do a TV show, the resurrected "Name that Tune."

One night Tony called me. He said, "You know what Cathy? We're going to make it. We're going to make it in this world and we're going to get off the drugs." That night, Tony died in his sleep. The grief I experienced was severe.

There was a part of me that thought, "If Tony can't make it into this world, how can I?" Within two weeks of Tony's death, I started to become allergic to everything. I felt disoriented. I couldn't get out of bed or even go to Tony's funeral.

Fortunately I had become a Christian several months previously. Prior to this experience I had been into a lot of Eastern thinking. I was going out to the desert to enlightenment intensives, trying to find out who I was. This was during the time of the Beatles and the Maharishi Yogi. Everybody was looking toward Eastern religion for finding a way out of this world, trying to find salvation. I had never been brought up in the church. My family wasn't religious. So I really was open to anything. Eastern thinking was hip and trendy. But every time I'd go into these enlightenment intensives, I'd get sick. So the leaders started telling me it was because I really didn't want to know who I was.

Across the street from where I lived in L.A. there was a couple. A lot of times I would just look out the window and watch them. They were married and were so happy. I had never seen anybody in my life that had that kind of joy. They were crazy, but wonderfully crazy. Finally one day I met them.

I asked, "What are you guys into? You just seem happy all the time."

The guy, who was an actor and stunt man immediately said, "We're Jesus freaks."

I said, "Oh gosh, anything but that," and I went home.

As soon as they knew I was curious, this couple, Gary and Susie, was on me like a tick on a dog. They kept coming over.

One day I was talking with them about human suffering and how could there be a loving God. "If what you're talking about is the Truth, why is it so narrow-minded? Why is it the only way?" Finally Gary said to me, "Listen, what kind of God is he if he can't take away your doubts?"

That thought captured me. I thought to myself, "Absolutely. I'll listen, I'll buy that." I wanted to know the Truth.

"Listen," Gary said, "Let's pray. If the God we're talking about is true, then he can take away your doubts." We prayed that day that Jesus Christ would reveal himself to me. I really didn't expect anything to happen.

Over the next couple of days I started seeing bumper stickers that said "Jesus." I had never seen them before. And I thought to myself, "I'm not going to say, 'Like that's it. I believe in Jesus now.'"

One day I was having lunch at Canner's restaurant, which is a restaurant in the Jewish section of town in Los Angeles. It was about four in the afternoon. I was having lunch with a friend when the waitress came over and said, "There's a little old lady over here and it's her birthday. Would you come over and sing 'Happy Birthday' with me?" My friend and I sang "Happy Birthday" and I went back to my seat and started eating. The little lady, when she went to leave the restaurant, came over to the table. She stood and looked at me a moment. Then she said directly to me, "If you ever need a friend . . ." And she put a business card face down.

I kept eating my pastrami sandwich and thinking, "Oh, you know—she just gave me her name and number. Isn't that sweet." Later, I wondered what her name was. So I picked up the business card. It was a picture of Jesus. The Bible says that there is a time when God calls us. I knew that it was God calling me. I started shaking, and sweating. I put down my sandwich and told my friend: "I'm sorry, I gotta go." And I went to Gary and Susie's home. I got down on my knees and accepted Jesus into my life.

As a brand new follower of Jesus, no one told me that I needed to grow or learn what was in the Bible, so that that knowledge would help me in life. I didn't understand what it all meant, but I knew that I had an experience with Jesus and I knew that it was real. But it was probably a little bit of adding Jesus onto my life instead of abandoning my old way of viewing things and going on with him.

After I became ill, I went to Scripps clinic. I cancelled the shootings with Max Factor and the "Name that Tune" show. Scripps did tons of tests. They couldn't find anything physically wrong with me. They said, "It must be psychological." So I just left.

I remember leaving the hospital and driving away. The whole world seemed disoriented to me. I felt like I was going to flip out, like I wasn't going to make it. Back home, I tried various treatments. I became weaker and weaker. I was put in the hospital. But while in the hospital, I became even sicker.

I got down to sixty-two pounds. I lost my hair; I just had patches of hair left. I was in bed for the next three years. The muscles in my legs were almost useless. I couldn't leave my bedroom. I had a portable potty that was right there, because by the time I had walked (I had made this one room environmentally pure) from the bedroom to the bathroom, my body would have so many reactions that I was scared.

There weren't any foods that I could eat. I was put on a rotation diet. I would eat one kind of food every ten days. But then it didn't matter what I ate; I reacted to everything.

I couldn't touch a phone or my hand would swell up twice its size. When anybody came into my room with perfume or any kind of makeup on, or if he or she had had their clothes dry-cleaned, my throat would swell shut or my nervous system would violently react. I would shake all over, my heart rate would go a million miles per hour. After a little bit, I would become totally fatigued. It would be a fight and flight syndrome where my body was just trying to survive. I would get exposed to something and might sleep for two days—what they call allergic sleep where you go to sleep and you feel like you've been drugged.

Everything meaningful had been taken away from me. I had nothing. I couldn't walk. I looked horrible. I was totally yellow. I looked like death; I smelled like death. I couldn't wash what little hair I had left. I hadn't washed my hair in a couple of years. There weren't any soaps, even natural soaps I could use. People think that your hair would be greasy and smell awful, but when you get that close to death there are no oils in your body. You don't smell. You don't perspire. I didn't perspire for three years. Everything was totally sealed up.

I was allergic to television. I couldn't watch television because of the tubes heating up the plastic and the radiation. I could listen to tapes; that was the only thing that I could listen to. I couldn't read anything. I was allergic to ink, so I couldn't read the Bible. Eventually, at one point, a brother in the Lord made me a glass case, where I could put one page of the Bible at a time and read.

I knew I was dying. The doctors knew I was dying. I resigned myself to the fact that there was no hope. I was at the place in those days that when I got reactions, I would just lay quietly and I'd have peace. I would look out the window and at the birds and talk to the Lord. But I wonder now if it wasn't a false peace. I was too content to die. It wasn't really a good kind of peace. It was like a demonic disguise . . . 'We'll just kill her. We'll just get her off the planet.' There was a warfare over my body. It was like light and darkness fighting over me. And I would cry. I had peace at some points and a crazy fear at others.

Yet Jesus freaks started ministering to me. And I began thinking to myself, 'If there was a way into this thing, there's got to be a way out of it.' Yet people would tell me "Oh Cathy, I know that God is going to heal you." And I would think to myself, "Oh bless their hearts. They don't know." During this time I had one guy call and minister to me every night over the phone. He would read the Bible and take time with me. He was not content that I was going to die.

The church that Gary and Susie belonged to had a pastor, Kenn Gullicksen. He came to see me. Then he got the church he pastored to start praying. They prayed twenty-four hours a day that I would live and not die. Shirley Boone, Pat Boone's wife, told me that God would wake her up in the middle of the night and tell her to pray for me. I began to hear of Christians from all over praying that I would live.

Kenn Gullicksen came another time. He said, "You know what? There's a doctor that goes to our church. He's a natural doctor. And some members from our church go to him. He has a real gift from God. We would like to pay for him to come the first time. We really believe that God would like to use him to help you." I said, "Bless their hearts. They don't know."

The doctor came that day. I was very sick. I remember the silhouettes of people coming in the room, and walking around the bed, kind of talking and doing muscle testing and chiropractic ways of diagnosing. Dr. Wagner said that God had revealed to him where much of my problem originated. He believed he could get me well.

Every day Dr. Wagner would call me and say, "Do this. Don't do that." I'd go into some reactions and I'd start convulsing. And he would say, "It's okay. Do this and do that. Take a pinch of this." And immediately I would be fine.

After two months of going through heavy detoxification and accompanying torment, Dr. Wagner called and said, "Cathy, God told me that you can go outside." I hadn't been outside in the air for three years. My friend carried me outside and took me in the car. He put me in the passenger's seat. That day, we drove through Los Angeles with the skylight open, windows down, behind diesel buses and cars. I was as weak as I could get. But the feeling of freedom; there is no way I could describe it. I was crying and laughing, not believing what was happening. And I wasn't reacting to the pollution.

But Ed had only begun to work on my body. I was still

sixty-two pounds. I still couldn't walk. I still didn't have hair. I hadn't had a menstrual cycle in four years.

Yet, bit by bit, I healed. Ed would say, "Go out for a half an hour . . . then an hour." Pretty soon I could go out even more. I was eating more; I was putting on a little bit of weight. Now I could start to go to Bible studies. I started learning and growing in the Bible. I went to a Bible study or church every day or night of the week. You couldn't overfeed me. I was like a sponge. I just wanted to know what Jesus taught. And every time I met with Jesus' followers I felt the presence of God.

I was starting to get better, yet I still had incredible torment. I kept thinking "My sickness is going to come back." I was so afraid! One time I was at a meeting at Hollywood Presbyterian Church. I went up for prayer. I was walking by this time, and my allergies were definitely better. There were things that I was obviously still sensitive to. And my kidneys and many other organs didn't work. I was starting to have periods. But that made things worse. Once my body started to have periods, it caused stress on the rest of my body.

The woman leading the study had never met me before. When she laid her hands upon me, she said, "From this day forth, the torment is going to be gone." The power of God fell upon me. And from that day forward the intense fear that I would again get sick left me.

Then I went to another Bible study. And the power of God was there. The Bible teacher said, "God told me that there is someone here that needs new hair. God wants to restore your hair." Of course, all the men went for it because they were going bald. Yet I knew it was me. I had lots of hair before I was sick. He laid his hands on my head. The power of God was on me. Right after that, my hair came in.

I healed step-by-step. It took a good seven or eight years of God just healing. He also helped me through difficult areas of my life, building up my character. God wanted me to face things, and be free. When I would let Jesus come in and heal me of different fears and unhealthy mental patterns, my physical body, too, would get stronger. Step-by-step.

And through the years my doubts cleared up as well. I learned that God isn't immune to sickness and suffering. He didn't ignore it or shield himself from it. Rather all the evil in the world that deserved the anger of God—all of our own wrong choices and those of others—was judged on a cross. God became man, in the person of Christ. He bore the suffering of the world himself—that we might live. Jesus healed me in spite of my choices. Could there be greater love?

Limits to Healing

There were limits to Jesus' healing. When Jesus entered his home town of Nazareth ("A prophet is not without honor except in his home town and among his *own* relatives and in his *own* household") it is said that "He could do no miracle there except that He laid His hands upon a few sick people and healed them."[18] A disrespect for his authority may have stymied Jesus' purposes. This similar attitude of skepticism has been expressed by some. Yet throughout the world the name of Jesus continues to be an instrument of healing.

For example, according to an international magazine, "A recent survey conducted by the Church Growth Research Center of Sri Lanka reveals a 27 percent increase in the number of rural (Christian) churches in 1986. . . . Eloise Clarno, executive secretary of the ICFG's department of missions, said that besides the sovereign work of God, the only explanation for the rate of growth is the fact that . . . 'Most of our churches have been started as the result of someone being miraculously healed, or delivered from demonic powers.'"[19]

HEALINGS POINTED TO SOMETHING GREATER

What we see in the life of Jesus is an abundance of healings which exceed the boundaries of previous healings.

How might the type of healing Jesus practiced be explained? A look at Matthew sheds some light, "And when evening had come, they brought to Him many who were demon-possessed;

and He cast out the spirits with a word, and healed all who were ill; in order that what was spoken through Isaiah the prophet might be fulfilled, saying, 'He Himself took our infirmities, and carried away our diseases.' "[20]

According to this insight the prophecy of Isaiah[21] was to help the Jews (and Gentiles) identify the Messiah "the promised one" when he came. This fact is important because it may account for such rampant and arbitrary healing. Healing, though important in and of itself, pointed to something greater. Jesus sought to communicate to the world his power and authority—that he, indeed, was God.

Today, as in New Testament times, Jesus still validates his power and authority through healings, miracles, and provision. Cindy was seriously ill with lymphatic cancer. One day she involuntarily visualized a petri dish full of cancer germs. While picturing this in her mind she saw a large red check being placed over the dish. Cindy knew she had been healed. She sensed that God, or some "higher power" had given her another opportunity at life. While sitting in my living room she remarked, "I feel like I'm being led. I believe I was supposed to talk with you. Please tell me what you believe." I did. Cindy's healing opened the door to more important issues.

What an excellent way for God to demonstrate to this world his love and compassion. God became man in the person of Jesus Christ in order to experience our hurts and demonstrate the love and power of God to all. Jesus, according to millions who have profited, still heals the sick, provides for the needy, thwarts evil powers, loves, gives, and delivers. But none of this activity is equal to the greater purpose for which he came. That purpose has a bearing on sickness.

Points to Ponder

1. The life of Jesus isn't fiction. It hasn't been fabricated for the purpose of starting a worldwide religion. It is historically verifiable. There are excellent books to investigate. *Evidence that Demands a Verdict,* Josh McDowell, Here's Life Publishers; *More than a Carpenter,* Josh McDowell, Tyndale House Publishers; *Mere Christianity,* C. S. Lewis, Macmillan.

2. Have you studied the life of Jesus in regard to personal

healing? This may be a good study to consider. The book of Luke, a physician writing of Jesus, or the book of John, a more personal look at Jesus, is a good place to start.

3. Since the life of Jesus is pivotal to the discussion of this book, one might consider the evidence for the reliability of the biblical document, F. F. Bruce, *The New Testament Documents: Are They Reliable?*, Eerdmans Publishers.

CHAPTER ❦ 3

DOES ANYONE CARE?

*F*or two months I lingered. I was in the home of strangers. A fine couple had invited me to share their home for several months. I would be collecting interviews from around the country for my first book. Of course, they had expected a healthy woman to enter their abode. Instead, as I arrived on the heels of my trip to Tulsa, this generous couple hosted a very sick young woman who was unable to get out of bed.

My locale—northern Florida; my destination—Atlanta, Georgia. At least I had friends there! I packed as my fever rose. I loaded the light blue Maverick, shut the door, and leaned back in the seat, too sick to drive.

Yet drive I must. My welcome had worn thin. The stress of remaining in a home unprepared to house an invalid, especially one without means of support, was enough to cause me to seek another type of stress—the open road.

Gingerly I headed for the freeway to Atlanta. Minutes later I pulled to the side of the road, unable to drive further. I tried again. This time I lasted twenty minutes. As I again rested, the bright Florida sunshine warmed my car. It took over three days to cover a distance designed to take hours. I was constantly hugging the side of the freeway, irritating faster drivers who honked and occasionally yelled things as they passed.

Finally in Atlanta, I found a motel, registered for a room, and collapsed into bed. A healthy paycheck for previous journalistic work had arrived the day before I left Florida. How long could I survive on it?

A telephone call to friends had evoked concern but no help. "Let us know if we can help," they said. I had already sought their help. I told them I was desperate with no place to go.

"Well, we really hope you find something," they replied. And I'm sure they did. My extreme circumstances and their lack of understanding were a lethal mixture. I saw it clearly. I needed a miracle.

About the third day in the motel room I made a long-distance call. A well-to-do woman, whom I had met during my travels, came on the line. I told her my situation. She gave me the telephone number of a woman in Atlanta. I placed a second call.

Joyce Hopping answered and listened to my need. "I'll call you back." She did and responded:

"Linda, for several years I was very ill. Jesus Christ healed me. Since that time I have been praying that God would send me someone I could help get well. I believe you are an answer to prayer."

For the next two years Joyce housed me, fed me, financed me, took me to various people who began treating me. I did not improve during this time. But those confined years were made more sweet because of this remarkable woman.

Could There Be a Loving God?

Must one believe in the great God in order to receive his kindness? Don't we all experience the beauty of nature, the refreshment of rain, the companionship of pets, the beckoning of a new day with new opportunity, and a body whose normal course is to heal?

"Every good gift and perfect gift comes from above"[1] James, son of Joseph, wrote in the first century. For the sick, and those who love them, medical treatments, encouraging friendships, spiritual and mental ability to cope are included in the category of "gifts from above."

Yet is there "more" for the one who seeks God? Does God long to give; love to give—will he give to those who seek him wholly? The following pages contain my answers to these questions.

For years I had few answers. Many times during my bouts with illness, I had little appreciation that God or his gifts existed—

at least for me. I wondered if he cared at all. Could a loving God
allow such infirmity to wrack at my body and soul? Really?
Consider the prayer of an afflicted man:

> Lord, hear my prayer! / Listen to my plea! / Don't turn away
> from me in this time of my distress. / Bend down your ear and give
> me speedy answers. / For my days disappear like smoke. / My
> health is broken and my heart is sick; / it is trampled like grass and
> is withered. / My food is tasteless, / and I have lost my appetite. / I
> am reduced to skin and bones because of all my groaning and de-
> spair. / I am like a vulture in a far-off wilderness, / or like an owl
> alone in the desert. / I lie awake, lonely as a solitary sparrow on
> the roof ·. . . / My life is passing swiftly as the evening shadows. / I
> am withering like grass.[2]

Sickness definitely blurs our understanding. During a two-
year period of my illness, my nerves were so raw and my mind so
dulled that I could not fathom the whereabouts of the Almighty. I
cried to him, pleading my case time and time again; it seemed to
little avail. One night I frantically turned the pages of the Bible.

"Give me something. Anything. Just let me know if you are
there. Help me, please. Is there any hope for me?"

The silence at last was broken with one Bible verse literally
leaping off the pages at me. "It is only the Lord's mercies that
have kept us from complete destruction."[3]

What I came to realize, years later, is that the Lord's mercies
were ever present, caring for me in many small ways, protecting
me, even keeping me alive. But I could not see his loving heart.

Why? The human being is so constructed that a physical
blow to the body may have a downward pull on thinking. Severe
illness, even severe fatigue and grief over a lingering illness of a
loved one, is capable of prompting many negative emotions.
These may translate into impressions of being unloved, uncom-
forted, and uncared for. The next step may be to question God's
character: does he really love me?

Such is the experience of many sick and those who sit in fear
and trembling, by the beds of the afflicted. In fact, many who
reach out falteringly for God and are met with less than their ex-
pectation never reach out again. For them God is often a muddle
cloaked behind a heavy veil. At points of crises he has been described by various individuals as distant, indifferent, uncaring,
unreachable, and dead.

This questioning of God's love is a condition the ancient psalmist understood:

"For God Himself knows our frame; He is mindful that we are but dust."[4]

If God (Jesus) truly did create us, then he must know the disquieted nature of the ill; the pull of the diseased structure on the inner person; the anxiety produced by fever; the depression brought on by low blood sugar and poor oxygen supply; the tarrying despair. He must know everything about us. The psalmist wrote in the Old Testament:

"My frame was not hidden from Thee, when I was made in secret, and skillfully wrought in the depths of the earth."[5]

The psalmist may have understood God, but throughout the earlier years of my sickness I simply could not comprehend what people were talking about in reference to God's love. He, my life, my circumstances were an enigma to me.

Loved Regardless

As I deliberately—no, determinedly—sought out my Creator in my battle with sickness, I slowly grew to understand. The love of God met me at a deeper and deeper level. His love, as I've come to believe, can meet all of us, without exception, within the caves and crevices where we live. One woman's experience illustrates.

Shirley was always on top of things. She was a leader, known for her unfailing enthusiasm. She amazed everyone with her positive mental attitude no matter what the problem. Shirley never thought herself capable of anger. Even the doctor's verdict of leukemia provoked a certain semblance of acceptance. She, in fact, experienced deep resentment for almost a year without knowing it.

"I was not one who felt that I had a right to question. I kept things inside. I didn't even acknowledge the way I felt to myself until the doctors told me plainly that I needed to do some soul-searching if I hoped to get well."

That soul-searching led Shirley on a five-year path of honesty. "It was a great relief to me when I realized that the biblical God knew me better than I knew myself—and loved me anyway. I told him my fears, my frustrations, and my anger. It was a revelation to me when one morning I blurted out, 'I hate you, God, for doing this to me.' Actually it was not a new discovery, only a first-time admission. But what is so wondrous is how the Lord God can handle absolutely anything I feel, think, or express."

Many of those in crisis have learned that this universal God is big enough and strong enough to withstand our deepest woes, secrets, fears, cares, and declarations.

King David, of Israel, understood. He wrote around 1,000 B.C.:

> O Lord, you have examined my heart and know everything about me. You know when I sit or stand. When far away you know my every thought. You chart the path ahead of me, and tell me where to stop and rest. Every moment, you know where I am. You know what I am going to say before I even say it. You both precede and follow me, and place your hand of blessing on my head.

> This is too glorious, too wonderful to believe! I can *never* be lost to your Spirit! I can *never* get away from my God! If I go up to heaven, you are there; if I go down to the place of the dead, you are there. If I ride the morning winds to the farthest oceans, even there your hand will guide me, your strength will support me. If I try to hide in the darkness, the night becomes light around me. For even darkness cannot hide from God; to you the night shines as bright as day. Darkness and light are both alike to you.

> You made all the delicate, inner parts of my body, and knit them together in my mother's womb. Thank you for making me so wonderfully complex! It is amazing to think about. Your workmanship is marvelous—and how well I know it. You were there while I was being formed in utter seclusion! You saw me before I was born and scheduled each day of my life before I began to breathe. Every day was recorded in your Book!

> How precious it is, Lord, to realize that you are thinking about me constantly! I can't even count how many times a day your thoughts turn towards me. And when I waken in the morning, you are still thinking of me![6]

I Am With You

Surely, if God made me, he would wish that I see him clearly. Yet, thankfully I came to understand his love and care was not determined by my ability or inability to understand.

Just as in a loving family no requirements are placed upon the sick in order to receive care, God does not require "faith" and certainty in his care, in order to respond. In my own case he hastened to my need far more from desperate crying than from doubt-less understanding and faith-filled ardor.

In one critical period I became desperately ill. I knew all too well that my body was unresponsive. A faulty colon had shut down many other organs. I was in danger of losing one kidney.

Fear was my companion. I had no hope. I had no strength. I told God so.

In my distress I turned on the television hoping to distract my fear. The speaker on one program was discussing the names God is addressed by in the Bible. Somehow I sensed that I should listen closely. I tuned my ear and heard each name of this biblical God:

> Jehovah Jireh—God the Provider
> Jehovah Rapha—God the Healer
> Jehovah Nissi—God our Banner
> Jehovah Shalom—God our Peace

Listening to these many definitions of God's character en-couraged me but none really reassured me until the speaker began to relate the story of Ezekiel, an Old Testament prophet. Undone by war, Ezekiel was taken into captivity. On the long path away from his home to a strange city amid foreign people and foreign gods, the biblical God spoke to Ezekiel. Desperately, I listened.

"What is it, God? What did you say to him? How did you help him? Are you there? Help me."

"Jehovah-Shammah" Ezekiel was told. "God *is* with us."

God visited us in the person of Jesus Christ. And He was with me now. At my great moment of need God chose not to give me his promise of healing, help, or provision. Instead he answered my fears and open lack of hope by giving me his presence.

The physical manifestations of sickness are burdensome enough, but the real gall of sickness is the tragedy of feeling un-loved. The peril of aloneness—feeling deserted—is far worse than any surprise diagnosis or physical malady. Coming to a real, gen-uine God just as I was, I experienced his presence and tender care.

God Is Able

Many have personally witnessed the love of God. Mike Aldrich wrote me concerning a small precancerous sore in his mouth.

"I wanted you to know that your concern and prayers were

answered. As a matter of fact, they were answered in quite a miraculous way. I did go in for surgery. I was drugged and wired up in the operating room. The doctor came in, put on his gloves, grabbed the syringe to anesthetize the tongue for surgery. As he looked at the area to be excised he had a puzzled look and asked for more light, then a tongue depressor, and poked around for a good two minutes.

"At this point I was very concerned—I thought he had found that the lesion had spread and more serious surgery would be called for. Then he spoke: 'What have you been doing? There is nothing here to take out. It is healed!'

"My response was, 'It wasn't what I was doing. It was probably one-hundred to two-hundred folks who were praying for me.'"

An article in *Psychology Today,* analyzing a segment of the religious population, bears witness to the benefits of calling on the biblical God.

> *A Healthy Dose of Religion*
> *The way that Christians view their relationship with God may affect their health.* The view that "God helps those who help themselves" is probably healthier than believing that we're puppets on God's string.
>
> Christians can be divided into three very broad categories, according to psychologists Daniel McIntosh of the University of Michigan and Bernard Spilka of the University of Denver: Active Christians, who derive great meaning from religion and tend to see God as a partner to work with; passive Christians, who tend to be less involved in religion and believe that everything is preordained; and questors, who are still searching for the truth.
>
> McIntosh and Spilka asked 69 Christian college students about their religious beliefs and health history. In general, the active Christians were healthier than the others. They reported having fewer colds, headaches, ulcers, respiratory problems and other ailments.
>
> In contrast to those who believe that health is largely a matter of chance or God's will, active Christians believe that, along with God's helping hand, they have a responsibility to behave in a healthy way. Active Christians are also more likely to pray. McIntosh and Spilka note that *prayer has been found to reduce tension, and it is also a means of seeking control over a situation, providing that all-important elixir: hope.*
>
> *Stress reduction, a sense of control over one's life and opti-*

mism have all been linked to better health in a spate of recent studies. Active and meaningful prayer may be yet another means to these ends.[7]

Dr. Ian Gunn-Russell offers insights on what prayer can mean to a practicing physician.[8]

As a physician, I have always believed that all healing comes ultimately from God. But back in England early in my career, I thought that he worked only through the hands of health professionals and through the miracles of modern medicine. I'll never forget the time I learned otherwise.

It was in Newcastle-upon-Tyne, England, that day in the early 1950s when I was a new, young doctor. A cold North Sea mist blowing up the Tyne slickened the cobblestones as I anxiously climbed out of my Austin-Mini.

Hunching against the morning chill, I hurried toward one of the old red-brick dwellings lining the street where my patient Alfred Lawrie resided. He had only an hour or so to live.

I had first been called to see Mr. Lawrie, a paper merchant, a few days earlier and had found him a very sick man indeed. A seventy-year-old gnome of a fellow, he was propped up in bed on feather pillows, wheezing and gasping for breath. His gnarled fingers clutching the coverlet were blue.

A preliminary examination showed him to be suffering from heart failure and severe *bilateral bronchopneumonia* complicated by asthma. His legs, sacrum, and lungs indicated retained fluid, his pulse throbbed spasmodically, and his blood pressure was dangerously low. As I read his temperature, 102.5°, his pale blue eyes regarded me anxiously.

"It's hospital for you, my friend," I said, shaking down the mercury.

He waved a hand weakly. "Eh . . . I'll think about it, Doctor," he managed to reply through blue lips before he sank back on his pillow.

"What do you mean you'll think about it?" I asked,

as I searched for a vein in his thin arm to draw some blood. "I'll ring for an ambulance right now."

He weakly shook his head and closed his eyes.

As I put on my coat downstairs in the hall, Mrs. Lawrie revealed that she and her daughter, who stood quietly at her side, had promised her husband not to join me in urging him into a hospital.

"He has great distrust of hospitals, Doctor," she whispered. "In fact, you are the first doctor he has ever seen in his life. And then he only let us call you *because he heard you were a Christian.*"

I stared at her and the sad-looking daughter who mutely nodded. Because I was a Christian?

Quickly turning to the problem at hand, I set up a care procedure.

Since the mother and daughter would nurse Mr. Lawrie during the day, I hired a night nurse and began Mr. Lawrie's treatment: intravenous digoxin and aminophylline for his heart and asthma; oxygen to help his breathing; and for his pneumonia, injections of penicillin, an antibiotic which had only recently become widely available. I knew of nothing else I could do for this poor man who had several medical problems, any one of which could kill him.

I drove on to my next patient with Mrs. Lawrie's words still ringing in my mind: ". . . because he heard you were a Christian."

Where had he heard that? Then I realized he may have heard me speak in a local church or at the young people's meetings which my wife and I had started in our home.

But what difference could *my* being a Christian make to Mr. Lawrie? I wondered. The penicillin and other treatments I gave him would have been as effective if I had been an atheist. As I put the Austin-Mini into gear and accelerated into the mist, a thought came to me quite unexpectedly: *You can pray for him to be healed.*

The idea startled me. This certainly was not my normal course of action. Although I had accepted Jesus as my Lord and Savior, my firm conviction was that his

healings and those of the apostles were miracles wrought
by God in order to get his church off the ground.

No—I shook my head as the car's windshield wipers
flailed against the drizzle—Peter had healed the lame
beggar, but we had penicillin today, and that was miracle
enough.

However, the next day when the report on Mr.
Lawrie's blood came back, it was obvious he needed more
medical help than penicillin. His hemoglobin level was
thirty percent of normal, which could be critical for a
fellow in his condition. Emergency treatment for anemia
would be necessary.

I asked a colleague, a chest surgeon, to see Mr.
Lawrie with me. After the examination the two of us
consulted on the curb by our cars.

"The man is going to die," he said, folding his arms
in resignation.

"Do you see *any* hope?" I asked.

He shook his head. "Not unless you can get him into
hospital straightaway. Even then he will almost certainly
die."

"I don't think he will agree to go!" I explained
urgently.

"Well, Ian," he sighed, "I have nothing more to
suggest." He climbed into his car, stuck his head out the
window before pulling away, and added, "You're doing
everything possible, I know, but your patient is going to
die."

His words seemed confirmed the next morning at
eight o'clock when Mr. Lawrie's night nurse rang me.

"He's very bad, Doctor," she said in a low voice. "I
haven't been able to administer treatment this morning. I
don't think he'll last more than an hour."

I immediately drove to his house. Mrs. Lawrie and
her daughter met me at the door, their faces ashen and
tear-stained. Even as I raced up the narrow stairs, I could
hear Mr. Lawrie's harsh straining for breath. As I bent
over him it was obvious he would soon be gone. The room
was chill; in the household's anxiety the coals in the
fireplace grate had been forgotten.

I stared helplessly at him. The night nurse had done everything possible. Mr. Lawrie had been getting his oxygen and all of his medication, including the miracle drug, penicillin.

Why, oh why, Lord, can't we help him? I found myself praying.

Again the thought came: *You can pray for him to be healed.*

As I stood there looking at this ill man, words from the Gospel of Mark ran through my mind like a message on a theater marquee: "These signs shall follow them that believe; in My name shall they . . . lay hands on the sick, and they shall recover" (Mark 16:17–18).

With the night nurse looking at me anxiously, I faced my own crisis, just as Mr. Lawrie was facing his.

Then, with the uncertainty of Peter climbing over the rail of that boat on the Sea of Galilee, I climbed over my own threshold of faith. Though hesitant to pray openly, I visualized myself laying hands on Mr. Lawrie as I silently and awkwardly prayed, *Lord, in the name of Jesus, heal this man. He belongs to you. I don't believe he should die just now. Please heal him.*

Mr. Lawrie lay still, his eyes closed, almost in a coma. Behind me the fireplace grate rattled as the night nurse stirred up the coals.

Mrs. Lawrie and her daughter had come into the room, and I turned to them. "I've done *all* I can," I said huskily.

Something kept drawing me back to the Lawrie house that morning. After an hour I returned, wondering if my patient was still alive.

He was. He did not appear improved and his breathing was strained, but he was alive!

Two hours later I returned again. Mrs. Lawrie met me at the door. Was there a hint of relief in her eyes? Upon examining her husband I found his color slightly better. His breathing was still labored but his pulse had steadied.

It turned out to be the strangest day in my practice as I returned to the Lawrie house hour after hour, fascinated by Mr. Lawrie's progress.

That evening I was surprised to find him sitting in a chair beside his bed. He was still a very ill man but now very much alive. And though I was hesitant about expressing my feelings vocally, I silently gave thanks to God.

Mr. Lawrie continued to improve, and in six months he was back at work in his paper business. He lived another fifteen years.

Some might say the medical treatment finally worked. I believe it was God who healed Mr. Lawrie, and he did it in answer to my prayer.

From then on, although I continued to utilize the latest developments of medicine and therapy, I began to rely more and more on the healing power of prayer. And as my confidence grew I was soon able to lay hands on my patients and pray for them openly.

I am grateful for my experience with Mr. Lawrie because through him God was able to show me there is much more to healing than medications and surgery. And even today, though I'm retired from active medical practice, I can still prescribe the most powerful therapeutic treatment available: the healing power of prayer.

Talking with God has been the best part of twenty years of illness. In fact I would rather be sick and have this relationship with God than be well without him. And what was the result of my own prayers?

Things did not drastically improve when I was sick and seeking the Lord. Anyone who believes in God and has had to live with insomnia knows that the presence of the Lord, though precious and sweet, often does not erase the deep tiredness that cages an individual. Those with pain know the Lord may meet you—he may even deliver you—but often it is the aloneness in the pain that he satisfies. The pain may continue to wreak its torment.

Human love can make illness bearable, but God's love makes illness a gateway. Reaching out to God and finding him a joy prevails over the obvious stresses. When asked to describe how that love performs such a task, many are at a loss for words. Yet it is real, for their countenance, though strained from the battle, reflects peace.

As evidence of God's love, many attest that angels are constantly surrounding sick ones keeping watch. Pamela Rosewell, in *Five Silent Years of Corrie ten Boom,* writes:

> It seemed that every evening recently, Ruth had witnessed a shadow cast on the bed as if somebody had passed along beside the night light at the foot of the bed. But no one else was there. And there was a strong sense of comfort and peace in the room at the same time. "I think it's an angel," she concluded.
>
> "Really," I said. "That is very interesting," not adding what I was really thinking: Ruth was seeing things. Yet Ruth was a practical woman, having grown up on a farm, and she saw things very simply. In that way she reminded me of Tante Corrie. It was not like her to be imagining angels. *She must be very tired,* I concluded.
>
> The next day, however, Lotte mentioned that she, too, had seen a shadow in Tante Corrie's room. There was something wrong with the bulb of the night light, I decided, and exchanged it for a new one.
>
> "Have you seen any shadows in Tante Corrie's room?" I asked Bernice when she appeared for the weekend a couple of nights later.
>
> "As a matter of fact I have," she replied. "At first I thought it was headlights from cars on the street. But that can't be it, because there have always been cars outside and their lights have not caused this kind of shadow."
>
> The next day it was again my turn at Tante Corrie's bedside. In the near dark, I wondered if I would see an angel. Surely they could not all have imagined it. For quite a while I saw nothing unusual.
>
> But when I had stopped looking and was sitting quietly next to Tante Corrie, I saw what the others had seen. There was a shadow in the room—not a dark hovering thing, but, if it is possible, a bright shadow. And at once I was overcome by a sense of comfort and peace, like the times when you do not realize you have been tense, but, upon heaving a sigh of relaxation, realize you were.
>
> When we talked about it later, we agreed that God was reminding us that we were not alone . . . ."[9]

Love for the Lovers

The needs of those assisting the ill are no less met by our loving God. "The bills were staggering," one man told me. "As I placed our house on the market (the only home we had ever known), I sensed the Lord's caring presence sitting with me, beside me. It was as if my tears were his tears. It was a moment of tenderness that enabled me to face many more bleak months ahead."

One woman, Myra, explained the stresses of caring for an elderly aunt: "Bedpans, dressing sores, spoon-feeding and listening daily to someone complain were not my idea of how to spend mid-life. I thought that when the kids were grown and gone I would have time to myself. Raising intrinsically different children with all their demands was preferable to this responsibility."

Myra investigated alternatives. Money was scarce. A nursing home was out of the question. Professional nursing care proved too expensive.

At first Myra prayed, "Lord, help. I can't do this. I don't want to do this." Her attitude began to change as she asked God for help.

Another prayer, "Lord, I must have some time off." An answer, "My grace is sufficient." Myra learned to snatch time for herself. At other times she felt she might scream. She reached more determinedly for God's strength and grace.

She prayed, "Lord, if I'm stuck here, help me love her as you love her. Help this not be a chore but a service to you."

A further conversation, "Lord thank you that you have allowed me to help Aunt Jane. I do love her as you do. May I make the hours of her day more pleasant. Show me how I can help her deal with this disability. Help me be more patient."

"What I relearned through all this," relates Myra, "is that God knows better than I what is best. Had I not opened myself to God I would have exchanged outer stresses for perpetual inner stresses. As I continued to seek his direction for my life, outer frustrations were turned to inner fulfillment."

The Answer to Sickness

In the midst of sickness or caring for the sick God is with us. Many I talked with, who have sought him in their dilemma, saw small circumstances alter to miraculously meet their needs. There were:

- phone calls at the point of despair
- extra funds provided from an unexpected source

- a cessation of pain in answer to prayer
- a friend to assist
- a passage from the Bible coming to mind to undergird at a crunching moment
- a breakthrough in treatment in response to concerted prayer
- sleep coming at last and refreshing the spirit
- deep peace in spite of everything

Still others report that God healed them. Completely! God overruled troubling vexations. God spared financial burdens. God miraculously provided.

In twenty years of experiencing illness and observing others who are sick or have helped the sick, I conclude there is no substitute for a person reaching out to God for help. He is able to enable the unable. With his strength added to ours, or *in spite of* ours, we are empowered to bear, to survive, to surmount, to endure, and to ultimately win.

God Is Enough

One morning, about fifteen years into my illness, I was lying back in bed hunting through the Bible. A pack of blue jays was pecking at birdseed placed outside my window. The jays' shrill "caws," as they ate, never seemed to fit their royal blue garb.

While reading I came to the book of Romans in the New Testament. Here I read a familiar instruction from Paul, a follower of Jesus:

> I plead with you to give your bodies to God. Let them be a living sacrifice, holy—the kind he can accept . . . Don't copy the behavior and customs of this world, but be a new and different person with a fresh newness in all you do and think. Then you will learn from your own experience how his ways will really satisfy you. [10]

Prior to, and during my years of illness I had given God my life to do with as he wished. Even though I didn't know very much about this God, I had seen enough "joy" in some of his followers to want what they had. Further, I had saturated myself in the Bible realizing they claimed to hold the key to successful living. At one point I memorized most of the New Testament, sure that this investment would pay off in future well-being. It occurred to me that to the best of my knowledge, I had fulfilled the requirements of the first part of this verse—not holding my life selfishly for myself but seeking God and his trustworthy and lasting perspective of love and design.

Then I noticed something I had never seen before in these verses. The results of exchanging my self-will for God's higher plan would be a proof or vindication. Of what? That God's ways really *are* satisfying. Another translation of "satisfying" is "that which is good and acceptable and perfect."

After fifteen years of struggling with the question of God's purposes, the light went on. I was beginning to understand good and acceptable. In spite of illness, and sometimes because of it, there was a deepening sense of satisfaction. There were wonderful benefits about the way God was working in my life.

But *perfect?* Could that be true? If I gave my whole life to the biblical God and learned his ways, would I realize his ways were perfect? But this didn't make sense! Didn't "perfect" mean that the situation couldn't be improved? Surely sickness could be improved upon. Wasn't I waiting for health to appear in order to consider that God's good purposes for my life were complete? Wasn't I like many others who thought, "When I get married, things will be perfect"? "When I get a raise, then things will start cooking"? "When the children are finally gone, I can begin to live"?

Yet wasn't it also true that many healthy people were not satisfied? And that many who followed the Lord, though ill, were genuinely at peace? If this was true, then sickness or lack of it couldn't be the determining factor of happiness. Paul must have been talking about something other than external circumstances. Maybe real happiness takes place inside.

From that day, a load was taken off my shoulders. A certain frustration about "when was God going to deliver me so I could start living?" was put to rest. With that frustration gone, and with this vital lesson learned, that *God was enough—right now—*I began to heal. Over the next few years, one treatment after another was provided to restore my health.

A Life-Altering Contract—The Love of God for Me

The night of the healing service arrived. The church was small and jam-packed with many new faces. I sat close to the back in order to slip out early if I started feeling bad.

The evening began with music and praise. I sensed energy and excitement. The pastor explained that for some time he had felt burdened for the sick. He believed this night was ordered by the Lord. He was expecting God to work because he believed that God loved the sick and longed to heal many of them that night. "One of the reasons God came to earth in the person of Jesus Christ was to demonstrate his love for the sick and to triumph over sickness and death," he said. I hoped that God's love and power would be demonstrated to me that night.

My thoughts drifted back to a time just prior to a major sickness. I was twenty-two years old. Confronted with my need for wisdom, character building, and an intense desire that my life not be wasted I walked the streets. An intense conversation was taking place between God and me. "How can I be changed?"

I wanted to move from being a needy soul to a giving one, from being introverted to overflowing with love; from stagnating in doubt to walking in optimism; from dreaming great dreams to actually participating in them.

Around 8 P.M., I found myself on a curb. I can remember the surroundings as clearly as if it were today—the lush, green grass surrounding a large estate, overgrown weeping willows dragging their long limbs back and forth across the ground in rhythm to the wind, blocks of unlandscaped marsh, and overhead, a black sky with glittering polka-dot jewels.

There was no question in my mind that a life-altering decision was about to be made.

"God," I began, "I'm afraid of looking back on my life and wondering at all I missed, all I failed to do that really mattered. I couldn't stand that. I want to do something that lasts. Yet if you don't do something with my life, something drastic, I won't have a chance!"

I was thinking quickly now. I knew what I wanted. "I would like to make a contract with you. Please take my life and *do absolutely anything you want with it. I don't care how difficult it is, or how much it costs me . . . as long as you use my life to the fullest.*"

Things seemed momentarily still. A snapshot taken in time seemed to be framed and mounted in space. I knew I had been heard.

Within weeks I became ill!

As the years of sickness continued, intense suffering worked its purposes in me. Gradually a fearful, untrusting child came to lean back, stretch out, let down her hair, and relax in the love of God. I realized that the contract with God on a curb under a brilliant sky in Houston, Texas, had been honored. The specialness of the night, symbolizing the path I had chosen—"I'll pay any price if you'll use my life fully"—would remain my bulwark, my mantle, my destiny. I sensed its culmination more and more. Something was going to give!

I turned my thoughts to the healing service. At last Pastor Jim asked those who sought healing to step forward for prayer. "Lord, am I to go?" I silently asked. "Do you have something here for me tonight?" There was no response, no inner sense to participate. I waited.

"Lord, do you want me to do something, pray something, be prayed for?" I asked again.

All about me people were standing in lines to be prayed for. There was no big show in progress, no theatrics, just humble people coming to be prayed for and caring people to pray

At the front, church leaders would gently take the sick one's face, or hands, or lay their own hands upon the head of the ill. And they would pray; *earnestly* they would pray. I watched their faces of love.

Again I said in the quietness of my own heart, "Lord, whatever you want. Should I go forward for prayer? Do you wish to heal me tonight?"

I dared not move without the prompting of the Lord. Through years of sickness I had been in training to learn that very thing—God's will, not my own.

"Lord," I prayed, tears now coming helplessly to my eyes, "I've waited eighteen years. I'm forty years old," I sobbed. "Could you heal me tonight?"

Friends leaned over and smiled, giving me a hug, expressing their love.

"Whatever you want Lord. My life belongs to you. Whatever you want Lord."

Then it happened. No person except myself was involved. God spoke to me in my heart at that little church where people cared about the sick.

"You're healed, Linda."

I paused and reflected; the message was unmistakable. I rose and went forward for prayer. The greatest work was done—the love of the Father, the touch of Jesus. Now I could go and participate in prayer, praying for others as well.

In the months ahead I grew stronger—my confidence in God's touch growing. No longer did I ask for health. I thanked God for health and began praying for "extraordinary" health—health so vital that many would reap the benefits.

Yet my healing was packaged as an unusual "gift." To receive healing I had not sat around for twenty years waiting. I was forced to take inventory of my life—putting God on the throne where he belonged. I had to reevaluate priorities; whatever God deemed important needed to become my own personal bandwagon. I had to adjust my lifestyle—no more undisciplined activity, going where my needs were met. I had to learn to station myself at the feet of Jesus, get my needs met there, and obediently walk the exciting path he had chosen for me.

The flesh had to be put to death—a pattern to emerge where it was habitual to refuse its demands. This included junk food indulgences, late-night binges that short-circuited energy needed for the next day, taking the easy way—here was a challenge; many of the treatments I endured seemed worse than the disease.

Other efforts involved learning to not overstress myself, learning to pray and stand against forces of the dark, developing love, forgiveness, a positive, uncritical mental attitude toward others, and learning to find joy within no matter what the circumstances.

Am I not one of the most blessed persons alive? Instead of just healing me God allowed sickness to prepare and mature me. I received healing . . . *plus!*

But I believe there was another profound reason why God allowed me to endure a sickbed for such a length of time. He knew that many people are often at a loss as to what to do with the sick, how to pinpoint their situation—mentally, physically, and spiritually—and adequately address their needs. God gave me plenty of time to think about these matters: frustrations, fears, reasons for suffering, faith, presumption, perspectives concerning healing, treatments, and other subjects confronted by the sick. The next pages explain the rest of my journey—the things I needed to understand in order to participate in a healthy and meaningful life. I pass these insights on to you for your consideration.

Points to Ponder

1. Know that God loves you as you are. Come to him just as you are and seek his love, healing, and plan for you.

2. My prayer is that many will open their hearts to the love of God.

CHAPTER 4

WHY AM I SICK?

W hy had sickness come upon me? Why had circumstances converged in such a way as to encourage ill health? Obviously I was not the first to ask such questions.

Since the beginning of time the victims of sickness and those who bore the responsibility of caring for the ailing must have asked, "Why?" Yet, if there are answers to be found, there must be some source to which questions can be addressed. If I could be sure of the source, I reasoned, then I could have the best chance of healing. I came to understand that everyone had a source for their viewpoint on sickness and health—though perhaps not well-defined. Some sources prove reliable. Others don't. I discovered a reliable source, which I appreciated after the fact. Let me explain.

I met Sonja while at a health clinic. She was young and brilliant. As a college student she probed areas such as scientology, est, and mind control. She was taught that she was the product of her own making. It was up to her to exercise her mind in such a way as to reprogram bad behavior, tune out negative elements, and ward off disease. She was taught that anything was possible and under her own command.

At the clinic Sonja had opportunity to put that thinking to work. Her body was struck with cancer. Sonja's goal was to curb the growth the doctors labeled "inoperable." I was curious about how this lovely woman's mind worked. At first, Sonja was reclusive. When she finally ventured a conversation with me, she said, "Actually I thought I was handling my life pretty well. Now to be told I'm so ill . . . ." I could sense the stress she felt. She was wondering if her mental skills were sufficient to save her. I hoped they were. Sonja fought valiantly using mind techniques, meditation, and mind control. I applauded her efforts to try to take action against the cancerous invaders, knowing that positive attitudes make a difference. Yet I had seen people die prematurely in spite of their best efforts, and I wondered what Sonja's fate would be.

Dorothy Clark, of Walnut Creek, California, was only twenty-three when she was struck with cancer. Centered in her throat the killer carcinoma cells destroyed more than precious tissue; her hopes of singing professionally went as well. For five years she endured surgery and treatment. The vicious disease rankled her. When it came to asking, "Why am I sick?" the tables were turned.

"I didn't think much during those days," explains Dorothy, "except about my personal loss and the grief of my husband. By the time I was moved from the intensive care unit of the hospital to the terminal ward, I had come to terms with my own demise. I was ready, even eager, to leave this world."

But Dorothy would not die.

"Month after month passed as those surrounding me died. I lingered. The doctors were puzzled. I had no desire to live with a cut-up body, a voice that could barely speak, let alone sing, and without the ability to bear children. My body cheated me; it healed itself of the cancer. I became angry. In place of cancer, ulcers developed from my attempts to bury the bizarre and unexpected turnabout in my life."

The question of why she was dying was easier for Dorothy to deal with than the question of why she must live. "Picking up the Bible, I began to read. I needed answers."

Throughout my illnesses I've had the opportunity to observe many who are captured by infirmity. The patients' behavior and peace of mind have varied considerably, depending largely on the source which they chose. I know one man who burned with resentment over his ailment until the day he died. I watched a sick woman try in vain to find a place to rest her fears. One ex-marine endured nobly for the sake of others, treating his ailment and his departure as the last honorable act he would perform—until his last few nights when he screamed unceasingly. I have witnessed sheer grit overcome many obstacles; we are made in such a way that that is possible. I have known a man with eight children who cried in fright for an entire month after learning he had cancer. And I have seen many who possibly could have been healed who had no anchor to hold them steady in the storm. Fright and turmoil took their lives as much as any disease.

But as I met various people in homes, clinics, and hospitals, I have on occasion seen real "peace" in sick individuals or ones approaching their own demise. Such peace, I have observed, is often connected with an age-old source.

CHOOSE YOUR SOURCE CAREFULLY

The person who discovers a trustworthy source of instruction for life's adventures has many advantages. Confidence and certainty may be the lot of those who follow its counsel. Many feel that mortal beings are in need of something transcendent. If we can truly discover such a source of communication, we are on our way to deciphering and solving an array of enigmatic problems— one of which is illness.

I offer, for consideration, the Bible as a reliable source of answers on the subject of illness. You say, "How can the Bible make any difference in this modern age?" The late C. S. Lewis, a former professor at Oxford and Cambridge Universities and a one-time agnostic, is one of the most widely read authors of this century. This highly educated philosopher wrote:

> You may have felt you were ready to listen to me as long as you thought I had anything new to say; but if it turns out to be only religion, well, the world has tried that and you can't put the clock back. . . . Would you think I was joking if I said that you can put a clock back, and that if the clock is wrong it is often a very sensible thing to do? But I would rather get away from that whole idea of clocks. We all want progress. But progress means getting to the place where you want to be. And if you have taken a wrong turning, then to go forward does not get you any nearer. If you are on the wrong road, progress means doing an about-turn and walking back to the right road; and in that case the man who turns back soonest is the most progressive man. . . . There is nothing progressive about being pig-headed and refusing to admit a mistake. And I think if you look at the present state of the world, it is pretty plain that humanity has been making some big mistakes. We are on the wrong road. And if that is so, we must go back. Going back is the quickest way on.[1]

The Bible was written over a period longer than a millenium by more than forty different authors. Yet, with such diversity in time and writers, the Bible contains symmetry of thought. What great men of history have agreed on such vast fields of history, science, psychology, and philosophy?

In the areas of science, medicine, astronomy, archaeology, agriculture, psychology, and health laws, the Bible remains not only accurate, but enlightening. When one considers that the Bible was written during a period of time when others wrote nonsense about every aspect of the world (like "the earth sits on the back of an elephant") one marvels at its authenticity.

George Washington stated, "It is impossible to rightly govern the world without God and the Bible."

Thomas Jefferson, commenting on the Bible's effects on society and relationships, wrote, "I have always said, I always say, that the studious perusal of the sacred volume will make better citizens, better fathers, and better husbands."

Abraham Lincoln wrote, "This great book . . . is the best gift God has given to man. . . . But for it we could not know right from wrong."

Henry Van Dyke said it well:

Born in the East and clothed in Oriental form and imagery, the Bible walks the ways of all the world with familiar feet and enters land after land to find its own everywhere. It comes to the palace to tell the monarch that he is a servant of the Most High, and into the cottage to assure the peasant that he can be a son of God. Children listen to its stories with wonder and delight, and wise men ponder them as parables of life.

It has a word of peace for the time of peril, a word of comfort for the time of calamity, a word of light for the hours of darkness. Its oracles are repeated in the assembly of the people, and its counsels whispered in the ear of the lonely. The wicked and the proud tremble at its warning, but to the wounded and penitent it has a mother's voice. No man is poor or desolate who has this treasure for his own. When the landscape darkens and the trembling pilgrim comes to the valley named the shadow, he is not afraid to enter; he takes the rod and staff of Scripture in his hand, he says to his friend and comrade, "Goodbye, we shall meet again"; and comforted by that support, he goes toward the lonely pass as one who walks through darkness into light.[2]

Those who are sick or who love the sick may revel in the pages of the Bible. I have received help from its pages—whether peace, encouragement, faith, instruction, or hope. There is much good information available to help the sick. (I refer to the Bible as a primary source of help, not the only source.)

Origin of Suffering

What does the Bible say about the origin of sickness? Where does illness come from? Why does it happen?

According to my research, God, the Creator, desires fellowship with his creation—us. Made in his image we long for fellowship too. Our barren souls covet relationships, camaraderie, understanding, respect, adulation, and bonding. God wants an intimate relationship with his created ones above all else.

Why then all the sickness and turmoil in the world? Put succinctly, the biblical perspective is that although almighty God created and loves us, he does not superimpose dictatorship. Human beings have the power and responsibility to choose. They will also reap the consequences of their decisions.

In spelling out the program and design of earth, the Bible explains that every individual has great potential *and* defeating enemies. Enemies such as: a questionable lifestyle and attitude (operating contrary to good purposes); ignorance (we suffer for what we don't know); outside stresses (aggravated by a lack of inner resources); and indulgences (conducting ourselves in foolishness). Does sickness originate from these sources? Let's take a look.

LIFESTYLE

Popular viewpoints. How they can entice! Philosophy, psychology, lifestyle, perspective: how much of the way we live is determined by untested, sometimes destructive points of view? What is our *attitude* about life, others, work, relationships, children, authority, values, and leisure? How might these attitudes affect our lives' goals, mental outlook, and health?

When John D. Rockefeller was young, he had plenty of strength and vitality. As a young man he launched out into business determined to make something of himself. His dream was dominated by the desire to make lots of money. By the age of thirty-three he had made his first million dollars. To achieve this goal he drove his body and mind at a superhuman pace and lived a self-occupied life. When he was forty-three he had the largest business in the world. By age fifty-three he was the richest man on the face of the earth.

But Rockefeller exchanged his health and happiness for wealth. He developed alopecia, a disease that caused the hair from his head, eyelashes, and eyebrows to drop off, giving the appearance of a mummy. His digestive system could tolerate little more than crackers and milk. He couldn't sleep. He withdrew from those around him. And many of those acquainted with him hated him for his overpowering efforts to boost his own success at the expense of others.

When he was fifty-three, Ida Tarbell wrote of him, "An awful age was in his face. He was the oldest man that I have ever seen." At that time it was generally thought that he would not live another year.

One night as Rockefeller considered his life, he reasoned that none of his great empire of wealth would go with him when he died. Within a brief twenty-four-hour period he turned his direction from selfish consumption to helping others. He established the Rockefeller Foundation which resulted in untold benefits to universities, missions work, hospitals, and the underprivileged.

But the person who benefited most was John D. Rockefeller. His vitality returned as he began to practice an admonition which the Bible and wise men and women have propounded for centuries: "Give and it shall be given to you."

Is it possible that variances in attitude from a healthy point of view may lead to illness? Doctors have documented and tests have shown that a positive attitude increases the body's propensity to health. A negative attitude weakens the body. In one test the level of an individual's strength in correlation with his outlook was assayed. Volunteers were asked to think of various words: grief, death, anger, love, peace, hope. Those who concentrated on the positive words increased in strength. Those who focused on the negative words decreased in strength.

In another test, psychologists at Boston University showed a filmstrip of Mother Teresa in action. Students who participated in viewing the documentary boosted their immune system. Recent scientific studies are confirming how mental outlook affects health. The Bible explained this long ago in such statements as: "A merry heart doeth good *like* a medicine."[3]

The one whose mental attitude mirrors a self-centered system may expose himself to wear and tear which may not be reflected in the cheerful, giving soul. In *None of These Diseases,* S. I. McMillen, M.D., states, "From the moment man sinned and brought upon himself bodily and mental diseases, the Lord sought to succor him and mitigate the effects of disease. But man . . . has often brushed aside as worthless the very admonitions that could have saved him."[4]

What does the Bible admonish?

- "Let us have real warm affection . . . and a willingness to let the other person have the credit."[5] Can greed aggravate the body?
- "Be kind to one another, tenderhearted, forgiving one another."[6] Will unkindness and unforgiveness undermine the body's defenses?
- "Never act from motives of personal rivalry or vanity, but in humility think more of each other than you do of yourselves."[7]
- "Love is very patient and kind, never jealous or envious, never boastful or proud, never haughty, or selfish or rude. Love does not demand its own way. It is not irritable or touchy. It does not hold grudges and will hardly even notice when others do it wrong. It is never glad about injustice, but rejoices whenever truth wins out. If you love someone you will be loyal no matter what the cost. You will always believe in him [or her], always expect the best of him [or her], and always stand your ground in defending him [or her]."[8]
- "You shall love the Lord with all your heart, with all your soul and with all your mind."[9]

Can self-centeredness and pride short-circuit bodily functions? Will failure to give God proper place as Creator, and draw on his help, diminish intended strength, peace, and vitality?

IGNORANCE

The old cliché "Ignorance is bliss" may well be true. It's the *consequences* of ignorance that are unblissful. Ignorance can give one peace of mind. After all, what you don't know, you don't worry about. Such is the manner in which many conduct their health, business, even their future.

Someone has said that it may be better to be unborn than untaught, for ignorance is the root of almost every kind of misfortune. Samuel Johnson penned, "He that voluntarily continues to ignorance is guilty of all the crimes which ignorance produces."[10] The guilt and consequences of many in regard to ignorance of health laws are great. Never has there been so much information on subjects and such little regard for it by the masses.

Diane Williams sought to learn the source of her sickness. But she suffered greatly from the lack of a proper diagnosis.[11] Her story shows the result of not knowing the answer to a problem.

In 1985, Diane Williams first noticed signs of health-related problems. Symptoms, such as not being able to feel shower drops on her legs and recurring bowel problems, should have signaled the need to seek help. Diane, unaccustomed to "listening to her body," wondered at the changes in her thirty-eight-year-old frame, but chose to ignore them until the Monday before the Fourth of July. Upon awakening, she found she was losing feeling in both feet. Diane tried to jog, thinking a pinched nerve had attacked both limbs. Diane relates the rest of the story.

*T*rying to run was very difficult. My feet weren't connecting. Fear hadn't taken hold of me but it was knocking at the door. I didn't tell Roger, my husband, supposing that as other ailments in the past, this too would subside. I told myself that this was nothing to worry about and tried to put it out of my mind, not wishing to consult a doctor.

When I awoke Tuesday I could no longer ignore the symptoms. My entire lower pelvic area felt tight as if a vise had gripped it. I was partially paralyzed. My first inclination was to check with my gynecologist. I sat in the waiting room thinking, "I just can't handle this." The pain continued to increase even though the doctor could find nothing wrong.

Still determined not to deal with the matter I forced myself to drive to work on Wednesday morning. This was foolish as I was losing more control of my legs and ankles as well as my feet. When I arrived at the office it became all too apparent that I had a full-scale attack on my body. "This is serious," I told myself. I also felt a mental resolve to fight against whatever was wrong with my body. I picked up the phone and dialed my mother's neurosurgeon, Dr. Lloyd Dayes at Loma Linda University Hospital. "Have someone drive you over immediately and plan on staying," he said.

Tests commenced as soon as I was admitted. The fear I now experienced probably contributed to the further nerve impairment. Numbness had soon crept up to my waist. I was then probed, punched, and poked in all parts of my body by doctors and interns alike. Sometimes as many as thirty people at a time were analyzing my body.

Initial testing was to investigate several possibilities: a tethered cord, fibroid tumors, multiple sclerosis and other diseases.

One day after electrodes had been placed on my body and needles stuck in my legs to ascertain nerve reactions, I felt that I could take no more. The testing was intrusive, painful, and humiliating. When the milogram was performed (injecting fluids into my spine) I wasn't sure what was worse, the disease or the attempted cure.

After completing the first week of tests the doctor entered my room. He addressed Roger and me, "We have determined that you have fibroid tumors in your uterus which are putting pressure on the spine." An emergency operation was ordered. They gave Roger and me one hour to give our approval for a hysterectomy which would mean "no children" of our own. Though I was frightened, I felt that the doctors were trying to save my life. If we had only understood at the time that they were "guessing" rather than "certain," it could have made a difference in our decision. Nevertheless, a decision was made and an operation performed . . . with no improvement. The fibroid tumors weren't causing the problem! In addition my numb pelvis was at the same time highly sensitive. The operation and its results caused such pain that I was given high dosages of morphine for several days which kept me from screaming with pain. A bowel blockage also called for extreme measures.

More tests began. Even though I had every symptom of multiple sclerosis: extreme sensitivity to hot and cold, difficulty with bowel control, loss of the use of limbs, it took many weeks and costly tests before the doctors would write that diagnosis on the insurance forms. Lonely and frightened to be left alone I lay in the hospital wondering if I would ever get out, if I would ever walk again.

The doctors had their own point of view. They believed there was no cure or hope of recovery for anyone with MS. I was therefore sent in my wheelchair for occupational and physical therapy. After seven weeks I went home with the idea that I would be a cripple the rest of my life.

A ramp was built up to our 40-foot Fifth Wheel recreational vehicle where we lived. Here I spent most of my time in bed or in my wheelchair. The diet I received in the hospital had not helped my stressed body. I came home unable to keep down food, get restful sleep, or perform normal body procedures very well.

In late September my prayers were answered by a lovely woman, Linda, calling with encouragement. "You don't know me. But I think I can help you." She then began to tell me about a treatment offered at the Frederick Erdman Association in Havertown, Pennsylvania.[12] The circulation treatment had been known to restore many MS patients to a normal life. Too sick to visit the clinic, Linda taught me the treatment. She also suggested a nutritionist. I began both treatments immediately, sensing hope once again.

By Christmas of that year my health was stabilizing and my limbs were gaining in strength. A few months later I was able to walk with a walker and then a cane. It took about a year and a half to be able to resume a normal life complete with bike riding, aerobics and a full work load.

Had I known that fibroid tumors could be treated naturally I would not have needed an operation which prevented me from having children. If I had known that circulation treatments could restore nerve tone, I needn't have wasted weeks in a hospital learning disability skills and taking needless, damaging drugs. If I had known that diet made so much difference I wouldn't have further threatened my body by eating the high starch and sugar diet offered in the hospital. Thank God I learned how to best treat my body.

One day, after my great improvement, I was walking with a cane and a nine-year-old boy, Jay, came up to me at church. He said, "You don't need that cane anymore." He was right. And I haven't needed it since.

We have had an influx of recent interest on health care, but more often than not there is still much ignorance by default when it comes to nurturing our bodies. For example: Did you know that fungus growth accounts for many illnesses? Bet you didn't!

Neither did I know of many causes and cures of illness. In fact, if I knew at the beginning of my illness what I later learned, I would probably have avoided years of ill health.

OUTSIDE STRESSES

It is frequently noted that much illness can be traced to incurring stress. The fast pace of society, expectations of others, job pressures, time crunches, family stresses, and red tape—how outside sources can tax one's mind and body! No wonder there is a surge of interest in stress reducing measures. Granted, it is impossible to live stress-free, but people would do well to free themselves of unnecessary burdens.

There are people who reduce uncontrollable tensions by building up their inner resources. It was necessary for me to reconstruct my inner person to throw off sickness. This included four steps of reprogramming involving analysis, replacement, refocusing, and diversion. (These steps I outline in my book *Staying on Top When Things Go Wrong,* Barbour Books.) Building up my own resources helped me to withstand and tackle the stresses which weakened my body.

Stress is also the product of improper handling of the food we eat. Centuries ago a wise man, King Solomon, wrote: "There is a time to sow and a time to reap."[13] Many of our fruits and vegetables are picked before they have naturally ripened. Therefore they don't develop the amount of vitamins they should. Poor handling of the soil has greatly diminished food value. Consider the effects of pesticides, preservatives, additives, polluted water, toxic chemicals, smog, and radiation, and we come face to face with stresses that are corrupting health throughout much of the world. One can understand why experts in the fields of nutrition and ecology are alarmed at the breakdown of health as a result of diminished nutrition and increased pollution.

The medical community is concerned with the strengthening of many viruses and bacteria. Some contend that the overuse of antibiotics has contributed to stronger strains of such plagues.

Questionable attitudes, a self-centered lifestyle, ignorance, and outside stresses are not our only enemies.

TEMPTATION

Yielding to temptation may be another avenue for breakdown in our physical strength. To be free of indulgences of the flesh would be a blessing for most of us.

We know we shouldn't eat that extra dessert but lustfully engage—feeling deprived if we don't.

We know we should get enough sleep, but the late night movie is so enticing.

Exercise is needed, but that requires time and discipline.

Some let their sex drive control them, not only risking AIDS, syphilis, gonorrhea, and other venereal diseases, but potentially inviting guilt-ridden emotions which sap the body's strength.

I am convinced that much sickness is due to lack of discipline in caring for our bodies. To illustrate how far someone might go to satisfy their cravings I offer myself as a case study.

My husband, Rusty, and I were visiting my parents' home in San Diego, California. Their house is built on a plot of land overlooking Mission Valley. I had been working for some time on a project and completed it while at their home. Wanting to celebrate, I reasoned that I *deserved* to celebrate . . . and what better way than with a box of some of California's best confections?

At noon I drove myself to the candy shop and picked out one pound of assorted chocolates. I studied them when I returned home. My taste buds respond well to chocolate, my body poorly. I would probably pick up a virus within days of a binge. "Maybe I'll get the flu. At least I'm done with the project," I rationalized. "And how long has it been since I've touched chocolate? Many months," I thought, priding myself on my discipline.

My private festivities began. I slowly took only one bite of each piece of cream-filled, nut-clustered, minty, coconut, fudge, toffee, butterscotch, praline, and fruit-filled delicacy—careful to savor every morsel fully. Completing my allotted amount, I took the half-eaten box of candy to Rusty. "Eat what you like. Then go out on the edge of the canyon and throw the remains way down the hill where I can't get to them." Rusty understood. We had performed this ritual before.

An hour passed and I began to think, "If this is my only cheat day for several months, I want to do it big! Where's the chocolate?"

But Rusty had gone to run an errand; the chocolates had disappeared.

The search began—cupboards, suitcases, drawers—I looked everywhere for the remains of that box. Finally Rusty arrived back at the house.

"Where are the chocolates?" I asked.

"Linda, you told me to throw them down the canyon and that's what I did."

"How could you?"

Putting on my sneakers I dashed out the back door and headed for the steel fence that lines the canyon. Rusty had a look of amusement on his face. I actually climbed an eight-foot, wire fence with rough edges on the top, dropped myself into the canyon, and began a candy hunt. Thirty minutes later I had not found a single piece. My rampage was forced to a halt. I dragged myself about for several days as a result of the sugar and chocolate binge.

In his book *None of These Diseases*, S. I. McMillen wrote, "No one can appreciate so fully as a doctor the amazingly large percentage of human disease and suffering which is directly traceable to . . . immorality, dissipation and ignorance."[14]

Many studies support such findings. And many individuals can testify as well:

- A woman with prolonged suffering in her back controls her critical and complaining tongue. Relief is forthcoming.
- A man with outbursts of temper brings his blood pressure down when he finds a suitable way to deal with his anger.
- A teenager overcomes bouts of low blood sugar and fatigue when fat and sugar are removed from his diet.

• A woman wins her battle over alcohol, releasing her body to cure itself of liver ailments.

The list goes on and on. Every sick person or invalid, every susceptible individual and potential victim should take note: if you let your desires rule your person—a breakdown in health may result.

Where else does sickness originate?

HEREDITY

Heredity also plays a role in illness. The nature of genetic transference can predispose a person to one disability or another, or limit bodily functions.

Growing up I found out that two close relatives had been committed to mental institutions. After my mental afflictions I learned of four more who had been institutionalized until they died. One had killed himself. All were of my father's line—his mother, aunt, uncles, and brothers. I was the first, but not the only offspring of my father to display similar symptoms.

What is the reason for such a genetic deficiency? Does the Bible have anything to say concerning the passing of flaws and weakness from one generation to another?

Moses wrote: "He is God, the faithful God who keeps His covenant and His lovingkindness to a thousandth generation with those who love Him and keep His commandments."[15] One of the stipulations of this covenant is: "And the Lord will remove from you all sickness."[16]

Is it possible that health can follow generations which honor the Lord? Does that blessing extend to children and children's children? Then is the contrary true also—that sickness, however obtained, may be transferable down to descendants through genetic predisposition?

Is hereditary weakness reversible? In my case and many others the answer is yes. Many medical discoveries have been made in the twentieth century which allay formerly irreversible maladies.

Are there other sources of sickness? Yes and therefore answers for them. Get ready!

Points to Ponder

1. What are you looking to for answers in your life? Today it can be baffling for the sick and those who love them to choose the best source. With the cults, the occult, materialism, behaviorism, secular humanism, rationalism, spiritism, religion, and medical science each purporting to be "the" answer, one must look carefully. The sick individual is motivated to look "harder" for truth simply because time may be short and options (because of lack of opportunity) limited. Choose your source carefully. Your life depends on it.

2. Have you considered the impact your attitudes and life-styles may have on your health problems? Have questionable values, rather than the good "sense" found in the Bible, caused you to tax and stress your body? Learn what the Bible teaches about daily living and build on a solid foundation.

3. If ignorance is a factor in your health, learn all you can. Keep searching.

4. Stresses, which can be controlled, may be necessary to control. Make wise changes.

5. Are you a victim of your own appetite and indulgences? Perhaps you should make a biblical study of areas that have been defeating you.

6. If heredity has affected your health, recognize that much is available to cure the "incurable" today.

CHAPTER 5

GOD HAS THE LAST WORD

*I*didn't even hear the sirens! As I regained consciousness, the paramedics were arriving and a crowd was gathering. I tried to remember what had just happened.

It was a beautiful summer day—too warm and cheerful to stay indoors for long. I would take my moped to visit a friend. The trip took only a few minutes and I felt stronger on this brave day.

I prepared to start the bike: I coasted down the incline of my driveway, then cruised past several cabins, and onto the mountain roads fresh with the spicy scent of pines. How could I have known that my neighbor, who was building on the lot next to mine, was using a large truck that completely blocked the drive? Rounding the curve I saw a massive steel truck in front of me. To the left of the truck was a tree. To the right was a brick wall and steep drop. I veered to the right, braking, but not quickly enough.

I could hear myself scream seconds before my face hit the wall, turning my head almost behind me on impact. My first awareness as I became conscious was the taste of blood. My mouth was not right. A quick check revealed the upper front teeth gone; the impact so forceful they were dislodged, roots and all. I felt no lip either, the whole lower part of my mouth having been removed as well.

The bike had already been pulled off my body by a neighbor who vigorously ran for help; I had hit the bottom of the thirty-foot drop before the moped landed on top of me. Moments later I picked myself up and climbed the hill to my house, noticing that my hand was mutilated. In spite of all the blood nothing hurt very much. I was numb.

When the ambulance arrived my "sturdy" disposition took over. "Now Linda," I told myself, "this may be the only time you'll ever get to ride in an ambulance. Try to have fun." I quizzed the ambulance assistant as to the extent of my injuries. The state of my mouth made speech practically impossible.

The thirty-five minute ride brought me to Saint Bernardine's Hospital. Once at the hospital the wait seemed forever. No one hurried to treat me. I began to wonder if they had forgotten I was there. Stretched out on one of the tables, I listened for the next several hours to other trauma cases being brought into the hospital. My drama was interrupted by a hysterical child and a panicky heart attack victim. I worried that I was losing a lot of blood. Eventually needle and thread were sewing me back together, plans were underway to repair my broken bone, and cuts and bruises were being cleaned and bandaged.

When I got home the pain kicked in. Had someone placed a fifty-pound rock on my face? What was wrong with my neck? How funny I looked without front teeth. By morning my face was swollen to the proportions of a gorilla's. I started losing sleep. Painful shingles came and lasted six months; my neck would not be better for two years. It's hard to stay on top when your body is damaged. But this was disaster added to disaster.

Was God's love present even now?

My neighbor, a cross-country motorcycle racing champion in the United States and a veteran of eighteen accidents, thought so.

"Linda, you should be dead. When you hit that wall your head turned 180 degrees in the other direction. And how you survived that fall, with the bike on top of you—you must have had angels watching over you."

Why Doesn't God Just Heal Me?

Yet, if God could provide for me in the midst of an accident, why not prevent the accident altogether or heal me instead?

Glaphre Gilliland, in her book *When the Pieces Don't Fit,* relates this story about herself:

My condition has progressed more slowly than predicted . . . At every critical moment . . . when the doctors were the most gloomy . . . when I was too weak to even turn over in bed . . . when the pain was too great to take anymore . . . God intervened and granted me a reprieve. Until the next time.

I couldn't understand why he didn't just heal me completely—once and for all. It seemed a better conservation of his energy. It would take a burst of creative power, but then he'd be all done and wouldn't have to mess with it anymore.[1]

If God can heal people, why doesn't he do so? Surprisingly the answer is often linked to his love. To understand the complexities of this issue, we must first look at what the Bible has to say about God's character.

The Enigma

We live in a time when many enjoy the comfort of a largely theistic society. Perhaps during a crisis we hope that some of it might rub off on us. A benevolent "giver" might reach down and deliver us from the consequences of our own choices. However, this convenience attaches little allegiance, let alone obedience, to a divine Creator-Ruler.

Much of current popular philosophy encourages this irresponsible thinking by creating a comfortable God—ourselves— whom we can satisfy or not satisfy at our own leisure. What we "feel" becomes our standard of evaluation. We ask, "What do I want?" Then we proceed to carry out our own wishes. At best, an individual caught in the throes of this philosophy will rise no higher than himself.

Some of this pleasant, me-thinking speculation has overtones of a life force somewhere in the cosmos that we might connect with if we so desire. C. S. Lewis considers this position:

When you are feeling fit and the sun is shining and you do not want to believe that the whole universe is a mere mechanical dance of atoms, it is nice to be able to think of this great mysterious Force rolling on through the centuries and carrying you on its crest. If, on the other hand, you want to do something rather shabby, the Life Force, being only a blind force, with no morals and no mind, will never interfere with you like that troublesome God we learned about when we were children. The Life-Force is a sort of tame God. You can switch it on when you want, but it will not bother you. All the thrills of religion and none of the cost. Is the Life-Force the greatest achievement of wishful thinking the world has yet seen?[2]

How eager many in the Western world are to be rid of the Christian God. And this is part of the enigma. There are things we like about the Christian God: forgiveness, mercy, comfort, and love. And there are things we hate: justice, righteousness, sovereignty, and invasion. There are parts of us which want God—our need for security, forgiveness, peace, direction—and parts of us which do not want God—independence, pride, self-centeredness, lust, sinfulness.

Let's look more closely at who the Christian God is, particularly in light of how he relates to those who are sick and needy.

God's Character

The biblical perspective is that God has the following characteristics:

Sovereign—All circumstances are ultimately in his hand.[3]
Righteous—God has no sin.[4] He cannot sin against us.
Just—He is completely fair in all of his dealings.[5]
Loving—His love is all consuming towards his creation.[6]
Eternally alive—He desires that the human race live with him in joy forever.[7]
All-Knowing—He knows all about every situation in our lives. Nothing catches him by surprise.[8]
All-Present—There is no place where we are that he is not.[9]
All-Powerful—There is nothing that he is not able to do on our behalf.[10]
Honest—God cannot lie.[11] We can depend on God to do what he says.
Faithful—He is trustworthy.[12]

God will operate consistently with his character. What has his character to do with sickness? Many things. Let's first look at God's sovereignty and his legal right to inflict and cure sickness as he wills.

God Has the Final Say

God is sovereign. He is the King of the universe. He can do
whatever he pleases with creation, with or without our permission. Such was the message he demonstrated to Job.

Job was a good man, well thought of. In fact, in his generation he was the person on earth most attentive to righteousness. At
the end of a period of great difficulty and disease which God permitted him to experience, and after endless questions by Job of
the Almighty as to why such calamity would befall "a righteous
man," the answer given to him by God is unmistakable, "Shall a
faultfinder contend with the Almighty?"[13]

God did not seek to destroy Job, but sought his instruction
and understanding. Job's integrity was vindicated in the process,
but a greater realization came as well—God is the potter; we, the
clay. God is the Creator; we, the created ones. Can we really pass
judgment on his choices?

An encounter Jesus made illustrates:

> And it came about soon afterwards, that He [Jesus] went to a
> city called Nain; and His disciples were going along with Him,
> accompanied by a large multitude. Now as He approached the gate
> of the city, behold a dead man was being carried out, the only son
> of his mother, and she was a widow; and a sizeable crowd from the
> city was with her. And when the Lord saw her, He felt compassion
> for her, and said to her, "Do not weep." And He came up and
> touched the coffin; and the bearers came to a halt. And He said,
> "Young man, I say to you, arise!" And the dead man [the corpse]
> sat up and began to speak. And Jesus gave him back to his mother.[14]

Such are God's loving ways. And such are the "rights" of
God. Ultimately it is his sovereign hand that causes, allows, initi-
ates, impedes, produces, halts healing. God's sovereignty has
been a source of much query. Much of man's rebellion is against
such ultimate authority of God. I, too, had reservations as sickness racked my body. It seemed I, like Job, had little to say as to
what had come upon me. God's sovereignty, justice, love, and
truth were all "on the line" as far as I could see.

Obviously God was in the position to do whatever he pleased
with me. I could cooperate or fight him. Although my mind questioned constantly, rehearsing pros and cons, possible reasons,

whys and wherefores, I'm glad I had enough sense to lay down my arms in surrender. I might fight the sickness. But to fight the Creator was pointless!

In our own minds, we may weigh God's justice against our own sense of justice, but ours will be found wanting. We are incapable of seeing the whole picture, viewing the end from the beginning, even rightly judging our own hearts. God, if he is just, is the only one large enough to see the "big picture" and determine what is ultimately fair. Justice was his message to King Nebuchadnezzar. Nebuchadnezzar (king of Babylon, 605–562 B.C.) thought he had final and rightful say over his own affairs. God's justice was called into play. Daniel, a favored Hebrew in the Babylonian empire, wrote:

> The Most High God gave Nebuchadnezzar . . . a kingdom and majesty and glory and honor. He gave him such majesty that all the nations of the world trembled before him in fear . . . . But when his heart and mind were hardened in pride, God removed him from his royal throne and took away his glory, and he was chased out of his palace into the fields. His thoughts and feelings became those of an animal, and he lived among the wild donkeys; he ate grass like the cows and his body was wet with the dew of heaven, until at last he knew that the Most High overrules the kingdoms of men, and that he appoints anyone he desires to reign over them.[15]

How does the character of God affect illness?

God, who is sovereign and just, is also righteous. He shares no part in sin and, though patient with our willful and wandering ways, will not tolerate rebellion amongst his creation forever. Therefore, in some instances he responds to sin with punitive measures involving illness. Nebuchadnezzar developed mental illness directly from the hand of God—God's sovereignty, righteousness, and justice being exercised. Let's look at some other instances of this:

- Zechariah was struck dumb by one of God's angels for failing to believe the word of the Lord.[16]
- Gehazi was smitten by God with leprosy in response to his avarice.[17]
- King Uzziah was punished for his presumption. "But when he became strong, his heart was so proud that he

acted corruptly . . . the Lord had smitten him. And King Uzziah was a leper to the day of his death."[18]

- Ananias and Sapphira were struck dead for lying.[19]
- King Jehoram was a candidate for divine retribution meted out in disease. "You yourself will have a severe sickness with a disease of your bowels, until your bowels come out because of the disease, day by day."[20]
- Miriam and Aaron experienced the direct hand of the Lord when he inflicted them with leprosy for speaking against his appointed leader, Moses.[21]
- The children of Israel were disciplined by the Lord when he sent serpents to bite them and inflict poisonous substances in their bodies.[22]
- The church is warned of incurring sickness and death from the Lord should they fail to meet the proper requirements at the Lord's Supper.[23]
- King Asa became diseased in his feet. "His disease became severe; yet even in his disease he did not seek the Lord but sought help from physicians."[24]

On a number of occasions in the Old Testament, God declared that he brings disease upon those who refuse to seek his way. Sickness is cited as punitive, "He will not put on you any of the harmful diseases of Egypt which you have known, but He will lay them on all who hate you."[25]

Sickness is also cited as a form of chastisement in order to motivate Israel to return to their God. In Leviticus 26, a fivefold plan of chastisement including illness—fever, consumption, plague—is revealed in response to not hearkening to the Lord.[26]

In Hebrews 12, we see a similar emphasis:

> My son, do not regard lightly the discipline of the Lord, nor faint when you are reproved by Him; for those whom the Lord loves He disciplines, and He scourges every son whom He receives. It is for discipline that you endure; God deals with you as with sons; for what son is there whom his father does not discipline?[27]

Jeannette Clift George, writing in *Travel Tips From a Reluctant Traveler,* addresses this delicate issue of God's sovereignty, justice, and righteousness. She writes of the disciples in the midst

of a ferocious storm—a storm into which Jesus had sent them—
and of Jesus walking on the water to meet them.

> They were scared. Oh, yes. But I think they caught on to something
> that we in the believing community occasionally forget. That Man
> walking on water has full authority! When we see Jesus coming to
> us through the storm, he is Lord. He has not come to take orders.
> He has come to take over.
>   It isn't always easy to turn the boat of our dilemma over to
> him. He may not honor our idea of how to resolve the dilemma. He
> may expect our submission just at the time we plan to exercise our
> authority! It's not always easy, but it's the only way out of the
> storm.[28]

To deny God his rights and his workings is not the solution.
To bow to his majesty and submit to his fairness and integrity
makes much more sense.

In a society that espouses permissiveness and a "nobody is
going to tell me how to live" attitude, it is important to remember
that God is the sovereign King. And if it is true that God is sovereign, wouldn't it be better to come to terms with the idea and seek
peace with God rather than to ignore reality?

Time and time again Scripture cites that punishment, chastisement, and discipline involving illness may come from the hand
of the Lord. Yet in spite of such evidence, there is a great urgency
among some to denounce the possibility of God's bringing disease
upon the human race.

Such a philosophy, which curtails God's choices, has limited
appeal. For what has not been reasoned into the equation is this: if
God cannot put sickness upon an individual—what gives him the
right or power to remove it? If he has no reign over one, what
exactly gives him the reign over the other? In other words, if God
cannot start/stop in this area of illness then he in fact is not all-
powerful. Even Satan has the power to start/stop illness. Is Satan
more powerful than God?

Who Is This Satan?

What exactly *is* Satan free to do in and amongst God's creation, and what has this to do with God's sovereignty? To understand we must first look at some history recorded by ancient
biblical writers.

Put succinctly, the biblical perspective is that Almighty God had, in eternity past, established fellowship with other beings he had created—a magnificent angelic race. Given the free will to choose their allegiance, one-third of this finely shaped and molded host rebelled. Under the leadership of Lucifer (Satan), who had previously been God's right-hand person, they set themselves against God—but not simply in opposition to God. This celestial race wished to supplant God and establish their own kingdom in his stead.

Earth and humans are God's program for resolving this angelic upheaval. God created us for fellowship. Yet he purposely left us free to say no to a relationship with him. He allowed sin, sickness, and suffering to continue in our lives (as the result of the fall of humans at earth's creation when a clear "no" was resounded by the human race), but in the hope that we would seek his fellowship.

As part of God's efforts to resolve this heavenly conflict, he has given Satan access to influence humans in his direction. God's love manifested to earth's population will be received, refused, or ignored as angels look on. In doing so God is allowing the rebellious legion ample opportunity to observe his justice concerning their deserved punishment.

This relatively short span of history in which this conflict is taking place will see a remedy in the not-too-distant future, according to the biblical perspective. In the meantime God, Satan, and humans coexist. Those who choose God find life everlasting; those who find Satan share his doom; those who find only themselves are the most miserable of all, finding nothing but themselves. Unknowingly they are also siding with the "evil one."

The Devil Made Me Do It

Years ago, many people in the Western world didn't believe in a devil. In the Orient and other places they knew him all too well. When sickness, death, or evil befell them, they blamed the devil and evil spirits. In the Western world, we blame God. Why the confusion?

Do Satan and his demonic cohorts still directly place illness upon a human being? Lauren Strafford, in her best-selling book, *Satan's Underground,* reports on the activity of satanic covens run by satanists which put curses of illness or bodily harm upon individuals. Geraldo Rivera, in his prime-time TV special on satanists, documented covert activity of demonic evil in the Western world. Such practices are growing worldwide. Satan is alive and active.

Exercising Authority Over Satan

It is well attested that many people, when exercising authority over Satan and demonic forces, have realized breakthroughs in long-standing health problems. For years I had sought to understand the invisible demonic world and how to defeat it. The subject seemed vague, hard to get a grasp of, and controversial.

At times I sensed that evil powers might be involved in my battles with ill health. This occurred when flus and viruses came upon me in spite of every human effort to prevent them, as well as mental oppression which at times was unrelenting. Frequently strange phenomena happened that stressed my mind and body at my most vulnerable moments. It easily resembled a sideshow: dogs barking incessantly making needed sleep impossible; rats invading my sleeping quarters; cats crying precisely at the point I would almost be in slumber; a neighborhood maniac on the loose; robberies; broken water pipes on the day I finally gathered strength to write; nightmares; well-timed interruptions; freak accidents; harassment and criticism; even huge cockroaches taking over my house, appearing on beds, pillows, couches, sinks, most aggressively and uncontrollably in spite of every precaution. I had little appreciation for how it all worked, no confidence that I could reverse the order. Until . . .

On a warm day in July 1985, Rusty and I were planning to fly from Denver, Colorado, to Dallas, Texas. We had been attending a conference. All week I had been riding a bicycle to and from meetings. My shoulders and neck were tight from using largely dormant muscles—the tension of steering the bike was too much for a fatigued body.

Shortly before boarding a plane to attend a bookseller's convention I noticed a sudden weariness come over me. I felt weak, as if my legs would not hold me. I could barely walk to the plane.

On the plane I grew rapidly worse. My arms would not obey my command. My legs felt like lead. Rusty brought me potassium and food to check mineral imbalance and low blood sugar. Still my brain and limbs did not connect.

Rusty wheeled me off the plane in a wheelchair and took me

to the hotel, my well-worn companion, terror, close at hand. Through the night I was unable to stand without assistance or turn over in bed. Yet miraculously, after only several hours of sleep I was able to attend the book convention to promote one book, *Secrets of Successful Humor,* and make contacts on another, *A Cord of Three Strands.* I had a sneaky suspicion that the enemy was in some way connected with this assault, particularly because of the importance of the latter book.

When I returned to Denver that same evening, my legs again became jelly; my arms ceased cooperating. For the next two months I was often unable to experience any use in my limbs and got no relief from treatment.

One evening I received a telephone call.

"Linda, my name is Vicki. You don't know me but the Lord has shown me that I am to pray for you until you are well." Vicki Carson did pray. And with what authority! She addressed Satan and evil spirits as if they were in the room. She commanded them to take their hands off of me.

Over a period of weeks I was beginning to understand and reap the benefits of this kind of authority mentally and physically.

Jesus Christ referred to illness inflicted by the devil. Luke, a physician who wrote about the life of Jesus, refers to a woman with a sickness caused by an evil spirit.

> There was a woman who for eighteen years had had a sickness caused by a spirit; and she was bent double and could not straighten up at all. . . . And He [Jesus] laid hands on her and immediately she was made erect.[29]

In many other cases of demon-caused illness, demons were forbidden by Jesus and his followers to continue their attack.[30]

Worldwide societies recognize that the church building, the cross, the Bible, and exorcism in the name of Jesus have been used to stop Satan. Could the sick likewise learn to protect themselves in the name of Jesus?

Who Has the Last Word?

The most reassuring part of the discussion on Satan is that God is greater. God has the final say in a matter. Consider the following.

In the case of Job, Scripture is clear that Satan asked permission of God to test Job. God gave that permission. Satan then afflicted Job.

If the president or leader of a country gives permission for someone to do something does he not carry responsibility for whatever is done? When President Harry Truman said, "The buck stops here," he was indicating that the Oval Office took final responsibility for decisions emanating from that office.

Consider:

- Satan had to seek permission to inflict Job's life.[31]
- Jesus told his disciple, Peter, "Satan has demanded permission [obtained by asking] to sift you like wheat."[32]
- The apostle Paul relates, "There was given me [by God] a thorn in the flesh, a messenger of Satan to buffet me."[33]
- God sent an evil spirit upon Saul.[34]

Satan is not uncontained. He is on a leash. In these passages God has the last say concerning what Satan is able to do. This is not to say that God is behind Satan's evil. One must not define evil, punishment, discipline, and suffering the same. God is not evil, yet he can punish, discipline, and cause appropriate suffering, difficulty, and challenge, much as a parent might. Otherwise, why would God give his children limited authority over demonic power? We know Satan is allowed access to God's creation, but that God's intent is that his works be destroyed. For Jesus came to make inoperative the works of the devil.[35]

Catherine Marshall wrestled with this paradox.

> . . . I had felt myself to be in accord with God's will in asking for healing. I loathed the idea of disease and of being sick and had self-righteously set myself not to submit to illness. Thus in my mind there was the sharpest kind of dichotomy between, on the one hand, disease and sickness—the Destroyer's territory, and on the other, wholeness of spirit, mind, body—God's kingdom.
>
> Yet back in 1943 a year and a half of asking on the basis of that dichotomy and of "believing" to the limit of my ability (what I thought was faith) had resulted in—nothing. The reason was, I perceived now, that God would not allow me to get well UNTIL I SAW HIM EVEN IN MY ILLNESS . . . . Blame it on Satan, I might, but see God IN it, I must. He would hold me at that point until I did.[36]

FEAR OF GOD

I have learned that my life is finally and securely in the hands of God, not the hands of the enemy, not even ultimately or finally in my own hands—that is the best news of all. I did not come to this conclusion easily in my own experience.

What is behind this confusing thinking that seeks to limit the Creator from exercising his sovereignty in this area of illness? Perhaps a conversation I had with a young man will enlighten the issue.

During a two hour exchange I sought to explain my position—that God indeed had the right to inflict illness, or give Satan the right to inflict illness, or allow our own neglect or sin to run its course in producing sickness. Each effort to point out God's sovereignty, justice, and righteousness was met with a volatile reaction.

I began to notice that the young man could not contend with the idea of God's having that kind of power or will. His arguments did not rest in biblical reasoning but in fear. That fear was that God might afflict *him*.

But changing doctrine—the doctrine that God may do as he wishes to his creation for his own purposes and in response to his character—to suit oneself will do no more to thwart the plan of God than telling oneself that the rules of a well-played game do not stand. In both situations the game continues as ordered; those who win must play by the rules.

What was missing, as is so often missing in this discussion, are God's other character traits besides sovereignty, justice, and righteousness. God may be the last word, a divine arbiter, and without sin or tolerance for unrighteousness, but he also *loves* his creation. He knows our situation. He is always present to aid us. In fact his many-sided character will dissolve the fear (terror) of those who really seek him. We need never fear one who loves us.

GOD—A LOVING PARENT

Why insist that God cannot inflict illness unless we are in dread and fear of this person and his plan? As long as we turn from our rebellion and indifference, we do not need to fear God any more than a dutiful child fears a loving parent. Caring parents do not shield their child from every difficulty. The younger the infant, the more protection is given; yet as the child matures, the parents carefully lift the shield, instructing the child, and standing with the child, but allowing the son or daughter to encounter life's difficulties. How else can that child grow?

Sickness is only one of the difficulties a wise Father knows is loaded with hearty teaching material. For what reasons would he shield us from its lessons?

Amy Carmichael, who experienced illness the last twenty years of her life, expands this idea:

> What does a child do whose mother or father allows something to be done which it cannot understand? There is only one way of peace. It is the child's way. The loving child trusts . . . . The faith of the child rests on the character it knows. So may ours; so shall ours. Our Father does not explain nor does He assure us as we long to be assured . . . . But we know our Father. We know His character.[37]

The bottom line is that sometimes we have misplaced our fear. We need not fear God who allows and may even bring sickness across our paths for his purposes. The only thing to really fear is missing out on something God has for us—and that may include illness and its many benefits.

It may also include the opportunity of seeing God's great love in spite of a fallen world and its consequences.

Sharon Chrisafulli shares her experience of God's loving concern in the midst of a frightening circumstance:

"*G*ood night, Jason." I leaned down and gently kissed my eight-year-old son's forehead as he snuggled under his comforter. He was wearing his favorite baseball pajamas. His hair, always a little too long, fanned out over the pillow. His eyes were already closed when I turned to leave. But as I was pulling the door shut, he called to me.

"Mom? I just had a dream."

I returned to Jason's bedside. "Honey, you haven't even been to sleep yet. How could you have had a dream?"

"I don't know, Mom. It just came to me right after I said my prayers." His brown eyes held a serious expression. "I was in school, at my desk," he said in a strange, matter-of-fact tone. "All of a sudden, I fell over onto the floor. People were staring at me. I was dead."

I sat with Jason until he fell asleep. His "dream" was disturbing. It seemed more than just a child's imagination.

Several times in my life I'd had similar experiences. I remember suddenly knowing my grandmother would die. Though she appeared to be perfectly healthy, she passed away three days later. And I remember being certain a seemingly happy couple were having deep marital difficulties. I don't know how I knew; I just knew. Outwardly they were the picture of marital bliss. A year later they admitted they had been near divorce at the time.

I went to bed wondering what Jason's dream was all about. Was it some kind of warning?

By the following week, however, the incident had been pushed to the back of my mind. Our home in Merritt Island, Florida, was a busy place, and I had plenty of other things to think about. Jason's school activities and caring for his lively three-year-old sister, Nicole, for example.

Then one night a week later, I sat up abruptly in bed, wide awake. It was after midnight, and Jack, my husband, was sleeping soundly. For a moment I thought it was he who had woken me. But before I could give it another thought, I was overwhelmed with the need to pray—to pray for Jason.

As I eased out of bed, I felt tears streaming down my face. I crept into his room and gathered him into my arms. I cradled his warm body against mine as I prayed. I rocked him as I had when he was a baby. Jason slept soundly through it all.

Then it was over. The need to pray ended as suddenly as it had begun.

The next night it happened again—the sudden need to pray for Jason. And again the night after that.

There was a time in my life when I would have felt silly praying the way I did. There was a time when I would have been afraid. But now I knew it was time to pray and so I prayed.

By the third morning my midnight prayers were
becoming as predictable as the other routines of my life.
As usual, I spent the few minutes before the children woke
up sipping coffee and savoring the quiet. Nicole was
usually the first to rise. But this morning she was still
snoozing even after Jason was up and dressed for school.

It was gloomy and overcast. As I looked out the
window, I was seized by a sense of sadness. Even as I
made Jason's breakfast, my heart grew heavier by the
moment.

I walked Jason to the end of our driveway. Right on
time and with a whoosh of air brakes, the school bus
pulled to a stop across the street, its red light flashing.

Jason and I both looked up and down the busy
highway. I gave him a quick kiss and he was on his way.

He never made it to the bus. His left foot had barely
touched the pavement when a speeding station wagon came
from nowhere and slammed into Jason, hurling his body
fifteen feet into the air. He came down hard, headfirst.

It all happened so fast. Now there he was, lying in
the middle of the highway.

I fell to my knees beside him. His eyes were rolled
back. His tongue was swollen and protruding. In a matter
of seconds his right leg had swelled, straining the fabric of
his jeans. His left arm was bent at a grotesque angle. I
leaned close to his face and realized he wasn't breathing.

"No," I whispered. Then I lifted my head and
screamed, "No, no, Lord, you can't let him die!"

A crowd gathered. They were all staring, horror-
struck.

"Somebody call an ambulance!" I was amazed at the
sudden control in my voice. "And get my husband. He's
working in the orange grove down the road."

I bent over Jason and prayed aloud, "Dear God, I
know you've raised people from the dead. Please raise up
my son!"

I don't know how many people were in the crowd of
onlookers, yet in their midst I suddenly felt a distinct
presence. I glanced up and found myself looking straight
into the eyes of a bearded man standing a few feet away.

He had reddish-brown hair and stood relaxed with both hands in his pockets. Though it was only a second or two, it seemed like an eternity before he spoke in a surprisingly soft voice: "I have oxygen in my car."

Moments later the man knelt beside me and gently placed the mask over Jason's face. Almost instantly, Jason gasped and drew a long breath. Weeping with relief, I leaned over and whispered into his ear, "It's okay, son, just think about Jesus. You're going to be okay."

But when I turned to thank the mysterious stranger, he was gone. And although the road was jammed in both directions, no one saw him leave.

Jason was in the hospital for months. His thigh and arm were broken. He had a severe concussion. But amazingly, there was no permanent damage.

Now, ten years later, I still shudder when I think about what might have happened if I had not heeded those urges to pray, and pray hard. You see, I know that the bearded man who saved Jason's life wasn't just some passing motorist. He was part of something bigger. Something that involved Jason's dream. Something that required my waking three nights in a row to pray for Jason.

That mysterious man was part of a heaven-directed rescue, and he was there in answer to my prayers.[38]

For the one who has yet to place his or her personal faith in Jesus of Nazareth, the resurrected Christ, please consider the following.

"The wages of sin is death,"[39] Paul wrote to the Romans. This is one of the strongest warnings in the Bible. In fact it makes clear that sin leads to the body's final demise.

Whatever form it takes, the body will fail in some manner; some organ will cease, causing all others to malfunction; some system will terminate, causing the others to desist and expire. The Bible makes clear that ultimate deterioration is the result of sin. But physical death is transitory, leading either to spiritual death or spiritual life. According to biblical perspective we will either enter heaven to enjoy the benefits of fellowship with God forever, stripped entirely of disease and difficulty . . . or we will enter hell, alone, separated from all others and separated from the God whose provision of Jesus Christ we refused.

In the meantime how gracious the Almighty is to allow glimpses of such penalty (such as illness) as warning signs to those who have not believed. How gracious he is to let us see discipline and punishment as a means of "waking us up" to divine choices. This is why ill health can actually be a blessing. It leads us to see our own weakness and God's greatness, our inconsistencies and God's faithfulness, our need and God's supply. Further, sickness causes us to confront our own mortality in a manner that few areas of life can. It forces us to consider "the other side."

Let's look again at God's character and see how it relates to areas of sickness and ultimate death.

GOD'S SOVEREIGNTY

God is the King of the universe. He created us. He is the One who will take us off this earth. While we're on earth he, in his sovereignty, has given us free will . . . to a point. He has left us free to acknowledge him, follow him and cooperate with him. However that free choice involves consequences that God as King will carry out. God's desire as King of the universe is that we might live forever with him.[40]

GOD'S RIGHTEOUSNESS

God is perfect. There is no sin in him. We are imperfect. There is sin in us, sickness and decay. A righteous God cannot have true "fellowship" with unrighteous humans. We are apart from him as much as criminals, who desire lawlessness, are apart from those who love integrity. The problem is we are all criminals in God's sight—even the upright (religious, do-gooders, benevolent)—fall short of God's standard whereby intimate fellowship is possible.[41]

GOD'S JUSTICE

We do not naturally seek after God. The purest of us miss the mark time and time again. As the upright long for justice for those who violate the human code of goodwill, God, too, has a sense of justice whereby the guilty are punished. Problem: We are all guilty. How might God's justice be meted out?[42]

GOD'S LOVE

Have you ever wondered what was so right or necessary about Christ's death? Someone needed to bridge the chasm between God and man. Someone needed to make fellowship between a perfect God and "imperfect" humans possible. Love caused the invisible and Holy God to humble himself and become a human being. That human being, both God and man, took the punishment for rebellious and indifferent human beings. All the anger of God which should have been poured out on wayward man was poured out on Christ instead.

Jesus Christ was punished for us. As a result those who acknowledge and believe in the work of Christ on their behalf can be clothed in his forgiveness and righteousness. God's justice and righteousness is satisfied because God himself took the punishment for our sins. Is there any love greater than this?[43]

Eternally Alive

As part of the package, Christ's atoning (payment) death (in our place) and bodily resurrection opened the door for us to live forever with the God who is eternal.[44] Far from simply contending with temporal and failing bodies we can one day have a new, healthy body—one which will last forever.

All-Knowing

God knows all about us. He sees deep into our hearts. More than wanting our current ease and deliverance, God longs for our eternal companionship. The Lord knows who has called upon him for his gracious forgiveness through Christ.[45]

All-Present

Right now God is all about you. He promises his comforting presence to those who come to him. He wants to provide for you right where you are.[46]

All-Powerful

If God did the utmost by sending Christ to die for you—how much more can he do for you if you become his child by placing your faith in Christ?[47]

True

You know truth when you find Christ. He is truth. His word is truth. Jesus said "I am the way, and the truth, and the life; no one comes to the Father, but through me."[48]

Unchanging

Our bodies, minds, and hearts are not dependable. God is. He is trustworthy.[49]

C. S. Lewis comments:

It is after you have realized that there is a real Moral Law, and a Power behind the law, and that you have broken that law and put yourself wrong with that Power—it is after all this, and not a moment sooner, that Christianity begins to talk. When you know you are sick you will listen to the doctor. When you have realized that our position is nearly desperate you will begin to understand what the Christians are talking about. They offer an explanation of how we got into our present state of both hating goodness and loving it. They offer an explanation of how God can be this impersonal mind at the back of the Moral Law and yet also a Person. They tell you how the demands of this law, which you and I cannot meet, have been met on our behalf, how God Himself becomes a man to save man from the disapproval of God. . . . Of course, I quite agree that the Christian religion is, in the long run, a thing of unspeakable comfort. But it does not begin in comfort; it begins in the dismay I have been describing; and it is no use at all trying to go on to that comfort without first going through that dismay. In religion, as in war and everything else, comfort is the one thing you cannot get by looking for it. If you look for truth, you may find comfort in the end; if you look for comfort you will not get either comfort or truth—only soft soap and wishful thinking to begin with and, in the end, despair.[50]

Elise Blair kept an open mind to spiritual truth:

*W*hen I was born Elise Mathisen Blair at Los Angeles' White Memorial Hospital in 1942, no one suspected that anything was wrong. I was an unusually athletic child. My body was lithe and I could get it to do almost anything I wanted. My first love was the California beaches where I swam and resisted the waves with glee. My second love was the violin. I finally opted for the violin, and the practice time required to meet my own standards of excellence resulted in leaving the ocean behind.

I was fortunate to be accepted into the University of Southern California music department. My college career was a joyful experience except for periods when I had difficulty with my arms and legs, and later with severe headaches. Though my endurance was affected, no doctor had the answer. Friends and family were sure that hypochondria explained my frequent periods of fatigue and my need for fourteen hours of sleep at night.

I was elated when, through the recommendation of a principal, I was selected to be one of the first female orchestra conductors for the Los Angeles Unified School District. Here I reveled in the art of working with students and producing fine, harmonious sounds. I was pleased when others throughout the district commented on my unique ability to produce beautiful works of music. Other groups, outside of school, soon called on my talents.

God was important to me. I believed in him. When I stood before orchestras I became keenly aware that he had blessed me with a unique gift. I felt deep gratitude. Such respect for a powerful, loving being helped me endure during a time of personal crisis. Ron, my fiancé, was diagnosed with cancer. I determined to be his comfort and support. In a round-the-clock vigil, I and Ron's family never failed to be with him for nine continuous months until his death. We always made sure someone was there.

On that last day of his life I had an unusual experience. While holding his hand, a favorite nun, Sister Teresa, entered the hospital room. It appeared as if she were wearing a shining halo. At that precise moment a strong light seemed to enter the room. Ron's spirit left its shell. I said my last goodbyes in private. The light remained until others hurried into the room.

After the funeral I traveled to help soften my grief. My Eurorail pass took me to magnificent countries throughout Europe. In Greece an accident was to set me on a downward course. The top bunk to which I was assigned on a Greek passenger ship was without a protective rail. I fell from this bed during the night and suffered a concussion, a broken nose, and a smashed face. After walking around for two weeks with the concussion, I landed in a Greek clinic and spent the next several months there. When I returned to my teaching and conducting, my body showed progressive signs of deterioration. In my seventh year of teaching I was hospitalized and diagnosed as having multiple sclerosis.

The thought of discontinuing my conducting was as oppressive as a death sentence. I mustered any strength I could find to continue my teaching. I still walked but with incredible pain. The stress of hiding my symptoms in order to continue my vocation added to my burdens. I lived a moment-to-moment existence. I did not think to pray.

Finally I knew the battle was against me. I was losing. In September of a new school year I knew my days were numbered as a conductor. I set as my goal, my "finish line," a Christmas musical program; it was the last time I conducted. I retreated to my room. I acquired a wheelchair. I still fought but was forced to retire to a sedate life.

My temperament was not prone to introspection. I did not mull over the "whys" of my disease, feeling such an endeavor was useless. I did not have a need to search out God or philosophical answers. I was occupied with the day-to-day fight for survival. My sister, Trudi, was more in tune with the spiritual side of things. She recognized my need for inner strength and solid answers and encouraged me to attend a Bible study meeting. Despite the fact that I resisted, this effort increased my awareness of the spiritual universe. Later I began to attend church. Here the most dramatic incident of my life occurred.

Each Sunday people who had not previously done so were encouraged to make a public acknowledgment that they believed in God and believed in Jesus. I felt this unnecessary because I had believed all my life. Trudi kept gently insisting that something was missing in my life and that this step would make a difference. I never could quite understand what the problem was and how publicly acknowledging Jesus as my own personal Savior had anything to offer me. Little did I know how great the difference would be between a general belief and an act of my will to call Jesus my own provision for my sin and my single access to a relationship with God.

I made the decision. It could have happened in the privacy of my own car or bedroom. But when I declared Jesus as my God and Savior, it was a vague concept becoming a clear reality. Jesus linked me to God, fully satisfying my spiritual void. My spiritual life began at that point. Whatever frustrations I have incurred since that time—an unresponsive body, the insensitivity of people about me, the financial distresses, fears and shame—Jesus has stood in the gap for me. My inner life, the permanent life of my person, grows despite difficulties with my body. I am a victor by the grace of God.

You can place your faith in Christ. Acknowledge that you, by your own efforts, cannot establish a relationship with God, nor bridge the chasm that exists, due to sin, between you and God. To experience fellowship with your Creator acknowledge that Christ made a relationship with God possible by taking the penalty of sin on the cross for you, and then rose again to prove his victory over sin and death and bring newness of life to you! Personally accept the free gift of forgiveness.

You may wish to make this decision by praying a simple prayer:

"Lord Jesus, thank you for dying for my sin—wrongdoing, failures, mistakes, lack of caring, insufficiencies—and for rising from the dead in order to bring me newness of life. I accept your free gift of forgiveness and ask you to enter my life. I acknowledge you here and now as my personal Savior from sin."

Believing God

Did you ask Jesus to be your personal Savior from sin? Did he do it? He did (if you asked) because he said he would![51] So you can believe your relationship with God has begun. The chasm has been bridged. Your sins are forgiven.

Don't worry if you don't feel different (or if you *do* feel differently now but the feelings go away in a short time). The follower of Jesus Christ lives by faith in God's trustworthiness and in his promises, not by feelings. Feelings can come and go. Sometimes they are a result of believing God by faith. At other times they reflect more the complexities of human personality than the work of God in one's life. The important thing to remember is that Jesus will never leave you once he has entered your life. He said, "I will never desert you, nor will I ever forsake you"[52] and "I am with you always."[53] He gives you eternal life the moment you acknowledge him as your Savior.

> God has given us eternal life, and this life is in His Son. He who has the Son has the life; he who does not have the Son of God does not have the life. These things I have written to you who believe in the name of the Son of God, in order that you may know that you have eternal life.[54]

Points to Ponder

If you have just received Christ as your Savior, I would like to send you some materials that will help you begin to grow in your relationship with him. God has so much more for you! Send me a postcard or letter at the address below, telling me you have made this decision. I will send more information to you. My address is:

> Linda Raney Wright
> Arrowhead Springs
> San Bernardino, CA 92414

1. Have you asked God to heal you? He may be waiting for you to come to him. If you have asked and you are not yet healed, consider his rights and his purposes. Many, it appears, wait before the Lord in regard to healing until they have acknowledged that it is the Creator's right to do as he pleases. Such is the case of Job.

2. There is no problem in life that an understanding of the character of God cannot deal with. It may be helpful to review his character and how that applies to your present situation.

3. Some of the best news in the world is that God has the last word. Rather than seeing Satan with such enormous power, begin to see him rightfully on God's leash. Acknowledge your authority over Satan in Jesus' name.

4. There is *never a need to fear God*. The Bible speaks of a "fear of God" akin to reverential awe that is entirely appropriate. However, fear of God's punishment (if you have acknowledged that Christ bore the punishment for you) is not appropriate. It is true that when we are fatigued and diseased, it seems that God is far away. But in fact he is very near. He has your best interest at heart. Fear of God for one who rejects Christ's provision is another matter. The biblical perspective is that either Christ pays for your sin . . . or you do. There is no greater decision you can make than placing your trust in Christ to deliver you from the penalty of sin (eternal death). If you haven't made the decision of inviting him to be your personal Savior I hope that you will make it soon.

5. This generation needs to understand much about Satan to know how to defeat him. I have written a booklet on spiritual warfare to help you begin to understand this area. It is available by writing to me at the address given above. Send $5.00 for the book; postage and handling included in price.

CHAPTER 6

WHAT FAITH CAN DO

O n one occasion I was fearfully ill. I called a woman for prayer. She came immediately. Up the rose-carpeted stairs she walked to my office. Seating herself in my well-used rocking chair next to a turn-of-the-century handmade quilt, she took my hands and looked straight into my eyes. Her message was surprising.

"Linda," she began. "What God wants you to do is stop taking all vitamins, supplements, and medicine and trust him alone to heal you."

The message confounded me. My mind and heart were in no way prepared for such a directive.

"I'll have to pray about that," I returned. At the time I was fighting a serious infection and a prolonged case of strep. I had been extremely weak.

"You don't need to pray about it," she returned. "At some point you will have to come to 'faith alone' in order to be healed. If you don't do it today, sometime in the near future you will have to let go of everything but God for your healing."

The words sounded very spiritual. She had spoken them with such authority. Of course, I would have loved to go off all outside remedies which often seemed a nuisance and expense.

But instead of sensing the rightness of this direction, I was filled with panic. Would I be living in unbelief not to carry out what this woman said to me? Was "faith only" required? What did this mean?

On another occasion another person proposed, "What you need is faith in yourself. You can overcome sickness if you try."

During years of sickness many asked questions about my health—my lack of it being obvious—and ventured to advise me concerning the matter of "faith." Much of the advice, though well-intended, was polarized and of the "one rule fits all" variety. It didn't help me as much as it confused me.

One woman, Sharon, called often. Each time her message was the same. "Linda, if you just had 'faith' you would be healed." I was certainly willing to be healed, eager to be healed, even desperate to be healed. I prayed every kind of prayer I knew. I asked God for more faith. I meditated on the faith-builder, the Bible. I asked giants in the faith to pray. After receiving several calls with the same theme—if you just had faith you would be healed—I became agitated and depressed with the repetition.

I recalled biblical teaching which suggests that healing faith can come from someone other than the sufferer. The burden of faith needn't be entirely mine.[1] The next time Sharon called I was ready.

"Sharon, are you aware that in the Bible the prayer of faith can bring about healing, even if it isn't offered by the one sick?"

"Yes."

"I've got a deal for you. How about your taking responsibility for a while? If the faith of a friend can do the trick, then you believe for me. Let's see if you can do any better than I."

Sharon prayed with faith. I remained ill.

On another occasion, I had been hospitalized for two weeks. After my discharge I went for prayer at a local church near the hospital. This church was known for great faith and miracles.

"I used to pray for everyone to be healed, believing that was what God wanted me to do," the pastor explained. "But I have learned not to limit the Spirit of God. God may have a higher purpose for you. If it is not the Lord's will that you be healed now, the Lord cannot direct me to pray in faith for you."

Kathy came to visit me at another time of great difficulty. "You're not seeking health zealously enough. You must be like the woman with the issue of blood who never gave up."

"I sought health with my whole being for many years." I explained. "I believed in God for healing. Now I'm trusting him for greater things. I'm tired of seeking my own agenda without results. If God brings me health I'll praise him and use it for his glory. If he does not, I'll praise him anyway."

Life and Philosophy: Do They Match?

Some people live in two different boxes. One box is called philosophy or doctrine and the other is called life. The doctrine or philosophy box (that teaching or experience one assimilates into his mind) goes unquestioned or unchallenged until . . . one day life does not respond to that particular position. Then we begin to question.

True philosophical perspective works in life. We may not always see immediate results. But if rightly understood and applied, it does work. If not, then our perception of some truth must be false or incomplete.

For example: let's say that one is taught that all power for healing resides within. Yet our best efforts result in a progressively worse diagnosis. What if one is taught that if he asks in faith he will be healed? After continuously exercising his faith (and remembering that Jesus said faith the size of a mustard seed would do) he is not healed. At that point a dichotomy may take place between perception of what we think is true and reality. Maybe the perception is 180 degrees off or only 1 percent off the mark. But when one's philosophy is viewed and assimilated correctly, it will ultimately stand the test. The person is no longer required to deal schizophrenically between life and philosophy.

One result of being sick and seeking answers is that sick persons look harder at the case for healing. We have to! Ample opportunity is given to test perspective on healing in real life. Discrepancies between life and philosophy become more apparent—more difficult to ignore.

My own conclusion, after many years of searching, is that putting the whole health puzzle together takes much prayer and determination. One must resist the impulse to:

- make the part the whole (Jesus healed the paralytic; Jesus heals all paralytics)
- exaggerate certain teaching to the detriment of other teaching (Mind control is the ultimate answer.)
- twist principles to get what we *want* ("*Whatever* we ask we receive")
- create philosophies or doctrine based on our own experience

- let current cultural thinking (which comes and goes more quickly than the tide) determine our perspective.

I have seen individuals attribute healing to nearly every type of philosophical and psychological perspective, from adhering to a guru . . . to making *themselves* the ultimate healer. I have seen people use one sick case to mandate what will happen to all others. For example, if Jesus abruptly healed a person they may launch into a crusade—"A great wave of healing is coming to the world." Just as often, a much prayed-over case which was not healed results in a point of view which purports that Jesus does not heal today.

We must investigate the subject of "healing" carefully and humbly, lest we use our own case, or someone else's case, our prejudices, or our lack of experience with the subject, as the ultimate pattern.

Cheer Up; Just Believe

The hype and fluff from the popular emphasis on faith— "Cheer up; just believe," might sour in the mouths of the long-term ill and those who love them. Feeling forsaken, and the "exception" to the rule, some have understandably turned their backs on God. They believe "God's quick-fix system" is true but come face-to-face with the reality that something is amiss.

Others realizing their error modify their views. They replace the drive-through and order up what you want perspective with let's sit and dine at the feet of Jesus. In doing so, they find out God is broader and finer than the self-service God they previously sought.

George A. Buttrick wrote to a war-torn America in 1942 from his best-selling book *Prayer:* "Thus the plea that nearly all our petitions are answered . . . not only is unconvincing, but leaves us morally and spiritually uneasy. For who can be sure of human wisdom, and who could worship so indulgent a God?"[2]

Some others do not relate to God, sensing little reason to speak into the unknown, having even less energy in sickness to search out matters that occupied little of their time in periods of health and leisure. They don't see God as a bellhop or benevolent grandfather; they do not see him at all.

Buttrick continues,

> God is still the Almighty "Other," and "clouds and darkness are round about him." But the pleas that no petitions are answered, and that prayer is only aspiration—perhaps toward some "external power" or perhaps toward "some part of our own nature . . . ordinarily submerged" . . . is also unconvincing . . . We must still "cry out," when the weaving of the tapestry of life's terror and triumph seems to cut across our fondest hopes, for we are still creatures and defenseless.[3]

What Is Faith?

There is probably not a person alive who has not believed earnestly for something, only to receive a different answer than expected. Efforts to claim a passage of Scripture for oneself, organize a prayer vigil, meditate, or seek faith in earnest have often been unproductive. When what we prayed for hasn't been gathered in, there are always those eager to inform us that our "faith" is not great enough.

Jeannette Clift George writes:

> They told me that I didn't have enough faith. So I tried to have more faith. I'd go to my room, and I'd try to look like those people looked when they said it. (I hadn't learned that if you don't have the fact of faith, the look of faith doesn't make any difference. So I worked hard on the look I'd seen in others.) Their faces were perfectly calm until they got to the word *faith*. Then many magic and muscular things happened to their faces. They said, "Jeannette, what you need is more *faith*, and their eyebrows shot up to where I assumed halos were rooted. Their eyes rolled to indicate a heavenly attitude. Apparently, the activated halos caused tension because their voices became breathy and high-pitched. Oh, how I wanted to have just as severe a case of faith.
>
> I figured it began with muscles at the back of the neck. "I'm going to have *faith*." Up went the eyebrows, *"Faith."* Back tossed the head. "Faith." Out with the chin. I practiced. The furrowed forehead. The tension in the scalp line. Nothing. I had a headache but no faith![4]

Believing in What?

Let's look at how faith might apply to the contemporary cultured thinking. Faith is involved in every system of religion, philosophy, cult, belief, position, or creed. Whether one adheres to materialism, spiritism, satanism, humanism, New Agism, or other "isms", faith will be exercised in some measure. One may say that to believe in money doesn't require faith. No, but to believe that money will make you happy is a belief system. Likewise to believe in man's existence doesn't require much faith, but to believe that a human determines his or her own destiny is a faith system. However, faith is not reliable *if* the object of faith is not reliable.

Belief in oneself, is that a reliable faith system?

It is appropriate to believe in oneself *within the limits* that God has designated. God has built humans in such a way that we have resources within us on which to draw. However, God may strip us of the provisions he has built into us in order that we might understand that our resources are from him. But to go past our limitations, believing that we have powers we do not have, is delusion, a misguided attempt at faith.

Many systems or philosophies in which people put faith, even though these systems may temporarily help or solve a problem, may fail in the end. Why? If we take a look at the nature of faith we will find our answer.

What is faith? Faith is a nonmeritorious system of perception. Faith, in and of itself, earns no rewards from God.

Faith, though intrinsically different, is categorized alongside rationalism and empiricism, which are other means of perceiving. For example: rationalism determines truth by means of logic—if it is reasonable it must be true. Empiricism determines truth through the senses—if it can be felt, seen, heard, tasted, or smelled it must be true. Faith, by contrast, relies neither on reasoning nor senses; it *accepts the word of another*; rationalism and empiricism often support such faith.

Why should we "feel proud of ourselves" for exercising a system of perceiving that we live with daily and which requires no real effort on our part? And why should we applaud or belittle another whose "faith" is not strong when faith is simply a vehicle of perceiving which everyone exercises. After all, we sit in a chair because we "believe" it will hold us; fly in a plane because we have "faith" in its ability to keep us airborne; accept the fact that Russia exists "by faith"—most of us never having been there. All these perceptions employ faith.

Object of Faith—The Issue

Faith becomes significant because it can direct itself to various objects. For example: a person can believe in Hinduism or Christianity. Both require faith to accept that particular system as true, but on crucial issues (such as the means of salvation, for example) both cannot be true. Christianity states that it is the only way to God, not one of many ways. If Christianity is true—which isolates it from other religions—other religions must not be true on this point.

What becomes vital is not faith itself, but the object of faith: Is Hinduism the truth? Is Christianity the truth?[5]

One of the trickiest misconceptions to unravel is the idea that "faith makes it so." *Faith* (focusing, meditating) *does not change what is to what is not or vice versa.* One can believe all day that a piano is a chair, and the piano will remain a piano. Or one can believe that a certain viewpoint or philosophy is true, but it continues to have no reliable basis. This type of error in judgment, our minds determine truth, is being perpetuated today.

Johnny had sought health for several years. He talked of faith and his need for it. But as I listened to his emphasis on this perception vehicle—faith—I became disturbed. The idea of "believing" had become very mystical and self-contained to Johnny. To him it was an entity in itself, as if it held some power. The illusiveness of the subject only fed his inability to master the topic. What Johnny erroneously tried to adhere to has confused others as well.

We are never told in the Bible to believe in nothing. We are always instructed to believe in *something* . . . God's plan, God's power, God's justice, God's wisdom. *God can change what is to what is not and vice versa. Faith cannot. We place our faith in God who can move mountains and act to accomplish his will.*

Let's look at misguided faith. "I am believing that God wants me well," a friend told me.

"Has the Holy Spirit convicted you to pray in that manner?" I asked.

"I don't need the Holy Spirit to lead me as I pray," came the light rebuke. "God has already said in the Bible that it is his will that all be healed."

"If God has clearly said it, then you have good ground for believing. Exactly where is this Scripture?" I asked.

At first she quoted 3 John 2, "Beloved, I pray that in all respects you may prosper and be in good health, just as your soul prospers."

"I think that is a wonderful way to pray for someone," I responded. "It's a desire I have for others just as John had. But how does that Scripture confirm that health, especially 'right now,' is always God's will?"

Next she pointed out a verse from the Psalms which said, "As for the days of our life, they contain seventy years, or if due to strength, eighty years."

"It's a great concept," I conceded, "but where is the guarantee?"

She quoted, "With long life I will satisfy him."[6]

"I hope it's true in your case. I really do," I returned.

Finally she quoted, "And everything you ask in prayer, believing, you shall receive."[7]

"You are missing a piece to the puzzle," I answered. "Life is more complex, more grand and encompassing than you are perceiving it." Using the Bible in which she believed to reason with her, I continued. "The angel of the Lord made Jacob lame in order to humble him. Would 'faith' have prevented this or healed him if God had other purposes? The twelve disciples never lived out their lives—eleven of them died as martyrs—only one lived a full life. Did something go wrong with the plan of God?"

Peter, who was tested severely offered this advice to others: "Beloved, do not be surprised at the fiery ordeal among you, which comes upon you for your testing, as though some strange things were happening to you."[8] What happened to the so-called promise of prosperity?

Job was plagued with boils. Until God's purposes were served all of Job's believing for healing would not avail a miracle. Paul wrote that our outer man, the body, is decaying.[9] Will believing prayer alter the aging process or ultimate death, or alter any fixed norm of the Bible? Further, can you move God when he has ultimately declared otherwise?"

What the learned student of the Bible realizes is that life is complex and the Bible is broad enough to meet it. The determining factors of truth do not lie in single verses, structural philosophies or isolated doctrines, but in God, a person and in the whole of his revealed will. When it comes to the subject of faith, the unseasoned in this discipline may be guilty of exercising presumption, not trust; self-fulfilling prophecy, not faith.

How does faith apply? The New Testament presents an interesting illustration of faith in the experience of Jesus and the centurion.

> And a certain centurion's slave, who was highly regarded by him, was sick and about to die. And when he heard about Jesus, he sent some Jewish elders asking Him to come and save the life of his slave. And when they had come to Jesus, they earnestly entreated Him . . . .
>
> Now Jesus started on His way with them; and when He was already not far from the house, the centurion sent friends, saying to Him, "Lord, do not trouble Yourself further, for I am not fit for You to come under my roof; for this reason I did not even consider myself worthy to come to You, but just say the word, and my servant will be healed. For indeed, I am a man under authority, with soldiers under me; and I say to this one, 'Go!' and he goes; and to another, 'Come!' and he comes; and to my slave, 'Do this!' and he does it."
>
> And when Jesus heard this, He marveled at him, and turned and said to the multitude that was following Him, "I say to you, not even in Israel have I found such great faith." And when those who had been sent returned to the house, they found the slave in good health.[10]

This particular episode sheds light on the meaning of "faith." The centurion understood that Jesus had authority because he was "under authority." As a soldier of the Roman Empire, the centurion knew that he could give commands and Rome would back him up. Hence Jesus, whose kingdom was from above, could give commands and heaven would back him up. That perspective spelled the kind of faith God has in mind. Faith in Jesus, whose kingdom is forever, is where healing has its best chance.

It is equally important to note what the centurion did not have. Though he was sure that Jesus "could" heal his servant, he was not adamant that Jesus "would" or "must" heal his servant. Rather he expressed humility, "I am not fit for You to come under my roof."

Neither does the centurion command Jesus to meet his need, rather the Greek language makes it clear that he implored him, "for this reason I did not even consider myself worthy to come to You, but just say the word, and my servant will be healed."

Nor apparently was any emotion poured forth as an evidence of "faith," nor positive assertions, "I believe, I do believe, I will believe." Rather the centurion *understood who Jesus was*.

Faith's Foundation

What is faith's foundation? According to the biblical perspective, faith's foundation is what God *is* and what God *wants*. "And this is the confidence which we have before Him, that, if we ask anything according to His will, He hears us. And if we know that He hears us *in* whatever we ask we know that we have the requests which we have asked from Him."[11]

Evelyn Christiansen, author and lecturer, tells of a situation that occurred at a church where she was speaking. The mother of one of the members of the congregation was ill. The congregation prayed fervently for her healing. She died. The church members wanted to know what went wrong. "Nothing," Evelyn replied. "The prayer we must all be willing to pray is for God's will to be done. The first prayer to pray is, 'Lord, what is your will?' Then, 'How shall I pray?' "

Get in Line with God

Jesus commanded us to pray, "Thy will be done on earth as it is in Heaven."[12] And Isaiah explained:

"For My thoughts are not your thoughts, Neither are your ways My ways," declares the Lord. "For as the heavens are higher than the earth, So are My ways higher than your ways, And My thoughts than your thoughts."[13]

God's desire for us, which is better than our noblest desire for ourselves, can be carried out in the lives of those who seek God wholly. Our part is much bigger than claiming any principle or setting our will to garner what we think we have coming, or insisting that God respond to our "faith." We must get in line with the will of God. We must seek his face and bow to him as our Lord and God. Only then, can we have the Scriptures personally opened to reveal his strategy and purposes. Only then can we be given "faith" to pray and believe according to his will, becoming assured of the results for which we pray.

Author John Edmund Haggai and his wife had anticipated a son who might follow John in helping others. So when the hours grew close for that son to be delivered they had high hopes. Shortly after labor began the medical specialist who was to deliver the baby could not be found. Hours later he entered the hospital. John, upset by the doctor's nonchalant attitude at an extremely difficult pregnancy, did not notice the alcohol on his breath. An error in judgment, fostered by this inebriated doctor culminated in the birth of a retarded child.

In his book *My Son, Johnny,* Dr. Haggai struggles with the possible death of this handicapped son. John and his wife Chris finally prayed, "We place him by faith on Your altar. If it's Your will that he die, take him. But if it can be possible in Your sovereign will, we ask You to heal him. If he lives, whatever the circumstances, we trust you to show us Your plan for his life."

That life of twenty-two years was to have a profound impact on the life and ministry of the Haggais. John later wrote:

> The older Johnny got, the more we saw his disability as a circumstance rather than a handicap. I believe that God endows everyone with the physical and mental traits needed to perform His will for that individual's life. Who can be sure that with a healthy body Johnny would have served God more effectively than he actually did?
>
> Some people might accuse me of being glib about Johnny or say I'm only trying to veneer the painful facts about him. But not so. People assess misfortune in direct ratio to their world and life view. A materialist would see Johnny as a tragic genetic mistake. But God helped Chris and me to see—with clarity and in awe—that Johnny illustrates how unimportant the physical side of life becomes when we measure it beside what is eternal within us.[14]

The Haggais did not trust the air, an idol, a creed, their inner self, a premonition, a saying—"Everything will turn out all right"—, their own prayers, chants, repetition, or the hopes of the doctor; nor did they have faith in a Bible verse or even in faith itself. They placed their trust in God. To state emphatically, *for best results our faith is not initially placed in any one principle or Scripture—but in God himself who does all things well.* This is the God we learn about through the Bible and in whom we place our trust. From that correct starting point he can then direct us as to how to pray and believe.

Positive Confession

What do we make of another popular teaching on healing?

The essence of teaching on positive confession (chanting, repetition, meditation) is that confessing our healing mentally or verbally will bring it about. Some may modify that to read, "may help" bring it about. In some ways this is similar to forming a perspective and making it come about by sheer vocal or mental repetition. Concerning positive confession there are both positives and negatives.

A good attitude can promote health; a bad attitude can impede it. To think positively concerning healing will aid the body by spiriting its defenses. To repress negative feelings, or simply cover them over with antithetical words—the feelings headed one way, the words another—may backfire.

I was disturbed to observe one critically ill woman seeking to relate her fears to a visitor, only to have every negative word rebuked. She would say, "I'm afraid I'm going to die." Her visitor would respond, "Don't say that."

I understood both points of view. The tongue has power, bringing blessing or cursing according to James in the New Testament.[15] That means we can use our mouth to our advantage. Speaking positive words of truth aloud can cement our faith. In contrast, I have seen the concept of positive confession move from an asset to a legalistic requirement inviting fear in those who veer from its course.

One day I tried to maintain a positive outlook. I decided that I would refuse every negative thought and word. I was a basket case within hours. Have you ever tried to center on your thoughts and words indefinitely? As your mind tires, you work harder and harder to make every thought a perfect one. Suddenly a fear enters, or a discouraging chain of thinking. You panic! "I'll die if I think this way." Thinking this is itself a negative confession. You force your thoughts back on course, terrified of your own mind.

What's wrong with the overemphasis on positive confession and much of the confession and chanting encouraged by New Age practitioners? Focusing on positive confession may generate fear when placed as a requirement, and it may also stymie the honesty that is needed for growth. If one looks at illustrations concerning healing in the New Testament, on no occasion did someone come to Jesus saying, "I am well, I am well." Everyone came realizing, admitting, and voicing his own sickness. Each may have expressed that Jesus or the disciples could bring about healing—but none ever denied his state of being.

Who gets the glory for self-healing through positive confessions and chanting? Many claim the glory for themselves by insisting their own efforts made them well.

No one gets well if God doesn't allow it. He has the right and power to take anyone off this earth anytime he chooses. (By the way, the death rate is still 100 percent. No one has ever beaten the odds . . . except Jesus!)[16] How thankful I am that my healing was not dependent on my ability to stay on top with my thoughts and my words. However, speaking the truth aloud was often a great encouragement to me.

One reason positive confession may have results is that a large percentage of illness is psychological. If positive confession works for you, fine, use it. It may strengthen your body's defenses and give you hope or it may alert the enemy (Satan) that his attacks are meaningless. A positive mental attitude is as essential to healing as medicine. But if you are not completely cured using positive confession, God is greater than your ability or inability to voice your faith. If you do get well it is *only* because God permitted it. Health is a gift. So thank him.

Seeking God in Prayer

Many prayer intercessors, initiated into the deeper things of God, understand the principle of letting God direct in prayer. Rather than deciding what verses to claim and what to confess, they seek the mind of God on each matter. A friend, Larraine, commented, "People are always coming up to me and asking me to pray for this miracle or that or to pray for deliverance from a certain problem or for healing. Don't they know that I cannot just press a button to make faith and power ooze from me? God must work in my heart to produce his power in prayer for whom he intends and in what manner he wishes."

Jesus Christ worked under the same principle. The physician, Luke, said of Jesus, "and the power of the Lord was present for Him to perform healing."[17] Could Jesus carry out his own will, or had he come to do the will of the Father? And was it not the Father who legislated when and how his power would be used?[18]

Many of those who pray for healing in large groups make an interesting comment. One woman remarks, "I don't know why some get healed and some don't. I pray believing prayers for all. God knows why some prayers are answered and some are not. That's his department."

The most important ingredient when it comes to faith and prayer is to pray in line with the Spirit of God. Is it possible that some group praying for individuals with different types of healing needs, could impede this singular directive of seeking God's individual will? On the other end of the scale (regarding group healing) isn't it possible that believing faith is evidenced and more active when men and women of biblical faith gather together in strength?

What about the exciting healings that are taking place in the name of Jesus today?

Power and Authority

In a recent article in *Christianity Today* on the increase in Christianity, it was reported that the message of Jesus of Nazareth is spreading most quickly and widely where healing in his name is occurring. Boonma Pathasri, director of a Christian ministry in Thailand, was asked why the message of Christ in Thailand was spreading at one of the fastest rates in the world. "Easy," he answered, "we do what Jesus did. We share the gospel, cast out demons and heal the sick."

The church of Jesus Christ has access to this power.[19] What if it is neglected? What if Peter, one of Jesus' followers, had suppressed his initial urge to command the lame man to "walk!"?[20] That man would not have leapt. He would not have exploded with praise to God or known the powerfully loving touch of God in such an intimate way. Others looking on may have missed the astonishing moment as well as its messages of hope and call to salvation. What a loss that would have been!

Many of us come to this level of faith and conviction—healing in the name of Jesus—slowly. Life's bumps force us to constantly reexamine the Bible. How fortunate to grow in faith, first by realizing what Jesus did to restore our relationship with God and then by learning more of what God has provided. Those of us who know Christ wish to carry forth his love—in whatever manner God may wish to display it—throughout the world.

There is no need to wait for a "gift of healing" in order to pray in faith for the sick. The directive to heal is given to some by way of a gift,[21] but many believe it is given to all who follow Jesus by way of authority granted them by Jesus.[22] We are commanded to pray for the sick regardless of our viewpoint on gifts or authority.[23] Faith may be cultivated by the least of us.

A further reminder: some people have substituted God's power for his purposes. That is, healing is everything, character is nothing. Some go to the other extreme. God's power is exchanged for God's purposes. Character building is everything. Miracles are for another age. God has power and God has purposes. We dare not minimize either or rationalize them away, but seek the mind of the Lord in each direction!

Jesus' Pattern

Note Jesus' pattern of helping others to know him.

> And Jesus was going about all the cities and the villages, teaching in their synagogues, and proclaiming the gospel of the kingdom, and healing every kind of disease and every kind of sickness. And seeing the multitudes, He felt compassion for them, because they were distressed and downcast like sheep without a shepherd. Then He said to His disciples, "The harvest is plentiful, but the workers are few. Therefore beseech the Lord of the harvest to send out workers into His harvest."[24]

Can Jesus' message of love and forgiveness take place without healings? Of course. But who is rightfully going to question that healing in Jesus' name is a wonderful impetus to pointing people to the Savior?

Does Everyone Get Healed?

To set the issue of "faith" right we must grapple with several other questions. First we must come to terms with a common statement expressed today. "Jesus healed all who came to him." This statement poses a set of questions: "You mean anyone who sought his healing, at all times?" "Were there any exceptions?" "What are the ramifications for today?"

On several occasions the New Testament writers wrote that Jesus healed "all" who came to him. In each case however, it is specifically stated about a certain locale.[25] Unfortunately there is no all-inclusive statement made that during his public ministry Jesus healed everyone who wished to be healed or sought to be healed.

The story of the man let down through the roof by his friends illustrates the extremes that individuals went through in order to pass by the large crowds and reach Jesus.[26]

In the midst of those who were seeking Jesus' healing we find Jesus going about his business, often seeking out certain individuals for healing: the synagogue official's daughter, the son of the widow of Nain.[27] In the case of the lame man at the pool of Bethesda, Jesus approached him and asked if he wished healing. The Gospels record only this one incident at a pool where hundreds gathered daily to wait for the angel to ripple the waters and bring healing. "Now there is in Jerusalem by the sheep gate a pool, which is called in Hebrew Bethesda, having five porticoes. In these lay a multitude of those who were sick, blind, lame, withered."[28]

Tiberius was also one of the healing centers of the known world at that time. Here people gathered from every part of the Roman Empire. Yet Jesus did not choose to minister there. Just a cursory reading of the Gospels will exhibit how many times Jesus sought out those who needed healing. But not all who sought healing were helped.

Why is it important to clarify that Jesus' healing is not "guaranteed" for everyone? Why does it matter?

For years I have watched the sick submerged in guilt and loathing because of inaccurate teaching. This happens where our "own" ability to control our destiny is taught at the expense of acknowledging God as our only true hope. Religious superstition suggests that following a creed, earning points, doing penance, or the like will bring about the healing we seek. Unfortunately this teaching happens in some Christian circles where some are guaranteed that Jesus will heal all who truly seek him. The real harm of saying that Jesus healed "all," if in fact he did not, is not just in the facts alone, but in what is made of them.

A preacher I listened to one morning dogmatically asserted that all who sought Jesus out in the Gospels were healed. He then used this argument to assure his listeners that anyone who seeks Jesus today would be healed. He concluded, "If you are not healed, then you are not seeking Jesus. It's as simple as that."

To hearty "amens" he continued, yet I turned to see a young woman sink her head in shame. Had she not prayed and sought out the Lord? Had she not attended healing service after healing service? Hadn't the elders prayed for her tirelessly?

There are principles which if applied will aid the sick. God also has supernatural power that can turn the sick around. But there are no promises that healing is guaranteed to all. Nor have we the ability to manipulate earthly or heavenly forces to serve ourselves at will.

Jesus—The Same Yesterday, Today, and Forever

Another question to consider regarding the area of faith is: "Do those whom Jesus heals ever get sick again?" There is no evidence that those Jesus healed in the first century did not get sick again. In fact Jesus told the lame man at the pool of Bethesda, "You have become well; do not sin any more, so that nothing worse may befall you."[29] Didn't those Jesus raised from the dead die again? Since we still have the ability to make choices even after Jesus has healed us, there is no guarantee that those healed by the Lord will not become sick again.

Isn't the supernatural healing today "in the name of Jesus" different than the healing performed by Jesus two thousand years ago? Essentially no. It wasn't Jesus healing then and his followers healing now. Jesus' followers only have power to heal in his name. And Jesus Christ is "the same yesterday, today, yes and forever."[30] Anyone who states that the healings Jesus performs today are different from those performed in the New Testament has neglected to understand who the healer is.

Prayer of Faith—Elders

Having looked at some clarifying in regards to faith, what ways might one demonstrate healing faith?

About six years into my illness it was suggested that I heed the biblical admonition, "Is anyone among you sick? Let him call for the elders."[31] Two church elders arranged to anoint me with oil and pray for my healing.

We met after church in the children's Sunday school classroom. All about me on brightly decked bulletin boards were little hand drawings of Jesus. Bible promises were displayed so that small eyes could read and believe. How appropriate that we should meet in such quarters where the reminder was clear: the simple faith of a child was all that was asked. There, as I sat in a tiny chair, the words of faith and prayer were exercised over me.

In the next twenty-four hours, two significant things happened. First, a clear idea came to me which I believed was from the Lord, "Seek every reasonable means of getting well."

Second, a letter arrived from a clinic. This clinic would prove to be extremely instrumental in helping me regain health.

What of this exhortation to "call for the elders"? This is a clear command to the sick. James approached this idea by reminding his readers to observe the example of suffering demonstrated by the prophets who spoke in the name of the Lord. "We count those blessed who endured," James wrote. Then he points to Job who endured and how the Lord, who is full of compassion and mercy, rewarded him.[32]

"Is any among you sick? Let him call for the elders of the church and let them pray over him (or her), anointing with oil in the name of the Lord." James continues by saying that in response to the elders praying, "the Lord will raise him [or her] up, and if he [or she] has committed sins, they will be forgiven him [or her]."[33]

By the time an individual is promoted to church leadership it is expected that he or she should be schooled in faith and intercession. Sometimes this isn't the case. Churches should take note that this is a specific responsibility God asks of the local church. We may need to school mature Christians in this task. With the command to "call for the elders of the church"—would not the sick do well to make this call?

There is a further command given by James for the sick. "Therefore, confess your sins to one another, and pray for one another, so that you may be healed."[34] Sin in one's life should be called sin. We are to admit to sin's work in us, without rationalizing or denying its reality, and turn to God for help. James states this confession as a *precondition* of healing for believers.

This command, "Pray for one another that you may be healed," is given to the church at large. This type of prayer by men and women of faith can make a difference. What amazing power believing prayer can generate. Yet what discipline and sacrifice it demands as we seek not our own will, but that of our Father in heaven.

The Holy Spirit and Prayer

How can men and women of God draw on God's strength and Spirit in prayer? The following is essential to understand for receiving God's power in believing prayer for healing.

When an individual becomes a Christian, he or she enters a new dimension—that of the Spirit. The Holy Spirit enters the life. Who is the Holy Spirit? The Holy Spirit is a person in the same way that God and Christ are persons. The three—Father, Christ, and Holy Spirit—exist as one yet perform separate functions. Part of the Holy Spirit's job is to assist us in our relationship with Christ: producing right attitudes, helping us understand the Bible, causing us to honor God in all that we do, and helping us to share what Christ has done for the world with others.[35]

The invisible, yet real Holy Spirit is our helper in all areas of our life. He assists us as we allow him, in all matters relating to health. The Holy Spirit takes the Word of God and applies it to our lives. For that reason we should study the Bible and find out what is available to us.[36]

Even though the Holy Spirit indwells every believer at the moment he or she believes and receives Christ as Savior (Jesus promised this indwelling Spirit for his followers), he can work most freely in those who consciously and deliberately give him that freedom. Quite literally that means that we are allowing him to direct our entire lives, health and all other matters.

It is the Holy Spirit who inspires us to faith or to any effort that aids us and glorifies God. On one occasion I was visiting a shopping mall. My body was so stressed that I sensed a collapse in the works. If I went to my car I might be away from help, but in this busy shopping center I didn't feel safe. I was close to panic.

Suddenly it came to me through the Holy Spirit that this might be an opportunity to express my trust. I raised my eyes to heaven. I spoke aloud. (No one was watching me—except the angels.)

"Before all the angelic host of God I wish to state, 'I am trusting God in this situation.'" Within minutes I was face-to-face with a friend who helped me get back home.

COMMANDED TO BE LED BY THE SPIRIT

Christians are commanded to be filled with (led by, in obedience to) the Holy Spirit: "Be filled with the Spirit."[37]

We are also commanded not to "grieve the Holy Spirit"[38]—don't do what the Bible tells us not to do. And "Do not quench the Spirit"[39]—don't refuse to do what we know we should.

Whenever we seek to exercise "faith," search out the Lord's will, understand our situation, or need strength, we should ask God through the Holy Spirit to lead us and help us. Our daily attitude should be a respect for and yielding to the leading of the Spirit in our lives.

The need for teaching faith and the leading of the Holy Spirit should be balanced by teaching about the bigness of God. I am reiterating the inability of the sick to produce this or that attitude at times or meet this or that requirement. We are not always at a place to "line our ducks up all in a row." When it comes to dealing with ill health, or other difficult areas of life, we may find ourselves spiritually disheveled and groping. From this vantage point we may see God work in spite of ourselves, our understanding, our faith, our obedience.

GROWING IN FAITH

The Holy Spirit helps us grow in faith. One of Jesus' healings illustrates that "growing in faith" is as much the result of healing as healing is the result of faith. Consider Jairus.

And behold, there came a man named Jairus, and he was an official of the synagogue; and he fell at Jesus' feet, and began to entreat Him to come to his house; for he had an only daughter, about twelve years old, and she was dying. But as He went, the multitudes were pressing against Him . . . While He [Jesus] was still speaking, someone came from the house of the synagogue official, saying, "Your daughter has died; do not trouble the Teacher any more." But when Jesus heard this, He answered him, "Do not be afraid any longer; only believe, and she shall be made well." And when He had come to the house, He did not allow anyone to enter with Him, except Peter, John and James, and the girl's father and mother.

Now they were all weeping and lamenting for her; but He said, "Stop weeping, for she has not died, but is asleep." And they began laughing at Him, knowing that she had died. He, however, took her by the hand and called, saying, "Child arise!" And her spirit returned, and she rose up immediately; and He gave orders for something to be given her to eat; And her parents were amazed.[40]

There is an important lesson in this healing. The father was afraid. He mocked Jesus' power. He was encouraged by Jesus to believe, but after the healing he was still "amazed"; not usually typical of a solid faith—faith expecting to actually see results. Yet Jesus healed his daughter. His faith in Jesus' power grew in the process. In the case of the raising of Lazarus from the dead,[41] faith was specifically lacking as well.

Fear and faith need not be seen at opposite ends of the pole. Faith may bring about healing. But God may use healing to bring about faith even in the midst of our worst fears.[42]

I asked a number of sick individuals what they did to grow in faith and trust. The replies? Bible reading, Bible memorization, fellowship with faith-oriented followers of Jesus, praise, reading faith-oriented books, worship services, Bible studies, Christ-centered radio and television programming, inspiring music, praying the Word aloud, recalling God's faithfulness in the past, prayers of others, the confidence that their friends or church were standing with them in their time of need.

Growing in faith should be our goal. I used to pray daily, "Lord, increase my faith." God kept sending trials. He would deliver me. I grew in faith. An individual should be careful not to mix faith in the biblical God with a multitude of other "faiths." There is a subtle temptation to lump the trendy philosophies together and produce a recipe of enlightened confusion, at best, and serious, sometimes eternal consequences, at worst. If you really want answers that last, let the Bible and the biblical God be the standard by which everything else is weighed.

If I Had More Faith

I finally found an answer to the advice so often given me, "If you had more faith you would be well." I realized that it took far more faith to live with sickness than to live in health.

We are often called to believe "in the midst" of a situation and through all its stresses. God graciously gave me ample opportunity to use and stretch my faith. That faith—continuing with the Lord in spite of the obstacles—is what life is made of!

Our faith or lack of it is not the last word, as the father of the epileptic told Jesus, "I do believe. Help thou my unbelief."[43] How easy it is to understand this father's plea. Faith does not come easily to us. "Lord, help us to believe you!"

Jonathan Goforth was an evangelist and a missionary to China. His wife Rosalind writes:

> It was our third or fourth visit to Pengeheng, an important center, sixty li northwest of Changte . . . just as we arrived, the weather turned bitterly cold and windy . . . . Almost at once Mr. Goforth caught a severe cold which rapidly grew worse with apparently high fever (I had not my clinical thermometer with me), and severe pains in head and chest and difficulty in breathing. In spite of my protests he insisted on taking his meetings, but about the third day he came in at noon looking so very ill I became alarmed. He would take nothing to eat and lay down saying he would be ready for the afternoon meeting.
>
> I was in despair. Changte was too far away for help from friends there and the roads were almost in impassable condition. I could only cry to the Friend who never fails. Then thinking Mr. Goforth was asleep, I slipped out and sent a messenger around to call the Christians to the tent. When they had gathered, I told them of my anxiety and of Mr. Goforth's symptoms. As I ended by saying, "Oh, pray for him!" I broke down and wept. Oh, what prayers then arose—earnest, heart-flow of prayer such as I had never heard!

As I listened my heart was comforted and I thought, "Surely God will hear such prayers!"

This continued for some time, then fearing Mr. Goforth might arrive, I gave out a hymn. A few moments later he walked into the tent in his old brisk way, looking quite well. As soon as I could get to him at the close of the meeting I said, "Jonathan, you seem quite better." He replied "Praise God, I am." He then told me how a short time after he had heard me go out the fever seemed to leave him, his head and chest ceased to pain, he could breathe easily and he felt quite well. The symptoms did not return.[44]

FAITH WITHOUT WORKS IS DEAD

The Lord showed me an additional insight about faith, as a result of my friend's visit (mentioned in the first part of this chapter). She had said to me that until I came to "faith alone," without treatment, I would not be healed. The phrase "faith only" sounds like the ultimate in healing—the *summum bonum* of healing and answered prayer. Perhaps it is. I may be a bit too practical.

The Bible has as much to say about how we *live* as how we *believe*. Let me illustrate: I look upon my body as a house structure encasing a person. I realize that just as actual houses are of varying size and soundness, so bodies are the same. If I believe God to protect my house, cannot I also fortify my windows, patch the cracks, and lock my door?

If I cover my house with the blood of Jesus should I not also strengthen a faulty foundation? Are the two incongruous? Does "faith" limit human responsibility?

As I pondered the removal of my therapies, in response to "faith alone," I reasoned that probably everyone took some precautions. Even the healthiest person has to eat sometime. Would not faith alone include total abstinence? Even the most trusting one needs sleep. For the ill it may be a matter of degree as to what is required to maintain the house—what additional things may be added to fortify the temple. We need more nutritious meals and more sleep. We may also need therapy. These don't need to be at odds with faith.

Of course there is plenty of biblical precedence for such a directive. John, one of Jesus' followers, wrote of such a healing. A blind man was brought to Jesus by his followers.

Jesus said, "While I am in the world, I am the light of the world." When He had said this, He spat on the ground, and made clay of the spittle, and applied the clay to his eyes, and said to him, "Go, wash in the pool of Siloam" . . . And so he went away and washed, and came back seeing.[45]

It is interesting to note that a natural element was added to this healing—clay and washing. This is not an exception to New Testament healing. In the book of James it is written, "Is anyone among you sick? Let him call for the elders of the church, and let them pray over him, anointing him with oil in the name of the Lord."[46]

The oil used in this passage is the same kind of oil used by the disciples, "And they were casting out many demons and were anointing with oil many sick people and healing them."[47]

Some believe that the oil may have symbolized the Holy Spirit. Others have suggested that the oil may have symbolized medicinal care since this same kind of oil is used in the story of the Good Samaritan representing a medicinal use, "and bandaged up his wounds, pouring oil and wine on them."[48]

This point may not be conclusive, but it causes one to consider whether Jesus promoted healing using God's provisions within nature.

How Complete Is Healing?

Within the framework of "faith," how complete is healing?

My friend Gwen shares the story of her friend who had multiple sclerosis. This woman later acquired cancer. In a special prayer service she was instantly and completely cured of cancer. A doctor verified this, but also confirmed that she was not healed of MS. Was Jesus playing guessing games with the woman?

Ten years later the woman's cancer recurred. Why? Possibly because there was no change in diet and lifestyle or no growth in taking authority over disease and demonic influences. Maybe certain stress patterns in her life were never addressed. Perhaps God's plan was not diligently sought by the woman, leaving her vulnerable to the world, the flesh, and Satan. Maybe it was simply God's time to take her home. The reason may not be revealed to us.

But shouldn't we keep on searching for answers? Shouldn't we also beware of using catch-all statements such as "It was God's will" or "It was for the best" when we haven't done our part to deal with our own bodies, minds, and lives, or even seriously considered what Jesus may have to do with the matter?

Catherine Marshall, who writes of her healing of tuberculosis after Jesus appeared to her,[49] suffered nonetheless with lungs which worked only slightly above 60 percent capacity for the rest of her life. Yet Catherine contends that Jesus healed her of tuberculosis.

What might the Bible mean by healing in light of these two instances of partial healing? Francis Schaeffer, theologian and philosopher, coined the phrase "substantial healing" to explain biblical healing. There is good basis for this view. The apostle Paul, inspired by the Holy Spirit, wrote that our outer body is in the process of decaying.[50] This pretty well sums up the direction we are all heading. Total healing—a new body altogether—is promised to all those who look to Jesus, the Savior, but only in heaven.[51] For now we need to make do with an earthly vessel which can and does easily go astray. It must be carefully maintained.

Anyone receiving healing or working toward healing will never come to the place where neglect is advisable. The term "substantial healing" is appropriate in light of the anticipation of a new and completely healed body some day. Thank you, Jesus, for what you've accomplished for us all. Help us maintain that which we've been given.

The ways of our God are such that we must return to him again and again. In the last analysis our lives do not fully stand on faith or leading or treatment. They must stand on God himself. Though we must seek to continue growing, understanding, and exercising principles of Scripture—and are at times seriously hampered when we do not—it is always consoling that God gives ear to our cry.

More on prayer follows . . .

Points to Ponder

1. Do you have trouble between what you believe and what works in life?

It might be good to think through exactly what you believe. Get a Bible and search that out for yourself asking the biblical God to aid you in your study and open your eyes to understanding.

2. Is faith (focusing, channeling, chanting, meditating) a legalistic exercise to you? Is it mystical and without power? Remember it is the object of true faith that should have our attention. You cannot help but grow in workable faith if you are seeking the true God and his revelation through the Bible.

3. As you think through your own "faith" ask yourself, "What is the object of my faith?" "What do I believe is the most important element of my faith?" "How have I been praying concerning my health?" "Does it have a basis in the Bible?" "Is my faith in a person, a principle, or both?"

4. Are you seeking God in prayer or are you merely seeking health? Is your "faith" a cover for selfish ambition, a platitude you're used to using—"I think everything's going to work out all right"; or is there real substance to your faith?

5. Have you sought the prayers of others? Prayer chains? Church elders? Men and women of God? Group meetings?

CHAPTER ❦ 7

PRAYER AND HEALING

*H*ow did I survive?

How is it that with so many serious ills I am alive and healthy today?

Answer. The Lord got me through. His assistance was moment by moment as well as day by day. At pivotal and life-threatening moments, he instructed me and gave me sure guidance. What do I mean?

Led by the Spirit

Divine guidance seems to be the common denominator by which many touch the garment of God in regards to healing. The New Testament reports that the "mature" son (or daughter) of God is "led by the Spirit of God."[1] The New Testament makes it clear that individual guidance is the norm for Christians.[2] Such leading is also the proper foundation and assurance of healing. God can and does instruct those who seek him in the ways of healing.

Rees Howell, a leading Christian statesman, whose fervent prayers affected the outcome of world events, writes concerning health and inner guidance, "To tell other people not to take medicine, when we are not sure of our guidance, is nothing less than tragedy, if they die. But I know of cases where people were guided not to take medicine and had victory all through their lives."[3]

I use here a diagram to help the reader understand the nature of Spirit leading in regards to health. God leading us and the Holy

Spirit leading us are used interchangeably in this discussion. Following is how I was directed.

Veiled Plan of God   Believing Prayer

> Spirit-Led Life

Obedience to God's   Spiritual Authority
Revealed Will

In the center of the box is my relationship with the Lord. By his Spirit he would lead me day by day—even hour by hour—in the direction that was best for me. In response to my prayer for help, God would direct me to various corners of the box—whichever provided the answer.

VEILED PLAN OF GOD

In the left-hand upper corner was the VEILED PLAN OF GOD. This corner referred to a "higher plan" which I was not capable of knowing or understanding at the time. Though God's purposes were veiled, I could still be assured that he was in control. The directive, should his Spirit alert me to that corner, would be to "trust" and "wait." God knew best. He would provide at the proper time whatever was most helpful to me and glorifying to himself. Many times in twenty years, this was his word to me:

"My times are in Thy hands."[4]

"In my own time I make all things beautiful."[5]

"Rest in the Lord and wait patiently for Him."[6]

"And we know that all that happens to us is working for our good if we love God and are fitting into His plans."[7]

Regarding this corner (the veiled plan of God) many saints throughout the centuries have written of the adequacy of God, the personal growth, the preparation for ministry which has transpired in their lives, of long awaited prayers being answered, of higher purposes performed in response to a season of illness.

"God is never in a hurry but spends years with those He expects to greatly use. He never thinks the days of preparation too long or too dull."[8]

"There are two ways of getting out of a trial. One is to simply try to get rid of the trial, and be thankful when it is over. The other is to recognize the trial as a challenge from God to claim a larger blessing than we have ever had, and to hail it with delight as an opportunity of obtaining a larger measure of Divine Grace."[9]

"When God delays, he is not inactive. He is getting ready His instruments, He is ripening our powers; and at the appointed moment we shall arise equal to our task."[10]

One afternoon I received a letter in the mail from a well-known Christian leader. I had written this man because he spoke with such confidence that God's will is for all to be healed. How amazed I was to open his letter and hear from him the same message that God had steadily put on my heart. He wrote, "I believe God has a purpose in your illness. Wait on the Lord."

Another woman struggled with this issue:

"The many approaches I took towards healing did little more than lead me into deeper introspection and more frustration," writes Ruthe White in her book, *Touch Me Again, Lord*.

> I tried everything! Having accepted Christ as personal Savior at the age of eight, I could quote Bible verses like a spiritual pro. As a teacher active in church work, I had quick answers to everyone's needs. As a Christian I was trying to put the puzzle of life together, and some of the pieces were missing!
>
> Then one Sunday afternoon when my husband and our two daughters (who had lovingly cared for me during my long illness), had gone to church, I found myself alone and desperate. I dropped my tired body onto the floor and began to weep. Finally, I grew weary from my crying. Too weak to pray, I just lay there quietly. All sense of time was lost in the solitude of the moment . . . . My thoughts took me into the biblical account of where Christ appeared to His disciples, as they were on the Sea of Galilee. I visualized His coming to them in the midst of the storm. He spoke "peace" to them. That was what I needed! I wanted His peace to calm the troubled waters of my soul. Suddenly I knew that even though I didn't understand life, I did know Him! I asked to know His peace, and He gave it to me!
>
> The knowledge of His presence brought with it an inner psychological and emotional healing. The turmoil inside me was gone the very moment *I became aware of his touch* . . . . But there was no instant physical healing. No visible change took place in my life and it was three years before my health was restored.[11]

Ruthe White travels widely today, speaking and writing on many topics.

When God has a plan for good in the making, we can be sure that our lives are in good keeping! Is he saying "no"? Is he saying "wait"? God's plan may be veiled from you . . . it's not veiled from him. If you know Christ as your own Savior and are seeking the Lord's will, then you can confidently wait on God. God knows best! Trust him!

BELIEVING PRAYER

Concerning the same prayer for God's will, God may direct me to the upper right corner Believing Prayer. "I am healing you. Stand on my promise to you. Do not waver. Trust me alone."

Such direction from the Holy Spirit was often given to me, both for provision in spite of ill health, and to believe him for the full return of health.

"No distrust made him (Abraham) waver concerning the promise of God, but he grew strong in his faith as he gave glory to God, fully convinced that God was able to do what he had promised."[12]

"For I, the Lord, am your healer."[13]

"Do not be afraid *any longer;* only believe, and she shall be made well."[14]

On one occasion Billy Graham stated, "I would have cancelled Sweden—the doctors didn't want me to go—but I felt I could trust the Lord and I went; and I think that God greatly honored it."[15]

I have been given similar direction. Invited to speak in two classrooms at Cornell University, I found that on the particular day when my second lecture was to be given, I felt unable to stir from my bed. I sought the Lord for his will knowing that if he led me, he would enable me, but if I foolishly neglected my health I might suffer serious consequences.

All morning I had talked with God about his decision—whether I should proceed or cancel the lecture. An hour before the talk I sensed that God was directing me to the believing prayer corner; I was to trust him for my speaking engagement.

I forced myself from bed and got dressed. A student picked me up from the quaint bed-and-breakfast inn where I was staying and drove me through the beautiful autumn-leafed town of Ithaca,

New York, to the campus. But my eyes weren't grasping the majesty of the scenery. Feeling that I might faint at any moment, I was concentrating instead on the promises of God.

I sat in the back of the classroom, head in my hands, my worried friends praying. When I was introduced, I stood, walked to the front of the class, spoke for forty minutes on "The Biblical Perspective On Women," and answered questions for an additional fifteen minutes. No one could tell I was ill. The response from the class was very positive. I was "given" strength. Within minutes after the class was dismissed I was rushed back to the motel, feeling as ill as before I spoke.

This kind of incident, believing God for specifics, happened so often to me that it became a way of life. I learned to count on God to raise me up to do his will no matter how ill I felt previous to some ministry.

But I also sensed God's encouragement to believe him for total healing—healing in spite of constant setbacks, unavailable treatment, mental discouragement, and difficult circumstances. Some of this encouragement came from others.

I am privileged to have several very special friends. Years ago one of them searched the Scriptures on my behalf. On the flyleaf of her Bible she marked my name beside verses on healing. For many years she never stopped believing that God would raise me up. Her faith has helped my faith.

It seems that at critical points there have been those "instruments" of God who have looked wide-eyed at my situation and pronounced, "Linda, God is going to heal you."

What if the sick person has no prayer support? I had also struggled with my lack of prayer support. At times I felt that if I had more prayer support I would be well. But I was encouraged to learn from the prayer of Hezekiah. Here is the story of a man whom God heard and healed:

> Hezekiah became deathly sick and Isaiah the prophet (Amoz'
> son) went to visit him and gave him this message from the Lord:
> "Set your affairs in order, for you are going to die; you will not
> recover from this illness."
> When Hezekiah heard this, he turned his face to the wall and
> *prayed:* "O Lord, don't you remember how true I've been to you
> and how I've always tried to obey you in everything you said?"
> Then he broke down with great sobs.

So the Lord sent another message to Isaiah:

"Go and tell Hezekiah that the Lord God of your forefather David hears you praying and sees your tears and will let you live fifteen more years."[16]

This is one of my favorite stories because God altered his message in response to an individual's prayer. (Some say that Hezekiah should have chosen death since two sons born during those fifteen years became antagonists of the causes of God. It is a reminder, of course, to be careful how we pray. But there is no recorded discourse on God's part which implies that the one prayer for healing produced the other wayward sons.) It should be encouraging that God has eyes and ears open to the pleas and prayers of his children. What should you be believing him for today?

SPIRITUAL AUTHORITY

Still another corner of the box the Holy Spirit might direct me to is that of Spiritual Authority. Perhaps the enemy was inflicting sickness or stresses contributing to my illness. Perhaps I needed to rise up against him and the infirmities within my own body, taking authority in the name of Jesus.

"I have given you authority over all the power of the Enemy . . . Nothing shall injure you!"[17]

"And [He] gave them power and authority over all the demons, and to heal diseases."[18]

John Wesley maintained that the church practiced this authority over demons and disease well into the fourth century, but largely lost it after that time due to unbelief.

Today, many practice this authority which Jesus made available to his followers. Viv Grigg, missionary to the Philippines and a former Navigator, writes of taking authority over the demonic world in his book, *Companion to the Poor:*

> Deliverance was coming to the community, but Satan was also a kicking, fighting antagonist who would not lie down. Usually on Saturday evenings before a day of such ministry, he would attack violently with sickness . . . *but he was never the victor.*

Grigg goes on to speak of the believer's authority to "bind the strong man" who often stirs up illness and infirmity.[19]

In her book, *Defeated Enemies,* Corrie Ten Boom relates

how God used spiritual authority in the case of one of her ill-nesses:

> What a joy it was to bring the good news of Jesus' victory into the darkness! But whenever I gave this message, I was so tired I could hardly reach my bed. My heart beat irregularly, and I felt ill.
>
> One evening I had a long talk with my heavenly Father. "I cannot continue like this, dear Lord . . . . Perhaps another month or two, and then my heart will give out!" Then in the Losungsbuck, a daily devotional book in German, I read, "Be not afraid, but speak, and hold not thy peace. For I am with thee, and no man shall set on thee to hurt thee" (Act 18:9–10). A short poem follows:
> Though all the powers of hell attack
> Fear not, Jesus is Victor!
> Joy filled my heart. This was God's answer! I prayed, "Lord, I shall obey. I will not fear and be silent. But with my hands on this promise I ask you to protect me with your blood, that the demons cannot touch me."
>
> At that moment something happened to my heart; it beat reg-ularly. I knew that I was healed.[20]

Corrie Ten Boom understood demonic power and how to bind the enemy from direct physical assault. In *Five Silent Years of Corrie Ten Boom* Pamela Rosewell writes of Corrie's last years. A stroke had taken her communication skills and left her vulnerable in other ways. Pamela writes:

> A regular part of life was the stand that it was necessary to take against the attacks of the devil. Tante Corrie went through some dark moments when she was confused and downhearted. One such moment occurred in the spring seven months after her stroke. She became agitated, and Lotte and I tried to calm her. Human effort was not sufficient. She remained upset.
>
> "Corrie," said Lotte, "I believe that this is an attack of the enemy. He would try to take away your joy. Let's pray."
>
> Tante Corrie consented immediately.
>
> "Father," prayed Lotte, "we come to You in the mighty name of Jesus Christ and we take authority over the devil who is trying to confuse and frighten Corrie. We resist him in Jesus' name and we pray that in the place of confusion You will bring Your peace and comfort. Thank You, Father. Amen."
>
> At once Tante Corrie calmed down and her tranquility was restored. It was one of many similar instances during those months.[21]

Many years into my own illness I began to think, "Did God want me to begin acting in faith against demons who might be inflicting me with illness? Did God want me to be aware of attacks by Satan on my mind and forbid him to do so?" The answer was yes.

Further, did God wish me to take authority over disease in my own body? But how could someone take authority over disease? A close look reveals that germs are alive. Watch their determination to invade and destroy, and one will get a better idea why we are to take authority over them.

I now ask the Lord if he wishes me to take authority over demons or disease in regard to health. So does a dear friend of mine. Kathleen's best efforts had proved futile at stopping advancing carcinoma. Even after her victory over cancer she entertained a "victim" mentality which she couldn't shake. Even Scripture reading and prayer failed to erase the gloom and fear. Until . . . she learned how to stand against the enemy. Kathleen forbade spirits of infirmity, guilt, hopelessness, discouragement, and fear to trouble her further. As a result, Kathleen's attitude changed drastically. Her "victim" mentality was replaced with a "winner" mentality.

Jesus said "first bind the strong man (Satan)."[22] If we learn preventive spiritual warfare—commanding Satan and his demons to get off our lives—*before* the onset of disease and related problems, many of us might be spared illness. Which brings us to our fourth corner.

OBEDIENCE TO GOD'S REVEALED WILL

Jesus said, "If you keep My commandments, you will abide in My love."[23]

Solomon wrote, "Trust in the Lord with all your heart, and lean not to your own understanding. In all your ways acknowledge Him and He will direct your path."[24]

This final corner—obedience to God's revealed will—was a frequent directive.

- "Linda, release the resentment and your body will do better."
- "Linda, you have been careless with your diet."
- "Linda, you are not trusting me with your schedule. You

are operating in the power of the flesh, not the Spirit. You have overdone and your body has paid the price."
• "Linda, work on this treatment now."

The ten lepers present an intriguing study of the place of obedience in healing.

> And as He entered a certain village, there met Him [Jesus] ten leperous men, who stood at a distance; and they raised their voices, saying, "Jesus, Master, have mercy on us!" And when He saw them, He said to them, "Go and show yourselves to the priests." And it came about that as *they were going,* they were cleansed."[25]

Obedience was required of the ten lepers as a prelude to healing. How serious is obedience? Hear this Old Testament story:

> The King of Syria had high admiration for Naaman, the commander-in-chief of his army, for he had led his troops to many glorious victories. So he was a great hero, but he was a leper. Bands of Syrians had invaded the land of Israel and among their captives was a little girl who had been given to Naaman's wife as a maid.
> One day the little girl said to her mistress, "I wish my master would go to see the prophet in Samaria. He would heal him of his leprosy!"
> Naaman told the king what the little girl had said, "Go and visit the prophet," the king told him. "I will send a letter of introduction for you to carry to the king of Israel."
> So Naaman started out, taking gifts of $20,000 in silver, $60,000 in gold, and ten suits of clothing. The letter to the king of Israel said: "The man bringing this letter is my servant Naaman; I want you to heal him of his leprosy."
> When the king of Israel read it, he tore his clothes and said, "This man sends me a leper to heal! Am I God that I can kill and give life? He is only trying to get an excuse to invade us again."
> But when Elisha the prophet heard about the king of Israel's plight, he sent this message to him: "Why are you so upset? Send Naaman to me, and he will learn that there is a true prophet of God here in Israel."
> So Naaman arrived with his horses and chariots and stood at the door of Elisha's home. Elisha sent a messenger out to tell him to go and wash in the Jordan River seven times and he would be healed of every trace of his leprosy! But Naaman was angry and stalked away.

"Look," he said, "I thought at least he would come out and talk to me! I expected him to wave his hand over the leprosy and call upon the name of the Lord his God, and heal me! Aren't the Abana River and Pharpar River of Damascus better than all the rivers of Israel put together? If it's rivers I need, I'll wash at home and get rid of my leprosy." So he went away in a rage.

But his officers tried to reason with him and said, "If the prophet had told you to do some great thing, wouldn't you have done it? So you should certainly obey him when he says simply to go and wash and be cured!"

So Naaman went down the Jordan River and dipped himself seven times, as the prophet had told him to. And his flesh became as healthy as a little child's and he was healed!"[26]

What if the ten lepers and Naaman had not obeyed? Are you waiting for God to tell you some big thing to do in order to get well? Have you pre-programmed your life that "such and such" must take place before healing can happen? You had best find out what God wants of you and begin doing it.

Some have testified that the Lord asked of them certain things in order to precipitate healing. Catherine Marshall was made conscious of righting the wrongs in her life. She wrote a series of letters asking forgiveness. Others have been directed to: begin walking a little more each day, change their diet, deal with wrong attitudes, change treatment, begin ministering to someone else, face a fear that has been avoided for a long time, admit to a particular sin in their life. The wise individual will pay attention to any call of God.

One such experience of the latter corner—Obedience to God's Revealed Will—came near the beginning of my illness in 1970, when I was a student at the University of California at Berkeley. God had provided free housing for me at the Baptist Student Union. This old building, situated two blocks from campus and one block from famous Telegraph Avenue, had been recently vacated. I was allowed to live there by myself in exchange for keeping the main rooms clean for various meetings held during the week.

Having my choice of any room in the four-story structure, I decided to occupy one on the second floor. A quilted spread, a coffee percolator, and vases of flowers picked from the property's unkempt garden were the only color and sole flavor in an otherwise dingy abode.

At the time I was living at the BSU I was also having trouble concentrating in classes, sometimes unable to put two and two together to get four. One evening, I felt especially helpless mentally. I got up and walked about the building. My mind was definitely not connecting as it should. In panic I cried out. "Lord, help me."

Immediately the thought "potassium" entered my mind. Having no previous knowledge of this mineral, I went the next day, after a fitful night's sleep, to have a potassium test made. Sure enough, a potassium deficiency was accounting for mental anguish and physical fatigue.

All of us, it seems, must abide by the rules our bodies set. No one seems to be entirely exempt from these physical laws. In the authorized biography of Billy Graham, John Pollack writes:

> The Billy Graham ministry has not been powered by a fit man's energy. Billy has paid a high price in strain on his health. For years he had a succession of "physical problems from time to time that have either weakened me or been irritating enough to humble me" . . . . He learned gradually to live more within the limitations of his strength until his health was better. . . .[27]

When I hear of individuals trying one treatment after another that doesn't help them or makes them worse, I am reminded that every clear directive of the Lord, every treatment he provided for me, worked to help my body in some way. But then I was seeking his will, not arbitrarily listening to this or that piece of advice.

One of the boulders in my road of faith came when a lump was discovered. For twenty-four hours I cried uncontrollably. When it was affirmed that the lump was definitely not a mere cyst—and was possibly cancerous—I lost all sense of time and space, unable to assess the situation.

The surgeon warned that an immediate operation was in order. Believing the Lord had directed me to try a natural treatment first, I traveled across the country by plane to a small clinic in rural Georgia. Special diet and other treatment were given to me.

When I returned home the surgeon checked me. No change. But I sensed that God was going to use this particular treatment to heal me of this lump. Periodic returns to the surgeon confirmed that the lump was decreasing. In five months it was gone. I reaped other health benefits as well from the strict dietary measures. Such are the benefits of "listening to the Lord."

Isn't it terrific that God works in so many dimensions. He has provided numerous possibilities of getting well, or triumphing regardless. I have observed "hopeless" cases and difficult diagnoses being remedied by medical doctors, preventive medicine, dietary changes, herbs, common sense, prayer, spiritual warfare, taking authority, etc. For this reason the Christian should be mindful to seek the Spirit concerning what specific thing he or she should be doing. No one is going to give you better advice than the Lord!

Putting It All Together

One woman's experience incorporates all four of the Spirit's directives—waiting on God's veiled plan, believing prayer, spiritual authority, and obedience. (God may use all four simultaneously.) Jane Prall of College Station, Texas, could hardly contain herself as she announced to me, "I've been healed, Linda. God has healed me." I was anxious to hear the story.

Jane's primary health problem existed in her colon. Sluggish at first, it soon produced impurities and infection. The next phase included an ulcerated colon with internal bleeding requiring hospitalization.

"I was seeking the Lord throughout this time," shares Jane. "I prayed, 'Whatever you want Lord.' I got worse!"

Doctors advised Jane that a colostomy was needed if she didn't improve. In the meantime she was placed on twenty-two tablets of medicine a day—twelve sulfur and ten cortisone. She weighed 145 pounds going into the hospital. Within weeks, due to the medication, she went up to 192 pounds.

In December of 1978, a brief time later, God sent a special woman into Jane's life. One would not expect the deep gifts of spiritual understanding to be embodied in such an unassuming woman. Perhaps, like Elijah, who would accept no gifts from Naaman for his healing and who wouldn't even come out of his house to make a big display of his healing power, this woman had no need of announcing her ministry. She simply loved Jane and ministered to her, explaining that she had felt led by the Lord to help.

Never had Jane experienced supernatural healing or personally known of anyone who had. Nor had she experienced anyone laying hands on her and praying in faith against the enemy. Her philosophy/doctrine had not embraced such possibilities.

February 8, 1979, was a decisive day. At 2:00 P.M. the woman arrived at Jane's home. She explained to Jane that she was being directed by God to pray for her healing. Jane knew nothing of the deep Bible intake and intercession on the part of this woman that had led up to this moment.

"She laid her hands on my head. She claimed biblical promises of healing for me. She commanded that my body function normally. She addressed spirits of infirmity, doubt, unforgiveness, and unbelief, commanding them to leave in the name of Jesus. I could sense the power of her words. When she finished I could tell no difference. That night as I went to bed I became more ill. All night I excreted foul-smelling feces—after not having a normal bowel movement in six months.

"In the morning I knew I was healed. My depression was gone. My doctor's appointment was that day. I walked in and announced, 'I'm beautiful today.' Testing confirmed that all putrefaction and infection were gone. Complete healing of the colon had taken place."

But Jane's story does not stop here. "After the healing God directed me to some specific health instructions: no coffee or sugar. Instead I was to praise Him." But Jane did not follow these instructions.

"I was high-strung. My nervous condition made me sharp-tongued with my family. I had constant problems with my weight. I did not understand the connection between drinking coffee, eating sugar, and the state of my nerves and obesity. But God did."

Several years later Jane finally followed the instructions. The weight came off; family relationships became more honoring to the Lord.

"The Lord didn't just want to treat my body," shares Jane. "My spirit and soul needed help as well."

The Ultimate Directive

The Holy Spirit may give still another directive. Reverend E. V. Hill is an outstanding Christian leader of this generation. It was my privilege to know his gracious, intelligent wife, Jane. I had the privilege of attending the twenty-fifth anniversary celebration of E. V. Hill's pastorate. At a lovely downtown hotel in Los Angeles I greeted Jane only to learn that she was suffering with pneumonia. She was heroic that evening, sitting at her husband's side in a shimmering gown, hardly able to endure the evening because of her malady.

While x-raying her lungs to determine why the pneumonia would not subside, doctors discovered a tumor. Later an advanced tumor was found in her liver. Jane participated in treatments for a long period of time. Then one providential morning her husband received the news from the doctors, "We've done all we can."

"I went to the hospital chapel and fell down on my knees," shares Reverend Hill. "And the Spirit of God had only two words for me . . . 'Trust me.'

"At first I felt that God meant to heal Jane. Then I wondered if God was saying something else. I argued with him, 'There's only one way I can trust you, Lord, if you heal her."

But in the days ahead Jane lapsed into a coma, in spite of Christian television advocating and enlisting prayer for Jane throughout the world, Reverend Hill knew God was saying, "Trust me, not for her healing, but in the midst of her death."

That is the same message for some today. "Trust God in the midst of your own death. Trust God in the midst of the death of your loved one."

But there is another reminder here as well. Death, for the Christian, is Graduation Day. As one daughter said of her recently departed Christian mother, "I wouldn't bring her back for anything in the world. Why would one want to?"[29] At death, the one who claims Christ as his personal Savior has everything he or she could ever hope for in the presence of the Lord.

Diverting Death?

Many in the social sciences, philosophies, and religious communities have gone a long way to divert the sick and the well from the finality and message of death with the "how to's" of proper dying. Today, many hospitals offer classes to the dying (even dying children) that negate the Christian message of hope. The reality of death and what it means to an individual is obscured in the dialogue.

Severe sickness and the process of dying are meant to alarm people into considering their final destiny which they have repeatedly put off. In some death and dying classes, this process has been coated with "meaningless distractions"; the misplaced goal—to "accept" death graciously.

This perspective has much of its roots in a book by Elisabeth Kubler-Ross erroneously calling death "the final stage of growth." Kubler-Ross, who admits to having spirit guides (demons), was grossly misguided in her attempt to assure those groping for answers that death is natural and not to be feared.

The Bible declares that death is not natural. It is an enemy. Only Jesus has power over this enemy. He will resurrect those who believe in him on the last day as he resurrected the son of the widow of Nain. Where will you go on that day? Do you know?

The one who does not acknowledge Christ as Savior—counting on his death to bridge the chasm between God and humans—is in serious trouble. Don't ignore what your own death means, and subsequently bypass your *only* hope—a last opportunity to decide your own destiny based on a decision for or against Christ. It's your choice. Don't be fooled!

Time and again there is no one at the hospital or in homes to provide a last hearing of the good news of Christ. As a result of a denial of death and occupation with the details of death, many move out of this world into an eternity of hell.[30] Many, however, do hear and respond.

If you share with others how they too, can know God's love and forgiveness, thousands may be grateful. Have you thought about visiting "terminal" wards bringing Christ's message of love and hope?

Are You Letting God Lead You?

S. D. Gordon wrote:

When we learn to wait for our Lord's lead in everything, we shall know the strength that finds its climax in an even, steady walk. Many of us are lacking in the strength we so covet. But God gives full power for every task He appoints. Waiting, holding oneself true to His lead—this is the secret of strength. And anything that falls out of line of obedience is a waste of time and strength. Watch for His leading.[31]

Rosalind Goforth writes about her husband, one of the greatest missionaries of all time:

> So many inquiries came to Goforth down through the years asking for a statement regarding his position on Divine healing that we give the following story of his early position and how he came to somewhat modify on this subject. About the time the Goforths left for China, Dr. A. B. Simpson's *Divine Healing* and Dr. A. J. Gordon's *Ministry of Healing* were being widely read. Goforth brought both these books to China and was inclined to take the extreme, or should we say highest view in favor of Divine healing. Sad experiences through which he and his wife had passed, had strengthened him in this position by the time the following experience occurred.
>
> A few months after settling at Changte, Goforth was suddenly taken ill, his symptoms all pointing to probable pneumonia; high fever, pains in head and chest, and difficulty in breathing. The nearest doctor was at Chuwang, but though Mrs. Goforth pleaded to be allowed to send for help, her husband absolutely forbade her doing so, saying he had taken the Lord as his healer. Anxious days followed for the wife as Goforth, white and still, consistently refused even the putting on of a poultice. The crisis passed and he began to recover, but before he had fully regained his strength, he was taken down with violent chills and fever. Regularly, every second day, the attacks came on him—first chills, then fever, followed by violent sweating and ending with a period of utter exhaustion. After the third attack, Mrs. Goforth became so alarmed her prayer now became the cry of desperation that help might come before it was too late.
>
> In the midst of praying thus Donald McGillivray returned from his touring and Dr. Menzies arrived from Chuwang. After seeing Goforth, the doctor said, "If he will not take quinine, and he says he will not, I fear two or three more such attacks as he has been having, will prove fatal . . . ."

Mrs. Goforth then pleaded with her husband who rescinded his decision and took the quinine, saying: "For your sake, I will take it. But we must face this whole question again, I am too weak now."

Mrs. Goforth continues,

> Later, the whole question of Divine healing was searchingly gone into, for Goforth realized that a "chain is no stronger than its weakest link." In discussing this question with others, he would never

dogmatize as to what stand others should take, but was content to say, "As for me, *I must leave my Lord to reveal his will in each case as it comes*. Sometimes we seem clearly led to use means and to regard a doctor as God's minister. Again we have seen God honor simple faith, and a miracle of healing was wrought."[32]

We dare not practice presumption rather than faith. Faith is no less the work of the Holy Spirit than grace or love. Therefore, as in all areas of life we are cast upon the Lord, to seek his face in every situation. He will show us what to do.

Points to Ponder

1. Holy Spirit: life is not trying by our own wisdom, power, or motivation to be what we should be. According to the Bible, we are to ask God what to do, ask him to empower us with his Holy Spirit and then be led by this Spirit as he shows each of us what God would have us do. This Holy Spirit is available to those who acknowledge Jesus Christ as Savior.

Have you ever considered this leading of the Holy Spirit in light of your illness or in light of attending the ill? Are you seeking God's face concerning matters, or are you operating out of your own point of view, that of a doctor, counselor, or someone else?

2. Veiled Plan: is the Lord telling you that he has a plan in your circumstances? Take heart! No plan of God's is harmful. Should you not praise him that he knows better than you?

3. Believing Prayer: is God leading you to stand on his promises? Are you to stand on them even when circumstances look the opposite, when physical feelings make possibilities seem impossible? Have you considered writing out biblical promises and taping them throughout your room? Can you mark them and date them in your Bible? Though I am not there with you I long to stand with you in faith for your healing. I have prayed over each person who will read this book. If you stand in faith, I'll stand with you. But more than this I pray that God will heal you for his purposes. May you soon to be strong in mind and body, seeking to honor and glorify God in all that you do.

4. Spiritual Authority: do you need to learn about the authority God has given you and use it? Can you say today, "Satan, in the name of Jesus, get your hands off my life and body?" Are

you ready to stand against disease in your own body? "I command disease in the name of Jesus to let go of my body."

May God want to teach those who love the sick in this area? For the sake of others would you use, if God so directs, your rightful authority in the name of Christ on their behalf?

5. Obedience: are you seeking to be obedient in the matter of healing? Are there opportunities for healing that you are not searching out? Have you been neglectful of basic health laws and health care? Don't bother to keep asking God for healing if you will not be obedient in the matters he is already showing you. Faith and works are part of the whole. Step out and do something about getting well!

CHAPTER 8

CAN THERE BE A REASON?

I met Rusty shortly after a bleak Christmas and a brutal heartbreak. The man I loved became engaged to someone else.

Who could blame my hoped-for suitor? What man would wed a sickly, bedridden woman with no promise of healing? To console myself I telephoned a friend. "Rusty Wright is coming to speak in our city," Linda Jo explained. "Ask him for a ride down to visit."

I did. During the trip from Atlanta, Georgia, to Auburn, Alabama, I empathized with leafless trees whose only hope was spring. I talked with this handsome young man about my illness, my dashed hopes, my faltering trust in God, and my determination to seek to live for God in spite of everything. Rusty drove more slowly back to Atlanta. He liked my company—enough to propose a few months after our meeting.

A romantic story. The Creator proved that he was over and above illness, providing for me in my bleakest hour. But there is more to the story. During our engagement, plans were briefly interrupted. It was a time of reflection.

"Linda," the Lord spoke quietly to my heart one night. "Are you willing to suffer that Rusty might grow?"

Not one to bypass a challenge, I responded, "Yes Lord, if that's what you want."

This commitment would prove very difficult in days to come. God, in his scheme of things, meant to use my own weakness to precipitate growth and change in Rusty. A close relationship would involve emotional confrontation. Being the weaker of the two, because of my illness, I felt the greatest blow. I had neither the health nor the nerves for these encounters. Suffering was heaped upon suffering.

Yet was there purpose? It did not look that way. Many times I prayed to die. Sometimes I even pleaded for Rusty, my source of irritation, to die. But Rusty was built as strong as an ox. There was not much chance of anything physical breaking down.

Divorce was out of the question. Divorce would result in condemnation by many who probably understood little about my suffering. It would be the end of me if pursued. As time passed I could see what God was doing. Rusty needed to be married to someone as dependent and needy as I was in order to break down his independence and build up his sensitivity. Rusty saw this too. I and my sickness needed to be a willing tool. So on bad days I submitted, kicking and screaming (not in rebellion, but in pain), to God's plan. On good days I reaped the rewards. At periods of spiritual peaks I actually thanked God for the plan. Doesn't this seem odd?

Content with Suffering?

"I am enthralled with suffering. I think it is terrific. I am privileged to have it. In fact it is one of the greatest assets of my life!" What would twentieth-century individuals say about a person who makes this kind of outlandish statement? What would your response be to such an outburst?

It may surprise many to know that this statement was made by the apostle Paul. It was recorded in the New Testament as a model of what our attitude should be toward sickness and suffering.

> Most gladly, therefore, I will rather boast about my weaknesses, that the power of Christ may dwell in me. Therefore I am well content with weakness, with insults, with distresses, with persecutions, with difficulties for Christ's sake; for when I am weak, then I am strong.[1]

Paul is one of many who have sung this seemingly ridiculous tune. Madame Guyon, writing about her illnesses and other sufferings, in the fifteenth century expressed: "I have no desire that my imprisonment should end before the right time; I love my chains. My senses, indeed, have not any relish for such things, but my heart is separated from them and borne over them."

Amy Carmichael, director of Dohnavur Christian Fellowship in India, during her twenty-year battle with sickness and pain, wrote of a certain "sweetness in the briar."

Poets have echoed this refrain: "Thy Jesus can repay From His own fullness all He takes away" (Bishop Moule).

Songwriters have again and again captured this melody: "When through fiery trials thy pathway shall lie. / My grace all sufficient shall be thy supply" ("How Firm a Foundation").

Oswald Chambers writes in *My Utmost for His Highest,* "The saint is hilarious when he is crushed with difficulties because the thing is so ludicrously impossible to anyone but God."[2]

Indeed Jesus tells us in the beatitudes to "rejoice in suffering."[3]

Why would anyone say such a thing? Surely health is to be envied; sickness, with all of its added and incurred suffering, to be cursed. Yet, is it possible that an arduous malady could be an instrument of God? Would a benevolent heavenly Father actually sift sickness, pain, and disability into his plan? Can there be good reason for afflictions? During many years of confinement I researched, contemplated, and wrestled with biblical purposes for sickness. What are they?

Displaying the Works of God

We may face illnesses, handicaps, and infirmities in order to help us see and understand God.

Moses wrote, in the fifteenth century B.C., "And the Lord said . . . 'Who has made man's mouth? Or who makes him dumb or deaf, or seeing or blind? Is it not I, the Lord?'"[4]

Jesus confirmed that God had formed the deaf, dumb, and blind when his disciples brought to him a man sightless from birth. An interesting dialogue took place between Jesus and his disciples. The disciples begin by revealing their mindset that sickness is the result of wrongdoing by the sick one.

"Rabbi, who sinned, this man, or his parents, that he should be born blind?"

Jesus' response surprised them:

"It was neither that this man sinned, nor his parents"; he answered, "but it was in order that the works of God might be displayed in him."[5] Jesus then healed the man.

I had explained to someone that God had demonstrated his character to me through my illness in such a way that others were helped by it. This person said to me, "People don't need to see you sick and God comforting you in order to believe in Christ."

But the truth is that many do respond positively to God as they see him helping his children in the midst of sickness and pain—the peace engulfing one who has lost a loved one; the good will expressed by one who has been cheated or maligned; the joy of one who has suffered a critical setback; the gentle courage of one enduring a disability. We receive encouragement and God receives glory in opportunities that cause his love and grace to be displayed, "For all things are for your sakes, that the grace which is being multiplied to more and more people may cause the giving of thanks to abound to the glory of God."[6]

Yet many have wondered about this thesis. Glaphre Gilliland, director of a worldwide prayer effort, writes in *When the Pieces Don't Fit:*

On one of my weekly trips to the clinic, once again I prayed for quick healing and footnoted all my reasons why this was a good idea. As I entered the waiting room, God reminded me of the opportunities He'd given me here to tell people about Him . . . doctors, nurses, technicians, even other patients.

My response was, "But, God, do I have to be a patient? Couldn't I just drop in at coffee break and tell them about You? That seems like a totally workable plan to me!"

A lab technician interrupted my thoughts by asking to talk to me. I followed him to the staff lounge.

"I want to tell you something," he said timidly. "Do you remember when I asked you how you could have so much peace when you know your medical prognosis?"

I did. It had been an opportunity to tell Rick about a God who brings peace in the midst of all circumstances.

"Well, I've been watching you all these months," he continued. "I was skeptical . . . I didn't want to accept what you said about God. I've never known anyone who felt that way about Him. But I've never known anyone who had such peace, either." Rick concluded, "I want you to know that, for the first time in my life, I believe in God."

The nurse found me in the staff lounge talking with Rick and took me to the treatment room. As she prepared everything, she said, "You know, I told Mom a few weeks ago I had this patient who had a peace like no one else I've ever known. Glaphre, I've come to believe in God, but I feel like I want more than that."

There in the cold, sterile treatment room, we prayed together.

That same day as I was leaving, one of the supervisors stopped me in the hall. I'd never seen this stiff, brusque woman look so nervous. "A lot of people come through this clinic," she said. "The patients are critically ill, and because they're scared and in pain, they can be extremely difficult to deal with. I've watched you . . . I've listened to you . . . and I've listened to what the staff has said about you.

"I've been a cynic all my life," she admitted. "I've never believed there was a God and have stayed away from anyone who did. But I want you to know, over the months you've been coming here, I've . . . well . . . for the first time in my life I believe there is a God." With that, she turned abruptly and walked away, wiping her eyes.

Glaphre continues, By the time I got to my car, I was sobbing. "O God, when am I ever going to learn that I'm in no position to guide my own life? I would have had me well long ago. Please forgive me for always wanting my own way. Thank You for knowing that most of all I want to honor You"[7]

God demonstrates his works, his glory, and his love through many means. If God is able to exemplify his eminence and love for us and others best through a sickbed as he did with Glaphre, the man blind from birth, and me—so be it! After all, who are we here to glorify? When God is glorified by our lives *we* reap the benefits.

God Gets the Glory

Many important contributions have resulted when individuals are confined to the sickbed to ponder and hear from God. George Mueller, who established many orphanages during his lifetime, experienced attacks of depression which made him dependent on the Lord and developed his ministry of prayer and faith. Charles Spurgeon, pastor and theologian, periodically confined to bed with the gout, was sharpened in thought. The apostle Paul and his team had the undergirding strength of God imparted to them *only* as their strength subsided:

> For we do not want you to be unaware, brethren, of our affliction which came to us in Asia, that we were burdened excessively, beyond our strength, so that we despaired even of life; indeed, we had the sentence of death within ourselves in order that we should not trust in ourselves, but in God.[8]

Twentieth-century individuals are familiar, as Paul was, with burdens that break us down physically. His body was ailing under such stress that it brought him to the point of physical death. Whether God answered his prayers by removing the burdens, strengthening him to meet them, or possibly both, we don't know. But we can be sure that God demonstrated his power and goodness to Paul and in turn Paul acknowledged God's majesty. Undoubtedly Paul saw a side of God's character he might not see under normal circumstances. After all, if a certain aspect of the Lord's care isn't needed, what will prompt us to search it out? The more experiences we have, the more we see various facets of God's wonderful character.

Cause Must Precede the Cure

"But it is the healing, not the sickness that gives God the glory," one individual protested to me. "Therefore how can you look at your sickness and say that God can use the sickness to demonstrate his love and works to others?"

"Simple," I responded. "If a person is not sick she cannot be healed. And the longer or more severely an individual is sick, the greater God's power in the healing. The problem is essential to the solution. Cause must precede the cure."

But God may have other plans for demonstrating his love and works and receiving rightful glory. The committed soldier has the privilege of participating.

Amy Carmichael wrote poignantly about this very thing.

> Another of those flying words addressed to the sick came in letters occasionally; it was about being "laid aside." It was the sort of thing one might say to a cracked china cup: "Poor dear, you are laid aside." But then the Lord's servant is not a china cup. He (she) is a soldier. Soldiers may be wounded in battle and sent to hospital. A hospital isn't a shelf; it is a place of repair. And a soldier on service in the spiritual army is never off the battlefield. He is only removed to another part of the field, when a wound interrupts what he meant to do and sets him doing something else.
>
> Only, as I have been learning through these months, the soldier must let his Captain say where, and for what, He needs him most . . . . A wise master never wastes his servant's time, nor a commander his soldier's—there is great comfort in remembering that.[9]

Why the Reservation?

One reason that this concept of glorifying God through illness is so difficult for some to see today is that the mindset of many is "me" centered. This boring preoccupation with self has many drawbacks. Pascal, the French philosopher, has stated, "There is a God-shaped vacuum in the heart of every man (woman)." There is a place within us designed for God alone. When we try to operate apart from our Creator, we will reap much disappointment. In fact self-glory always has a disappointing end.

Another reason that the concept of seeing God's works displayed and glorifying him is hard to accept is that some popular teaching has tended to focus on God's power at the expense of God's purposes. The fact is that at any given moment God may have more in mind than to keep us feeling wonderful. For many of us our focus is too narrow. In fact the Bible makes it clear: We should center on God's whole view of life—not just health.

What does God's view of life include? Consider the case of the Israelites. At a certain point in history, in God's scheme of things, the Israelites were given an amazing ability to reproduce their race.[10] Israelite women were having healthy babies—one right after another. The children were also growing up to be unusually vigorous.

In this instance God had a purpose in allowing bodies to work at maximum procreativity and endurance. He was intentionally increasing the nation of Israel to meet his objectives of marching them into the Promised Land.

At another point of history, and for a different design, one godly Jewish woman, Hannah, could not conceive children. God was using the delay to prompt Hannah to give her child (Samuel) back to him. Samuel, weaned by his mother and raised in the temple, became a great teacher of Israel.[11] Afterward God blessed Hannah with many children.

At some time, either now or in eternity, mankind will know that God's purposes are far superior to our own. This realization brings immense satisfaction and reward. As Amy Carmichael recognized, soldiers do not know better than their captains the best means of carrying forth the kingdom. He also knows, far better than we, what will ultimately satisfy us. Those who are sick, those who treat, minister to, or care for the sick, must see that each particular illness or a situation where an individual assists the sick, can be used to demonstrate the work of God and show his greatness to a world desperate to see something beyond themselves.

Be Happy with Problems

Besides sickness and suffering for the purpose of seeing God, the Bible reveals another reason for experiencing infirmities; it is to produce character. James, Jesus' brother, wrote to the New Testament church, "is your life full of difficulties? . . . Then be happy, for when the way is rough, your patience has a chance to grow."[12]

Is the building of our character important? Absolutely. Without character we lack the ability to fully enjoy life. But there is no guarantee when illness strikes that character will be the result. Why? Sickness is the means, not the end; the catalyst, not the finished product. We need to cooperate with our Creator while suffering to reap the benefits. James continues, "So let it [patience] grow, and don't try to squirm out of your problems. For when your patience is finally in full bloom, then you will be ready for anything, strong in character, full and complete."[13]

Sickness may be seen as an accelerated character building program. It's a trial that we can't duck out of or run from successfully. We are cornered, as it were, by the Hound of heaven.

When I was growing up one of my strong points was intelligence; my nickname was "Brainy Raney." My girlfriends were beautiful—attracting plenty of dates. Not as appealing to the opposite sex I became quite good at advising guys, who were goggle-eyed over my girlfriends, as to how to get their attention. Hence our joint title—my girlfriends and myself—beauty and the brains.

I was successful in classes where I at least opened the book, and often in spite of any reading, largely because I easily assimilated and retained spoken or printed information. During all of this educational intake, I knew little of God's wisdom and ways. Smart was not enough. Good grades didn't make life more fulfilling; nor did bright ideas bring one a richer relationship with others or God.

Isn't it interesting that *this* part of me, my thinking ability, which God intended to harness to help others and fulfill me, was severely crippled. For years I literally could not think without asking God to tell me what it was I should think. I couldn't respond healthfully in emotions without asking, "God, show me what I should be feeling."

One who has been sick in the manner I was may not understand how God could take a bright mind, test it, produce an utter lack of confidence in its ability, and resurrect it to serve him. But that's what he did. Painful as it was, I've been reprogrammed and set free to serve God.

God's kind of edifying process is constructed to produce wonderful benefits. Watch for them! If we can see the end from the beginning—the possibilities of character building, inner freedom, and being an instrument to demonstrate God's goodness to others—we'll get through the middle. If we can also remember that God has more in mind than whether our present moment is brimming with good feelings, it will help orient us to greater things.

Greg Anderson shares his experience of beating the odds—and finding something better.[14]

*F*our years ago I was told I was dying of cancer. I remember the doctor's exact words after surgery. He'd stood in my hospital room, awkwardly shuffling through his sheaf of papers. He finally gave up any pretense and looked me straight in the eye. "The tiger is out of the cage, Mr. Anderson," he said. "The cancer which used to be contained in your lungs has invaded your lymphatic system. Ninety-eight percent of the patients in your condition don't pull through."

Only those who have heard words like that can know how chilling they are, how they make a shambles of your world. As I look back now, though, I can see that those words began the journey that has changed my life for the better.

On that December day in 1984 the doctor went on to tell me I had only thirty days left to live. Nothing more could be done for me. I was told to go home and put my affairs in order, then wait to die.

I went through the classic emotions—guilt, denial, anger—mostly anger.

The day after I came home I was sitting in an easy chair in the den, supposedly going over bank statements and my will. But the letters and numbers were a jumble. I was so furious at God that I couldn't see straight. How could he let me die? I was a young man, with a young wife and a two-year-old daughter.

"God, take this cancer away!" I demanded. "Heal me!"

As I sat there, miserable, I saw our little Erica down on the floor by the sliding door to the backyard. She was gathering her toys around her. Just looking at her gave me immense pain. "Oh, God!" I cried. "I was going to love her *so much* as she grew up!"

As if in direct answer, a shaft of sunlight spilled through the glass, lighting up Erica's blonde hair. And in that moment it came to me. Three words: Love Erica *today.*

The force of those words and the force of their implication shocked me.

I was a busy man, with important work to do (running a church growth institute), and I was good at it. That was why God put us on this earth, I thought, to get something done. That was where my self-worth came from. I planned church time and family time as consistently as I planned everything else. Why should those words rock me so?

At the same time another idea was growing in my mind. Simply put, it was this: The doctors say that 98 percent of the people in my condition die. That leaves 2 percent who live. Maybe if I can find some of this 2 percent who beat the odds, I can find out how they do it. And if I find out how they do it, perhaps I can beat the odds as well.

The next morning, I went into my office at the Institute for Church Leadership. The staff gathered around solemnly.

"If there's *anything* we can do . . . ." started one of my associates.

"Yes, there is," I answered. "I'm not packing up yet. I'm looking for survivors, people who have lived when they were supposed to die."

"Then you'll want to talk to Mary Doremus," my associate Marge said. "She's making remarkable progress."

Two days later Marge's friend Mary came in. When Mary rolled off the elevator in her shiny black wheelchair with a red racing stripe, there was no way you could start to feel sorry for her. She wore cheerful, bright clothes, her white-blonde hair was knotted in a bun, and her smile was not just on her lips but in her eyes.

"I hear you have cancer," I said as we settled in my office.

"A degenerative illness of the nervous system," she said bluntly. "The doctors said it was fatal—there was no hope. I'd lose the use of my legs and arms as it progressed. But I'm *regaining* the use of my arms—and my legs!"

"How?" I asked.

"I've conquered my illness," she said simply, "and you can too."

"I've already asked God to cure my cancer," I said.

"That's a start," Mary said. "But I didn't say *cure* cancer, I said *conquer* it. That goes much deeper. Instead of asking God to change your physical circumstances—your cancer—you have to ask him to heal *you*."

Those words rang true. I used to think it was my doctor's responsibility to make me well, but that's not so. It's up to *me* to be a well person—emotionally, mentally, spiritually.

When God showed this to me, it changed my life. I suddenly saw the stresses, the negative emotions like anger and unforgiveness, and the barren spiritual life I'd been living. I saw that I wasn't being choosy about what I fed my mind. Even though I was a Christian, the fruits I wanted my life to bear were money and prestige, not faith and hope and love!

"Greg, I'll tell you the great secret," Mary had said in a clear, confident voice. "Your life doesn't change because you live through a serious illness. You live through a serious illness *because* your life has changed."

Did *my* life have to change? After all, I'd been doing "the Lord's work," even as a job.

Yes, my life did have to change. I needed to align my will with God's will. And when I prayed, "Lord heal me," I came to know that my physical healing might be the last thing on the agenda. Healing is about peace. Doctors are beginning to find out what a strong influence our spiritual and emotional well-being have on our physical bodies. If you have peace, you've conquered cancer instead of letting it conquer you. Then you can accept what happens, whether it's death or a life much fuller than the one you've known.

Now I could see how God's command to "love Erica today" could be a direct result of my prayer for healing.

Since that day, I started seeking out more and more survivors. I have met with hundreds of people who were beating the odds.

I can truly say that the people I met were more than survivors; they were *conquerors*. From one I learned the importance of having a good doctor, one who treats you as a partner, not a victim. Another emphasized the importance of healing broken relationships. Yet another showed me how stress cripples us spiritually as well as physically, and how we can choose our attitudes and guide our emotions.

Each person had his or her own style, but their messages were very similar. Collectively they reminded me of the verse in Second Corinthians which says, "Therefore, if any one is in Christ, he is a new creation; the old has passed away, behold, the new has come" (5:17, RSV).

The people who had conquered cancer were those who saw their illness as a message to change the focus of their lives. They had stopped fighting against God and had joined forces with him, and with the doctors, in order to become healed.

My fellow conquerors and I began holding group meetings, because we found strength in each other—we were each walking proof of God's love and healing power.

I admit none of this happened to me overnight. This kind of healing is slow and sometimes painful, because it means working through emotions, approaching people you need to forgive or ask forgiveness of, spending time in prayer, and giving God control of your life. These are all things Jesus commands us to do, because when we do, he promises to make us new creations. It took cancer to make me listen! It took cancer to save my life.

As I said, this journey started for me over four years ago.

Last time I went to the doctor—a different doctor, by the way—there was no trace of cancer. But I can honestly say that doesn't matter as much as my inner healing.

You see, we're all going to die. I've come to believe firmly that *how long* we live is not half as important as *how well* we live.

If we pursue God's inner peace, we'll change the world and those around us 100 times as much as if we

CAN THERE BE A REASON? • *163*

pursue money and prestige. Jesus has commanded us to live this way. If we ask him to help us, he guarantees that we'll be "more than conquerors" of disease, yes, but of all of life.[14]

Questions abound concerning the presumption that difficulties can be a great asset.

"The Bible says that Christ bore our sickness on the tree," one man said to me. "If Christ bore our sicknesses on the cross, we are not to have sickness. Therefore it serves no purpose."

We must take a look at Isaiah 53 to consider this proposition. "Surely our griefs [pains] He Himself bore, and our sorrows [infirmities] He carried."[15]

The word for infirmities is *astheneia* in the Greek. It is the same word that Paul uses when he says, "Moreover I will boast in my weaknesses (astheneia)."[16] This presents a dilemma. If Christ bearing our infirmities means we are to be completely free of them at all times, and God has no purpose in them, why was Paul glorying in his and contending that God had purposed it for him? The text gives us the answer—to keep Paul from exalting himself he was "given" this thorn in the flesh. We are also "given" many things—including infirmities—to encourage a godly character.

A similar verse should also be addressed: "By His stripes we are healed."[17] This is a great verse for the sick. If God so leads I would urge the sick to claim this principle for themselves. Just be sure to keep in mind other points of Scripture which have been addressed and God's particular purposes in your own situation. Christ's death opened the door to health, but he also opened the door for character building and service.

Purposes for Affliction

Author Ruthe White tells the story of surgery that was needed for a particular problem. Though she had experienced supernatural healing in the past, she was also mindful of the "ways" of God. "As I prayed over my surgery I sensed that God had a particular plan in mind for this hospital visit."

Such was the case. Ruthe roomed next to a famous movie star who was to experience the same surgery. This woman was frightened and depressed. Ruthe knew her hope rested in the Lord and radiated that belief. She was not afraid. The movie star's husband, learning of Ruthe's optimism, begged her to talk with his wife. She did and the woman heard the message of the love of God in Christ. Her countenance changed as she found peace and security.

Periodically I have heard a shortsighted comment. "Evidently you really need sickness to mature you." This remark is often said as if lack of character in the speakers' lives did not exist in sufficient measure to merit God's buffeting! Look around! How many healthy people are resentful, critical, proud, selfish, uncaring, greedy, vindictive, unforgiving, unyielding? God did not allow some to get sick because they were the worst sinners of all, requiring the greatest measure of pruning. Actually, the sick may be way ahead. Why? Because they're in God's pruning vineyard—cut back so their growth may flourish.

Rather than view the sick (or disabled) with disdain, the Bible takes a different view of God's special pruning and purging. One of my favorite poems explains:

> He sat by the fire of seven-fold heat,
> As watched by the precious ore;
> And closer He bent with a searching gaze,
> As He heated it more and more.
>
> He knew He had ore that could stand the test,
> And He wanted the finest gold;
> To mold as a crown for the King to wear,
> Set with gems of price untold.
>
> So he laid it there in the burning fire,
> Though our eyes were dim with tears;
> For we saw but the fire—not the Master's hand,
> And questioned with anxious fear.
>
> So the gold was laid in the burning fire,
> Though we vain would say him, "Nay";
> And we watched the dross, that we had not seen,
> As it melted and passed away.
>
> And the gold grew brighter—and yet more bright—
> As it mirrored the form above,
> Who set o'er the fire, though unseen by us,
> With a look of ineffable love.

Can we think it pleases the Master's heart,
To cause us a moment's pain?
Oh, no, but he sees through the present loss
The bliss of eternal gain.

So he laid it there in the burning fire,
With a love that is strong and sure;
And our gold did not suffer a bit more heat
Than was needed to make it pure.[18]

Eternal Perspective

We experience trials to center our focus on eternity.

Life is short. Eternity is forever. God may allow sickness to force issues: our eternal destiny, our course in life, our eternal choices.

One of the five crowns (rewards) mentioned in the Bible is designated for those who have been faithful to Jesus Christ, God incarnate, in the midst of suffering. We also have the privilege of reigning with Christ in eternity.[19] After Christ rose from the dead, he ascended into heaven. Someday we who have received his precious gift of forgiveness and eternal life will live with him. But those who have allowed a greater work of knowing, loving, and serving him, will reign with him. Some of our suffering is in preparation for that.

Dr. Earl Radmacher, author and president of Western Seminary, states, "No one had a larger list of problems than the apostle Paul, but he found tremendous deliverance by looking not at the things which are seen but at the things which are not seen."[20]

It is in light of eternity that we understand the concepts of long-suffering and forbearance. The reason that "long-suffering"[21] is listed as a fruit of the Holy Spirit's work in our lives is that it is *required* for effective Christian living. God's purposes include a predisposition to bear up under pressure *with eternity in mind*.

What about suffering with eternity in mind? In several temperament tests taken in my teens and early twenties, I scored very low in the area of perseverance. I was a great starter, but less than perfect on the finishing end. This was the result of obstacles discouraging me along the way. I had trouble focusing on the eternal—the temporary (difficulties, especially) were all too apparent.

As I observed what God was doing in my life I realized that he was giving me more and more difficulties. Each time it was with the hope, that from the beginning of the trial to the end, I could maintain an emotional equilibrium—ceasing from frets, worries, fears, and despair; becoming secure in the fact that *God would come through for me in the end*. Sickness helped me learn endurance, to stay at a task until completion. In light of eternity the present couldn't defeat me, nor were my efforts futile.

Dr. A. Berkeley Mickelsen recently retired as professor of New Testament at Bethel Theological Seminary. He shares his experience of illness and provision in light of an eternal perspective.

I was sitting on the radiator in my parents' home and shivering. I did that often during that fateful fall of 1936 in Wheaton, Illinois. Why was I always cold when no one else was? And why was I always thirsty? And why did I have so little energy that I didn't even feel like playing basketball with my high school classmates? Basketball had always been the love of my life.

A week or so later, one of my most loved teachers told me privately that I had very bad breath. I began using mouthwash several times a day but I still had a bad taste in my mouth most of the time. Although I had no aches or pains and ran no fever, I knew something was not right.

In February 1937, I went to a doctor and he delivered the verdict: I had diabetes. I would have to go to the hospital and be treated with insulin and then learn how to give myself insulin injections and how to regulate my diet. This was only fifteen years after insulin was first used for diabetics. Before that time, those who got juvenile-onset diabetes (before age twenty-five) simply died. Those who got it at older ages could sometimes control it with strict diets.

My parents were devastated (I was an only child) and thought I had very little time to live. On the other hand, I was relieved to know what I had! However, we knew enough people with diabetes to know the complications that often arose—blindness, kidney disease, amputations of legs and arms.

During my ten days in the hospital, the toxic effects of the uncontrolled diabetes were burned out of me by large, carefully monitored doses of insulin, followed by insulin reactions and large glasses of orange juice and sugar. Then I was taught how to inject myself, how to test my urine for sugar, and how to calculate and weigh food for the proper amounts of carbohydrates, protein, and fat. I began a lifelong study of diabetes and its treatment.

By the time I left the hospital, I knew a great deal about food, about diabetes, and about life and death. As an adolescent for ten days in a twelve-man hospital ward, I had firsthand encounters with pain, suffering, and sorrow. Pastors came to minister to me, and God also gave me some opportunities to minister to others. When I left to go home, I was feeling much better and I had matured by years.

When news of my disease spread, scores of people told me they were praying that God would heal me. My parents and I prayed for healing. We enlisted our church and other churches to pray for my healing.

I came home feeling good, both about the improvement in my health and about all the people who were praying for me. And wonder of all wonders, my diabetes began to taper off. Week after week, I needed less and less insulin to keep a normal blood sugar. God was answering prayer, we were sure. A year later, I was off insulin entirely. We had much for which to praise God.

I graduated from high school and entered Wheaton College. Still no need for insulin. God had healed! But by my junior year, I was feeling less well, and during my senior year I began to lose weight rapidly. By this time, I knew the diabetes had returned, and I would have to go back to insulin. Had God withdrawn his healing?

I did not learn until many years later that many juvenile-onset diabetics have a "honeymoon" period during which they can get along without insulin. But the diabetes always returns. Probably my doctors at that time were not aware of this fact and thus did not warn me.

Some people back in 1942 probably thought I was showing a lack of faith by returning to insulin. At that point, I could not worry about theological implications—I was fighting for my life!

Also, by then I had done my own study of the Bible about healing, and I knew that, while God sometimes heals miraculously, he often does not. I had seen the emotional pain and guilt that come from the teaching "If you have enough faith, God will heal" and from the belief that lack of healing is due either to lack of faith or unconfessed sin. I had read in 2 Timothy 4:20 that Paul, who *sometimes* had the gift of healing, had left Trophimus sick at Miletus. And God had not healed Paul's own "thorn in the flesh"—whatever that was. I also believed that medical knowledge and treatment were often part of God's way of healing.

And so I returned to the hospital for another balancing time. It was harder to get good control the second time—partly because I had stayed off insulin too long. I had only one hundred twenty pounds strung over my six-foot frame. Although I wanted to go on to graduate school, I had to stay out of school for a year to recover.

After I regained some degree of control, I began graduate school at Wheaton. I completed my Master's and Bachelor of Divinity degrees, and then enrolled at the University of Chicago for a Ph.D. program.

During those years I had difficult struggles for blood sugar control; insulin reactions were frequent. Once I had an insulin reaction on the train going back to Wheaton. The conductor, unable to wake me up, saw that Wheaton was my destination. My parents were alerted; an ambulance met the train, and I woke up at a hospital.

Despite my diabetic problems, in 1950 I completed my Ph.D. in New Testament and early Christian literature.

Now, fifty years after I heard that fateful diagnosis of diabetes in 1937, I have retired after thirty-six years of teaching at Wheaton College and Bethel Theological Seminary in St. Paul. My wife and I have two grown daughters; neither has diabetes. Did God work a miracle for me? Perhaps not, but he certainly did something out of the ordinary.

I carried a full academic load of teaching until last year, when I chose to retire at age sixty-six. I have spent my life poring over tiny Hebrew vowel points in the Old Testament Scriptures, studying Greek texts of the New Testament, and reading thousands of pages of students' papers. I rarely missed a day of classes for illness, and I often went to school a mile away on cross-country skis, wearing a huge backpack full of books and papers.

My eyes show *no* damage from my fifty years of diabetes. Circulation is still very good in my hands and feet, and my semi-annual examinations by a diabetic specialist have never shown kidney damage or any of the other common diabetic complications.

My diabetic specialists have had no explanation as to why I have not suffered the usual complications of juvenile-onset diabetes. I once participated in a tissue study at the University of Minnesota where researchers were trying to find out why a few diabetics like me do not get the usual complications. To my knowledge, there were no definitive findings from that research.

I have no explanation except the grace of God and perhaps my persistence in doing what I could to help control the disease. That meant a dogged determination to learn all that medical science could teach me. It also meant maintaining a daily exercise program whether I felt like it or not.

Diabetes taught me many things. One of the hardest lessons was to learn to admit I had diabetes and that I might need the help of others—students and colleagues. When I first began to teach, I didn't want to tell anyone about my problem. Later I learned to tell students at the beginning of each school term that I was a brittle diabetic and subject to insulin reaction.

I explained that if I drank a Coke in the middle of class, it was not because I was rude. I told them that if my speech began to slow down, become slurred, or if I seemed confused or began to perspire to quickly bring me a Coke and insist that I drink it. It was good for me (and for them) to know that I needed them and that days might come when they would have to minister to me or to others like me.

My colleagues learned to help me in the same way. Other people might nod off in faculty meetings and be politely ignored. I could never do that—two people would be beside me urging me to drink a Coke or eat a candy bar! In a few instances, an alert student or colleague saved me from very serious consequences or from death itself! My wife and daughters often rescued me. I have been constantly aware of my mortality.

My diabetes kept me from one temptation that plagues many others—the temptation to keep adding more activities and responsibilities. It is not easy for any of us to say, "No I can't add that—no matter how worthy the cause."

I rarely preached on Sundays and never took interim pastorates, though I often taught adult Sunday school class in my own church and in recent years my wife and I have team-taught in our church and in many churches of other denominations.

Perhaps everyone in our family is healthier because of my diabetes. A diabetic diet goes heavily on fresh fruit and vegetables, a minimum of sweet desserts and pastries, and a low proportion of protein and fat. All these things are now considered to be ideal for everyone!

So *did* God heal me? I believe he gave me the *degree* of healing I needed to fulfill his calling for me. He has preserved my eyesight so that I can see those tiny Hebrew vowel points and so that I can study my Greek text of the New Testament, using the scholarly tools he has given me to teach and to write.

Life-Changing Benefits

Along the way I have heard testimony from many as to the life-changing benefits of an experience with ill health when God was earnestly sought. They include:

APPRECIATION CAPACITY

"I used to take so many things for granted. Now I am more fully aware and more appreciative."

"I was a fretful person. Many things upset me. After the prolonged sickness of my child I realized that there were more important things to be concerned about. I don't worry like I used to."

"I learned to appreciate myself. Sickness demanded more of me than I ever thought myself capable of. The fact that I have emerged successfully has significantly aided my sense of self-worth."

UNDERSTANDING GOD

"I was a very capable person. I loved God, but I really didn't need him all that much. It took a major illness to expose my need."

"Since I could no longer depend on myself and others as I once had, I found God more than adequate. I can now say with personal confidence, 'God is able.' This experience of knowing God in deep difficulty has prepared me to dialogue and fellowship with him during less stressful times."

"I did not have the energy to continue my resentment, unforgiveness, and criticalness. It was either let God have his way in my thought life or possibly die from the burden of wrong thinking. It has been worth the sickness to be free of many wrong attitudes which kept me unhappy."

PRIORITIES REARRANGED

"I never seemed to have time to spend with God. Flat on my back was where God had to bring me in order to get my attention."

"My family and my work were the priorities in my life. But reaching out to others, sharing what I had found from knowing Christ, and helping those in need was not on my list. Since my sickness—personally experiencing what it is like to be afraid and helpless—I am seeking to be God's tool for others."

"Prolonged infirmity, during which time my own strength was not sufficient to serve God and others, caused me to learn to listen to the Holy Spirit of God. It is amazing how much service for God I did previously based on my own ideas and using my own energy to carry it out. No longer will I ignore God's Spirit."

"As I watched God work, where I could not, I grew in my faith. More and more I realized his power and goodness."

"I had asked God to increase my faith but had forgotten to look at Romans 5:3–5, which says that trials produce faith. In spite of the difficulties I have been grateful. I am not the same timid person as before. I have more boldness when it comes to prayer and other matters."

Other comments have paralleled scriptural reasons for infirmities:

- "I learned how to care for others." "Blessed be the God and Father of our Lord Jesus Christ, the Father of mercies and God of all comfort; who comforts us in all our affliction so that we may be able to comfort those who are in any affliction with the comfort with which we ourselves are comforted by God . . . But if we are afflicted, it is for your comfort."[22]
- "I began empathizing with others." "And if one member suffers, all the members suffer with it";[23] "Bear one another's burdens."[24]
- "I was motivated to study the Bible and find out what I could do about my situation." "It was good for me that I was afflicted that I may learn Thy statutes."[25]
- "I sinned less." "Therefore, since Christ has suffered in the flesh, arm yourselves also with the same purpose, because he who has suffered in the flesh has ceased from sin, so as to live the rest of the time in the flesh no longer for the lusts of men, but for the will of God."[26]

DILUTED GROWTH

Such growth as described above, is greatly diluted if we do not fill our minds with the right perspective. Suffering, in and of itself, will not aid anyone. It is combining suffering with proper perspective that changes a person for the better. Before I became sick, I heard a Bible teacher say, "Good times are to prepare for bad times. Study the Bible faithfully in prosperity and it will serve you in difficulty." The Bible, which filled my mind, is what made the biggest difference for me in sickness. The recipe is: We mix the promises of God with suffering to produce character and insight.

And be sure to *look* for God in the situation.

I recall a night, one of hundreds, when I just couldn't take my circumstances another minute.

"Lord," I asked, "how could you let things be so bad?"

Into my mind came priceless thoughts. "Linda, let me tell you what's *really* bad," I sensed God responding. "It's having the illness and the hardships, but—not having a friend who cares, not having a comfortable bed to lie in; not having sufficient food to eat; not having telephones available in emergencies; not having a sturdy roof over your head to keep out the elements and keep in the warmth; not having extra vitamins and supplements available; not having a little cat at your feet to cheer you, the mountains to look at, a cup of tea, sunshine, my presence and the promise of eternal life no matter what!"

I had thought that my situation couldn't get any worse, that I had met the ultimate foe. But there were still things for which to be grateful.

Growth for the Caretaker

During some of my years of illness I interspersed bed rest and travel. After marrying, one reason for going on the road with Rusty for university lecture tours was that I was too sick to be left alone at home. Still I looked forward to freedom from my bedroom walls.

The ritual seldom varied: the thought of traveling stressed me to the point that my shoulders burned with pain, my brittle nerves threatened to shatter. The plane ride never failed to terrify me, not because I felt the plane would crash, but over and over I would, for no apparent reason, visualize myself falling through the floor of the plane . . . and out. The lecturing I was able to do several hours a week was always a challenge—not to speak, but to be able to "stand" without blanking out, passing out, or vomiting in front of everyone.

In the areas where we traveled, there were few hospitals I had not visited, frequenting some sort of health care facility almost as often as the universities where we spoke. One incident stands out in particular. Rusty and I were in Albuquerque, scheduled to speak at the University of New Mexico. Having arranged to meet one of our sponsors from the university, I walked the block from our motel to a fast-food restaurant. Once there I ordered iced tea which proved to be too acidic for my undependable stomach.

Without warning I began to feel ill; I always needed to think fast and take quick action when this happened. I excused myself and started back to the motel. I got as far as the sidewalk, threw up, and collapsed. In minutes the paramedics, ambulance crew, and a crowd of mostly students stood around me.

Someone went to get Rusty. He was awakened from a nap. "I'll be there in a minute," he sleepily told the frightened woman. Then he went back to sleep.

When they got me to the motel, Rusty was a muddle.

"What happened?" he asked, still half-asleep.

"Well, I drew a good crowd," I responded. "But I was too sick to speak."

It seems difficult at times to explain how Rusty and I have survived sickness and its ramifications. It is to Rusty's credit that he stayed with me. The one who loved the sick (Rusty) has suffered and grown as much as I.

Hopefully as you explore God's purposes you will gain insight into your own situation and profit accordingly.

Fulfilling My Desires

Along the journey of my illness I have been told over and over that I should have died years ago; that my case was not promising; that I had far too many things wrong with me to survive.

One doctor said, "You have lived for years by sheer willpower. Your body has been far too weak to keep going."

Others have said, "It is a miracle that you are alive and healing."

God was fulfilling his desire for me and my true desire for myself—pulling out every temporal prop and replacing it with his eternal foundation.

Today I am traveling to the far corners of the earth speaking and teaching the great message of Jesus. I've got plenty of books in print and more books on the back burner than I know what to do with (God will show me). Wherever I go I have answers (real answers) for people in need. How satisfying!

Friends who have been with me in darkness, now rejoice with me in the light. A little cat sits at my feet while I write and follows me about the house as I work and prepare meals. A husband, who has been pruned as well as I, travels, speaks, and writes with me as a teammate. All this because God was able to use sickness to ready me for new heights.

We started with Paul's "boasting and tribulation." Let's hear him further on the subject:

> Yet what we suffer now is nothing compared to the glory he will give us later. For all creation is waiting patiently and hopefully for that future day when God will resurrect his children. For on that day thorns and thistles, sin, death, and decay—the things that overcame the world against its will at God's command—will all disappear, and the world around us will share in the glorious freedom from sin which God's children enjoy.
>
> For we know that even the things of nature, like animals and plants, suffer in sickness and death as they await this great event. And even we Christians, although we have the Holy Spirit within us as a foretaste of future glory, also groan to be released from pain and suffering. We, too, wait anxiously for that day when God will give us our full rights as his children, including the new bodies he has promised us—bodies that will never be sick again and will never die.
>
> We are saved by trusting. And trusting means looking forward to getting something we don't yet have—for a man who already has something doesn't need to hope and trust that he will get it. But if we must keep trusting God for something that hasn't happened yet, it teaches us to wait patiently and confidently.
>
> And in the same way—by our faith—the Holy Spirit helps us with our daily problems and in our praying. For we don't even know what we should pray for, nor how to pray as we should; but the Holy Spirit prays for us with such feeling that it cannot be expressed in words. And the Father who knows all hearts knows, of course, what the Spirit is saying as he pleads for us in harmony with God's own will. And we know that all that happens to us is working for our good if we love God and are fitting into his plans.
>
> For from the very beginning God decided that those who came to him—and all along he knew who would—should become like his Son, so that his Son would be the First, with many

brothers . . . he called us to come to him; and when we came, he declared us "not guilty," filled us with Christ's goodness, gave us right standing with himself, and promised us his glory.

What can we ever say to such wonderful things as these? If God is on our side, who can ever be against us? Since he did not spare even his own Son for us but gave him for us all, won't he also surely give us everything else?

Who dares accuse us whom God has chosen for his own? Will God? No! He is the one who has forgiven us and given us right standing with himself.

Who then will condemn us? Will Christ? *No!* For he is the one who died for us and came back to life again for us and is sitting at the place of highest honor next to God, pleading for us there in heaven.

Who then can ever keep Christ's love from us? When we have trouble or calamity, when we are hunted down or destroyed, is it because he doesn't love us anymore? And if we are hungry, or penniless, or in danger, or threatened with death, has God deserted us?

No, for the Scriptures tell us that for his sake we must be ready to face death at every moment of the day—we are like sheep awaiting slaughter; but despite all this, overwhelming victory is ours through Christ who loved us enough to die for us. For I am convinced that nothing can ever separate us from his love. Death can't, and life can't. The angels won't, and all the powers of hell itself cannot keep God's love away. Our fears for today, our worries about tomorrow, or where we are—high above the sky, or in the deepest ocean—nothing will ever be able to separate us from the love of God demonstrated by our Lord Jesus Christ when he died for us.[27]

Points to Ponder

1. Have you learned the lesson that suffering, mixed with seeking God and his Book, can be a great asset?

2. Are you willing to have God demonstrate his love and works in you? Can you get yourself out of the picture and allow God to be seen? Would you be willing to be God's instrument so that he can receive glory and others can know him?

3. Are you willing to ask God to help build your character by any means he would choose?

4. If you are suffering today, or living with or helping someone who is infirm, ask yourself these questions:

Have I asked the Lord to use this time to search my own heart to see if he has something to teach me? Is there anyone I need to forgive, anyone with whom I need to make something right? Is there something I should be doing that I have resisted and need to make a commitment to do?

Am I trusting God, allowing him to show me his love, provision, caring, and healing? Am I confessing my dependence on him, and him alone, to do what he wishes in my life? Am I thanking God in the midst of the situation for his presence and help?

Am I seeing the greatness of God in the situation and leaning on the Bible—God's revealed message to the human race—to instruct me in this time?

CHAPTER 9

WILL YOU TAKE RESPONSIBILITY?

A t eight years of age I informed my mother that I could finish a large bowl of cherry cobbler at one sitting. Mother protested, stating that the cobbler was *far* too much for a four-foot, fifty-five-pound little girl to eat. I insisted as only an eight-year-old can.

"Your eyes are bigger than your stomach, Linda," she cautioned.

The first few minutes I loved the heavenly taste of mother's cobbler. By the fifteenth bite the familiar taste of cooked sweetened cherries and melt-in-your-mouth crust began to lose its appeal. By the time I finished the bowl (my pride was at stake), I was hoping I'd never see cobbler again.

The biblical Scriptures tell us that "Foolishness is bound in the heart of a child." Why would I overeat? And why are we sometimes childish about the way we abuse the bodies God gave us?

One Problem Begets Another

Traits we often lack—patience, perseverance, discipline, hope, and self-esteem—are often connected to the problem of deteriorating health and our ability to preserve good health.

The first time I met Jackie she was in a deathly down cycle. Round-the-clock nurses, bedpans, enemas, spoon-feeding, vomit-drenched blankets, all signaled the marks of a critically ill person. Jackie wanted to live . . . but without paying the needed cost to regain normalcy. She would constantly refuse feeding or insist on eating food she could no longer digest. She loudly complained about each treatment or attempt to help her—like one being pampered at a beauty salon, rather than one whose life depended upon careful obedience to doctor's order.

Many people, such as Jackie, lack personal character qualities or do not find them in sufficient quantities when sickness comes. Health problems may worsen rather than be corrected. One woman had experienced years of sleeplessness and nerve problems. I encouraged her to visit a clinic specializing in balancing the body's chemistry. They found that she was seriously deficient in calcium. Within a few nights of receiving help she was sleeping through 'til dawn and her nerves were beginning to stabilize.

Instead of finishing her visit at the clinic, she insisted that she was fine and went home. Her body lacked sufficient treatment to maintain normalcy; within a week she began to miss sleep. She called me on the phone.

"I'm still having insomnia," she said. "Can you suggest anyplace else I can go?"

"Go back to the clinic," I said, "and stay until your body has stabilized."

"I've had enough of that place."

"Did they treat you badly?" I asked.

"No," she said. "It's just that I was there for over a week. Give me something that's quick. I don't want to be taking vitamins the rest of my life."

Victims of Our Own Making

These women are not alone in their shortsightedness. The U.S. government reports that there are over twenty-five million smokers in America. Based on interviews, it was reported that 55 percent of those smokers would not quit if they could. They are inhaling themselves to death.

In spite of numerous reports on the serious effects of obesity, the number of overweight people continues to grow. Junk food, for many, tops their list of consumable items.

In addition I know of:

- despairing wives who are watching their husbands drink themselves into early graves;

- husbands watching their wives starve themselves at the expense of their health;
- teenagers who choose pot over potatoes;
- workaholics giving little regard to physical maintenance;
- the elderly refusing to seek medical help for fear of confronting bad news;
- worried families watching a family member not follow doctor's orders.

I know people with allergies who won't avoid their worst food enemies, people with high blood pressure who will not deny themselves salt, people with low blood sugar who continue ingesting sugar in any form. We are often victims of our own making.

When sickness struck I knew little of caring for myself or of its importance. How could I resist foolish choices and impulsive behavior?

Where could I acquire the character I needed to care for my body?

Taking Responsibility

Taking responsibility for our lives stands as a great challenge to the least of us. Failure to take responsibility for our lives may be the number one reason for health-related problems.

According to Bernie S. Siegel, M.D., a practicing surgeon in New Haven, Connecticut, and teacher at Yale University, people who assertively take responsibility for their health are far likelier to have success at conquering invading diseases. He cites a study by Lydia Temoshok, Ph.D., who treated melanoma patients at the University of California at San Francisco in the early 1980s. The study showed that those patients who were extremely compliant and unassertive, and who did not deal with their emotions, had more severe cases and a worse prognosis.[1]

Further studies reveal that those who actively treat the whole person—body, soul, and spirit—have the best chance of coping with or winning over a debilitating invader. We must acknowledge our mind, emotion, and will as being intricately connected to our body's responses.

Observers from many faiths and philosophies have stated the

importance of our bodies and proper care for them. What importance does the Bible place on personal responsibility for body maintenance? King David, psalmist, military leader, and philosopher, understood the marvels of the human body. He phrased the complexity of our house structure, in the psalms in the Old Testament, as "fearfully and wonderfully made."[2] Paul, both a religious thinker and leader in the first-century Christian church, argues, "Your body is a temple of the Holy Spirit"[3]; therefore, "Like an athlete I punish my body, treating it roughly, training it to do what it should, not what it wants to."[4]

Detailed health laws involving food, sewage, contagious diseases, and so forth are spelled out in the pages of Scripture.

Ample illustrations of the practical need to care for our bodies abound in the biblical documents. For example, when King David was sick a young girl was summoned to lie near him and keep his body warm.[5] When Elijah had traveled far and was in excessive despair, he alternated rest and food until he regained his strength and perspective.[6] Exercise is also espoused in Scriptures: "Bodily exercise profits in some measure."[7]

Play by the Rules

Few shortcuts exist on the road to health. Basic rules of healing must be followed to produce positive results.

Rule number one: a person must want to get well. A defective volition, conscious or subconscious, will thwart the effort that is necessary to obtain and keep health.

It has been well said, "It's not whether we can or not; it's whether we want to." To have sufficient will to counter sickness an individual may need the help of others . . . and the help of God. In my uphill fight for life I would constantly ask the Lord to give me determination to be diligent. At times I prayed, "Help me to open myself up to receive health. Help me understand myself so that I don't work against myself."

Most of us learn things the hard way. We change when we're fed up with pain inflicted by our choices. One man illustrates. Used to a vigorous life, he, in his seventies, developed lung diseases—bronchitis, emphysema, inflammation. However, during the cold season, despite repeated warnings, he refused to wear warm clothing to protect him against the chill. Time and again he would contract a virus, flu, or bacteria, usually culminating in serious lung ailments.

Part of this man's difficulty was that in consenting to wear warmer clothes he was acknowledging his growing lack of vitality. He could no longer withstand the bitter cold of winter as in the past. His fear of aging and pride at admitting weakness led to tempting the elements. This man wanted to be well. But he wanted something else more—the security of denial.

One afternoon I was speaking with a beautiful young woman in the process of getting a divorce. She was also precariously close to a nervous breakdown. The divorce and nervous condition were partly the results of this woman's health problems. I knew the situation well and desired an opportunity to speak with her candidly.

I encouraged the woman by mentioning that the requirements of obtaining full health were not endless. If she applied herself diligently for a brief period she could get most of her stamina and coping ability back. I offered my assistance as I challenged her to practice the treatments she had learned.

Her reply, softly but firmly, was, "I'm not willing to do that. I tried the treatments once and found them difficult. I don't want to mess with them anymore."

"Look," I reasoned, "you don't have to live like you do—constantly feeling as if you're going over the edge. It makes sense to invest time in regaining your health now, before it's too late."

She listened. She thought. "I just want to be left alone," she said. "If people leave me alone, I'll be all right."

"You do need to cut down on stress," I assured her, "but you'll never avoid it indefinitely or altogether. It makes sense to build yourself up so that you can cope."

This woman had developed the pattern of "living for the moment." She wanted to feel better . . . but not enough!

Such conversations have caused me to appreciate the dilemma God encounters in the human race. We want free will. We want our choices. We want good times. But don't ask us to invest the required effort in assuring future stability. Then we wonder why God doesn't do something when everything caves in on us.

My friend, at many points in your illness the ball will be in *your* court!

Rule number two: You must be *determined* to get well. Consider a woman whom Jesus healed.

> And a woman who had had a hemorrhage for twelve years, and had endured much at the hands of many physicians, and had spent all that she had and was not helped at all, but rather had grown worse, after hearing about Jesus, came up in the crowd behind Him and touched His cloak. For she thought, "If I just touch His garments, I shall get well." And immediately the flow of her blood was dried up; and she felt in her body that she was healed of her affliction.

How did the Great Physician view such an effort?

> And immediately Jesus, perceiving in Himself that the power proceeding from Him had gone forth, turned around in the crowd and said, "Who touched My garments?" And His disciples said to Him, "You see the multitude pressing in on You, and You say, 'Who touched Me?'"
>
> And He looked around to see the woman who had done this. But the woman fearing and trembling, aware of what had happened to her, came and fell down before Him, and told Him the whole truth. And He said to her, "Daughter, your faith has made you well; go in peace, and be healed of your affliction."[8]

Many times God will honor such determination as this woman demonstrated. In fact Jesus taught that persistence pays off. *"Keep on asking. Keep on seeking. Keep on knocking. For everyone who asks, receives. Anyone who seeks, finds. If only you will knock, the door will open"*[9] (italics mine).

Two vivid experiences marked a turning point in my own healing. They both involved determination. After the church elders prayed for me I sensed a directive from the Lord to seek *every* reasonable avenue of healing. At different points this meant that I would actively pursue leads, endure difficult treatment, make the extra effort, and put out the required money, trusting the Lord to meet the financial need.

On a further occasion I made an important decision. Every available penny would be used to secure my health. Later, after marriage, I shared with my husband, Rusty, that there was *one* thing he could do for me that would mean more than anything else—help me get well. This meant car trips to clinics, seeking medical help, using funds conservatively in every area in order to allow money to be released for health purposes.

Such single-minded determination, whether it be in areas of financial focus, curtailing activities, searching out treatments, meditating on the Scriptures, or reprogramming our thinking, is often what makes the difference between those who get better and those who do not.

Many people will not make this required, sometimes sacrificial, effort to get well. They might spend money to repair their car, but their health goes unattended. One bedridden woman remarked, "I'd like to feel better, but right now we are buying a new home. We haven't got the money to invest in treatment." (She admitted the home was a need to "keep up with the Joneses." It was not a necessity.) Time, treatment, effort, money, prayer, soul searching—what are you willing to invest in your health?

A healing that Jesus performed speaks indirectly to determination and repeated effort.

> And they came to Bethsaida. And they brought a blind man to Him, and entreated Him to touch him. And taking the blind man by the hand, He brought him out of the village; and after spitting on his eyes, and laying His hands upon him, He asked him, "Do you see anything?" And he looked up and said, "I see men for I am seeing them like trees, walking about." Then again He laid His hands upon his eyes; and he looked intently and was restored, and began to see everything clearly.[10]

Healing by degrees is common to many of us. It was my experience not to have one healing but many. "Many are the afflictions of the righteous, but the Lord delivers him out of them all."[11]

Do you have staying power? One lady told me, "Until the bell rings signaling the end of the last round, I will just keep on fighting. I may get knocked down—there may be days that my body just won't cooperate—but Lord willing, as long as I'm alive I'm gonna get back up again and again." How determined are you to get well?

Rule number three: do something *now!* The more seriously sick the person the more that is required to get well. Prior to serious illness there are times we are given warnings. Small pains become big pains if those warnings aren't heeded. Little problems become widespread if precautions aren't taken in time.

"Don't ask me to stop drinking milk," one woman with milk-related allergies told me. "Maybe if things get really bad I'll stop. But they're not that bad yet." How bad does it have to get before one does something?

Another woman constantly talks of her bouts with arthritis, backache, indigestion, constipation, and fatigue. For her to make a change in lifestyle or eating habits is totally out of the question. Instead she calls anybody and everybody to have them pray for her, provide for her, and do for her. Exactly when, at what point, will she decide to take responsibility? How many will have to take time visiting her in the hospital, preparing her meals, taking care of her interests because when she could do something about the problem she would not?

To make a point, I said quite firmly to someone who "put off" taking responsibility, "Since you won't do what's necessary to correct your health problem now, you will get much worse. Don't come to me for help then. If you won't take responsibility for your own health now, don't ask me to carry it for you later." This conversation was not as far out as it may sound. God requires that we take responsibility. He may decide to withdraw his help if a person consistently ignores the warnings.

A minister, praying for a hospitalized emphysema patient, was startled when the man's hand turned cold and clammy. Unaccustomed to having someone die while he prayed, the minister questioned others as to the possible reason for this man's death. What he learned was that on four occasions the man had been healed of lung ailments through prayer, but eventually fell back into smoking. At age fifty-eight the man recklessly smoked himself to a premature death. He never got the message that *now* is the time to deal with the problem.

The act of seeking help while there's time is sometimes complicated by an interesting notion. Clyde was not part of a church fellowship, but watched religious television programming. One station in particular aired an abundance of programs on healing faith. In a day like ours faith teaching is a needed emphasis. But somehow Clyde had gotten it in his mind that he must be healed by faith alone. For six years this had been Clyde's stance. And for six years his ailment grew worse.

In Clyde's case the question was not whether or not God heals. Rather, Clyde was irresponsible about his eating, sleeping, lifestyle, and health care. He was using "a religious teaching" to maintain an ungodly and unaccountable existence. By postponing responsibility he lost six years of health.

Foresight seems removed from our generation. Who will later carry the responsibility for those who refuse to carry responsibility for their lives now?

Rule number four: *focus* on health. One must not arbitrarily grope for health. One must make a conscious decision to be open to treatments, lifestyle adjustments, an inner makeover by his Spirit, or whatever else may be required to regain health. This focus may be essential for the sick and those who care for the sick if healing, especially long-term healing, is to have a chance.

Focusing requires that we ask these questions:

Am I ready to pay a price for the state of being healthy? Am I willing to consider various treatments that may be difficult, time consuming, costly? Am I willing to sacrifice my pride, my active lifestyle, my enjoyments, in order to put the required effort into health care? Am I willing to retrain my eating and living habits? Am I in this for the long haul?

What is my reason for seeking health? Am I willing to let God have his purposes fulfilled in my life? Am I willing to work at health for the sake of others?

The exercise of focusing may do us all good.

Rule number five: we do our part; God does his.

Some take the responsibility of getting well seriously—too seriously! One woman had read so much material related to the causes and cures of cancers that she literally became weighted down with the encumbrance of personally preventing another cancer recurrence: was she eating, sleeping, relaxing, working, relating, and living right? Had she solved all the stress-related psychological and personal problems that could turn the foreboding of cancer into a reality? The frantic efforts to keep her lifestyle free of cancer causes increased her tension. This burden is not uncommon to the sick.

Is it *all* up to us? Where does a person find the incentive to act and live responsibly? Who will help the sick person and those who love the sick bear the burden and responsibility of getting well?

As I entered my teens and the onset of health problems I had many questions:

What was life about?

Who was I in this great cosmic universe?

On what basis should I make choices?

What was important?

Who would help me with the difficulties of health-related problems?

Fortunately, as I shared earlier, I found the source of these answers while facing my first serious illness. I did not find an illusive "higher power," a cosmic source, a great force, or an extension of myself. These would have done me little good as my mind got weaker and my physical strength was challenged.

The person who is sick finds it almost impossible to hold to a creed, live by a set of rules, please an invisible power, measure up to some standard, or imbue himself or herself with magical motivations. The truly sick know better. They are not capable of Herculean duration, effort, or attitude. They may not even be up to some of the rules of healing: motivation, determination, focusing. What they need is a FRIEND—someone outside themselves (and inside) who can love, strengthen, comfort, direct, change, forgive, motivate and help them be healed.

God's Responsibility

Then, what part do we play in our own healing? What part does God play?

We are to take responsibility for our own lives and choices: to seek God for his direction; to walk through doors that God opens to us; to obediently pursue what he has directed us in; to lean on him for strength and determination; to allow him to change us into the people we were created to be; to allow him to use our lives on behalf of others.

What is God's part? Open the Bible and read for yourself.

- "I have loved you with an everlasting love." [12]
- "God always goes before me. He is with me. He will not fail me. He will not forsake me. So don't be afraid or bewildered." [13]
- "Trust in the Lord with all your heart. Don't rely on your own estimation of the situation. In everything you do turn your attention to God, and He will direct your path." [14]

- "For it is God who is at work in you, both to will and to work for His good pleasure."[15]
- "And the Lord will guide you continually, and satisfy you with good things, and make your bones strong; and you shall be like a watered garden, like a spring of water, whose waters fail not."[16]
- God "is able to do exceedingly, abundantly, above all we ask or think."[17]
- "God is not deaf that He cannot hear, nor is His arm shortened that he cannot save."[18]
- "I can do all things through Him who strengthens me."[19]
- "Fear not; for I am with you. Be not dismayed; for I am your God. I will strengthen you; yes, I will help you; yes, I will uphold you with the right hand of my righteousness."[20]
- "They that wait on the Lord will not be disappointed or ashamed."[21]
- "When you pass through the waters I will be with you; and through the rivers, they shall not overwhelm you; when you walk through fire you shall not be burned, and the flame shall not consume you."[22]
- "Though I fall it will not be fatal, for God is holding me in His hand."[23]
- "I go to prepare a place for you."[24]

We are to take responsibility for our lives, and lean on him who is not flawed in character, nor limited in the value he places upon us, nor restricted in what he is able to do on our behalf.

When we seek the Lord and persevere, we observe the Lord's hand and grow in faith, understanding, and often health.

Points to Ponder

1. Have you examined possible thinking patterns, inappropriate behavior, incorrect philosophies, lifestyle, etc., which may contribute to present health problems?

2. Are you a victim of your own making? Are you allowing junk food, malnutrition, smoking, alcohol, lack of exercise, drugs, disregard of the effects of pollutants, pesticides, chemicals, etc., to affect your health?

3. Are you taking responsibility for your own health?

4. Do you want to get well? Are you determined to get well? Are you looking for shortcuts to healing—a pill, an operation, etc., rather than seeking total healing—body, soul, and spirit? Are you properly focused?

5. Are you procrastinating or persevering? Will you keep on asking, seeking, and knocking? The Lord longs to give, to show his kindness toward you.

6. Are you bearing your burden alone? Have the demands of illness or caring for the sick been too much for you? The great God who has revealed himself in the Bible longs to bear your burdens. "Cast your burden on the Lord and He will sustain you."[25] If you do not know God and his son Jesus, seek him out and rejoice in his everlasting love.

CHAPTER 10

OVERCOMING FEAR

I had recently moved into a mountain cabin. From the north side I could see well beyond the mountain ranges into the desert. The man-made lake at the bottom of the hill, often covered with ice and surrounded by tall white trees, was a picture of serenity in the winter. I loved it when icicles dropped from the roof, watching to see how "long" they could grow before the sheer weight brought them crashing down. In the summers the heat of the day and dazzling blue of the sky attracted many tourists who loved the fishing and swimming. If I was awake at dawn, as I often was, the wonder of the peek-a-boo sunrise never failed to amaze me.

Rusty and I had chosen to make our bedroom downstairs with the rock-imbedded fireplace, wood paneling, and many windows letting in the warm rays of light. On this particular evening I was clothed in my warm flannel nightgown and snuggled deep down in my bed. But even in my lovely surroundings I could not dispel the sickly downcast spirit in my soul and body that sickness had caused. Sipping tea, I pushed back negative thoughts. Finally, I picked up a storybook to read. Unfamiliar with the plot, I thought that a short, blithe story might prove a good distraction.

I threw myself into the story. Cheerful at first, the story line soon changed and the hero unexpectedly died on the last page. I was horrified. In my weakened mind, I wondered if it was a message to me about my own death.

I fought off fear—the fear of losing control to death—then seemed sucked right into it. I remember the pleasant room fading into a blur, reality becoming a swirl of darkness about me.

As a camera is able to center on one object, blocking out all others, so my focus became a tiny circle of doom. That which I feared—loss of control—had come upon me. Sensing I could no longer fight, I cried out to God to save me.

All of a sudden God entered the circle. I still was not aware of the room, but at the center of the darkness a presence had joined me. I was no longer alone. The need to keep myself alive or determine my destiny didn't rest on me, nor in that sweet moment with him did it concern me. When I lost control . . . he took control. When I could no longer hold on to him, God held onto me.

Growing Fear

Throughout childhood, fears pummeled my fragile mind. These fears were infinitesimal when compared to the terror of adult years plagued by illness. Illness rarely travels alone. Fear is its companion.

"Fear brings torment," a biblical writer explains. Torment is defined as anguish, vexation, torture, and pain in Webster's seventh edition. I could add my own list of nouns and adjectives—dread, harrowing, faint-heartedness, horror—and still feel inadequate in describing the siege of this hideous monster.

Fear and Sickness—The Tie that Binds

Fear in connection with sickness may range from little concerns to floating anxiety and foreboding doom. What seems within coping range while in good health soon appears overwhelming to a sick person. What was manageable becomes unmanageable.

Sickness often does not initiate fear as much as it propels it forward. In other words, whatever gnawed at us before now gnaws at our sense of peace. Whatever lightly pursued our thoughts prior to sickness now hounds them.

"I don't know what has happened to my husband," a gentle woman told me. "Ever since his operation he is irritable and snappy. I can't seem to do anything to please him. I feel like I'm living with a stranger."

I had an opportunity to talk with this woman's husband.

"My mind is constantly battling fear," he shared. "One minute I am thinking we'll go broke if I don't get better soon. The next I'm afraid my wife is going to leave me. I guess it is my anxiety that puts demands on her, always testing her. What has happened to the person I once was?"

This conversation lasted only twenty minutes, but this dear man must have referred to fear—afraid, scared, uncertain, worried, frightened—at least thirty times. No wonder. Medical science confirms that when the body is impaired, the mind is subject to many more fears.

Catherine Marshall writes extensively about the fears that accompanied her lingering illness. She writes,

> Last night I had a vivid dream . . . . While driving a car, I became terrified of what was ahead. With no clear idea of what the problem was, I could not seem to keep from doing the very worst thing possible—closing my eyes as I drove.
>
> Then I was driving over a concrete road with about three inches of very clear water on it. There was still overwhelming fear in me. I awoke in panic.
>
> As I pondered it this morning, the message of the dream would appear to be that my actual danger is very small—shallow water. Thus my real problem is fear itself.[1]

Not only can the state of the body make one more vulnerable to anxiety, the particular circumstances of the sick also propagate fear. Greg lived his own kind of war with asthma. Attacks of asthma could be brought on with any inner or outer stress, with a change of temperature, or a whiff of fumes, sprays or insecticides—so prevalent in our culture. Little warning preceded the sudden lack of breath, the gasping for air. The bronchial tubes needed constant watchfulness lest they shut down suddenly and fatally.

Joyce lived with a similar conflict. Her heart worked improperly. A ready supply of nitroglycerin tablets were with her at all times. Once she forgot them. Thinking they were in her purse she reached for them in an emergency. She emptied her purse nervously. Finding nothing she began to sweat. Her palms became clammy. Her heart rate shot up; the troubled organ was irritated further. Fortunately friends got her back home to her medication in time to thwart the danger. The trauma of the moment and the fear of its happening again stayed with Joyce.

The Body Affects the Mind

How might a person deal with the fears that accompany sickness? Since fearful thoughts are often the result of a negative pull of the body on the mind—the taxed brain being the real culprit—it would be extremely important for the sick to have knowledge of how the body affects the mind and learn how to deal with it.

Consider that even a healthy person who has missed a lot of sleep has a difficult time being optimistic. The saying, "Get a good night's sleep. Things will look better in the morning," is indicative of the fact that mental perspective is influenced by the shape the brain is in—tired, rested, stressed, relaxed, dull, alert. Watching a child's crankiness when he needs a nap, or observing the inability of a toddler to be sweet when teething are mini-studies in this dilemma.

When the brain is overstressed, fear becomes difficult to reason with. The very ill might respond when sudden fears assail them, "Look, I am worried because my body is weak and is affecting my brain negatively. Things are not as bad as they appear. God is still here watching out for me. Things simply look worse due to the physical state of my body. I will treat my body (sleep, nutrition, medication) rather than try to work out this fear. When my body is better things will look more manageable.'"

This technique has been employed by soldiers battling fatigue and emotional stress. When their bodies begin to shake, sweat, or behave uncontrollably, they are urged to treat the panic with reminders that this is a bodily reaction. "It will stop soon and I will get through this."

Understanding the workings of my body—hence giving me some control over the situation—delivered me many times from the trenches of despair and dread. To gain this education I asked questions of those experienced in the field and observed patterns within my body.

Karen lived with a cyclical apprehension—a bleeding ulcer. She knew that stress worsened her condition, yet her condition stressed her. She often found herself in patterns of worry and fear.

The stress cycle went as follows: Karen sought to relax herself so that the troubled stomach would heal. The stomach would be better for a minute, then she worried whether her stomach was all right. Immediately she felt her stomach tighten. At this awareness she feared for her stomach, not wishing to bring on vomiting blood. The additional fear caused her stomach to tighten further. She sought to relax. On and on this effort would continue until Karen feared she could not keep control of the situation any longer. "It was the worst nightmare I ever lived through."

Getting Off the Unmerry-Go-Round

Many fear cycles can be broken with understanding. During critical years of insomnia I came to fully appreciate the incapacitating fear of not sleeping. Others are mindful of this as well. One woman tells of her father's battle with insomnia. Originally business pressures caused him to lose sleep. After those pressures subsided, he still found himself tossing and turning into the wee hours of the morning. The more sleep he lost, the more fear took hold. The more fear took hold, the more difficult he found it to sleep. He grew to dread his bed, his bedroom—anything associated with sleep.

Many sleep problems were at last resolved for me as I learned several things. First, I learned that sleep is a natural process. An individual will eventually fall asleep. That took some of the sting out of fear.

Then I learned that if the body is not sleeping, there is usually a physical reason for it. Even if an emotional upset has triggered the insomnia, there is probably a physical reason which can be corrected: tension in the neck and shoulders, gaseous foods or gas provoked by tension, low potassium, low calcium, toxicity, low blood sugar, dilated arteries, TMJ (dysfunction of the temporomandibular joint), and so forth.

One should do all he can to treat emotional causes of stress and fear. Talking out the fear with a friend or counselor can be very beneficial. It is also comforting to learn that correcting health problems will enable the body to function more normally. For example, to treat insomnia, depending on the case, one might add potassium, calcium, magnesium, and other minerals to the diet, drink water to dilute toxins which tense muscles, clean the colon, massage upper torso, participate in vigorous exercise early in the evening, eat something light prior to sleeping, or avoid chocolates, caffeine, and alcohol. A sleep clinic may also help the insomnia victim.

Outmaneuver Fear

On the practical side, diversion has been used by many to outmaneuver fear. As quick movements and surprises may steer troubled children from what is upsetting them, so diversions may direct the sick away from their fears. Walks through nature may deflect fear as might a picture window, a good story, a visit with a cheerful friend, a pet, or a hobby.

Living in our scenic mountains as colors and seasons unfolded before me with an abundance of wildlife—squirrels, raccoons, bluejays, woodpeckers, owls, ducks, quail, coyotes, even bears—aided me through many trying years. In the early years of illness, drab living conditions agitated every fearful fiber of my being. All the more reason to assist the sick in providing comforting surroundings. A wise Creator provided the sky, grasses, flowers, trees, birds, wildlife, stars, beaches, deserts, and mountains to soothe and calm troubled souls.

There is a delicate balance between diversion and confrontation of fear. Looking wide-eyed at fear may magnify it—the very admission of its presence somehow enlarging its hold on us. The denial of fear may short-circuit the process needed to shoo it away. Frankly, as with other ghouls in our life there may be an appropriate time to do both—ignore and challenge the monster.

Diversion, then, may be an adequate foe of fear. However, the one who diverts fear continuously rather than facing it is liable to be endlessly locked in its claws. It is necessary to acknowledge fear and search out answers to it.

This strait poses its own kind of contradiction. One rarely jumps from a high place, not knowing if anyone will catch him or her. Facing a fear without solution can be the most arduous jump of all. As the guilty have a difficult time confessing sin until they are assured of forgiveness, so a fearful person may find it impossible to admit a fear before sensing extrication.

God Is Adequate for Today

A bit of practical advice concerning fear involves a biblical admonition, "Take, therefore, no thought for tomorrow."[3] Not much encouragement, you say. And nearly impossible for the sick. I agree. A sick mind often lacks the discipline to steer itself away from problems. But to live just for today discourages a lot of tomorrow's fears. It has taken me many years to appreciate the benefits of living a day at a time. Several insights helped me put this into practice.

First I realized that focusing on today, not tomorrow, is a biblical command.[4] The wise writers of the Bible did not suggest trusting God for today; they ordered it. The Lord isn't just hinting that our lives would be less fearful if we brought him our troubles day by day. He goes further—he knows it is vitally important that we *not fret* over tomorrow's possibilities. That includes the fear of what may become of us, and the fear of fear itself pouncing upon us at some point.

A second insight is that God would provide the necessary strength to do what needed to be done whenever tomorrow became today. Therefore, I was not to concern myself with the many details of life. He would provide. The Bible expands on this idea of sufficient strength to accompany specific responsibilities, "As your days are, so will your strength be"[5]—a promise that when the time comes to fulfill a responsibility or carry out the will of God, the needed stamina will be given to pursue it.

A final point made it easier to let go of fear about "tomorrow." "Do not seek the approval of others!" I have often seen those who are vulnerable to illness controlled by the needs to be accepted, approved of, or esteemed. Such needs, not deliberately and persistently given to the Father to satisfy, will cause the healthiest to waver under the pressure of pleasing others. I had to learn that if I passed out in front of others, forgot what I was saying, couldn't communicate satisfactorily, had to excuse myself and leave the front of an auditorium with all eyes on me, or quit a project I had agreed to do, that was acceptable. I mustn't overly concern myself with what others think. The whole world needn't and wouldn't understand. But that was all right. I could not meet everyone's expectations. I had to learn to say no without the fear that others would reject me (or at least not allowing the rejection to undo me). I also found that since I sought to please the Lord, he rewarded me with unfailing and understanding friends. To this day I consider them one of my greatest gifts from God.

Illness speeded up a needed process in my life. When a person is sick, every wrong attitude bears harder on the individual's health. It took a long time, but at last I stopped (at least I hope I've stopped) trying to meet other people's standards and measure up to God instead.

Source of Deliverance from Fear

There is only one ultimate source of deliverance from fear that I know. It is a Person. He is made known in the pages of the Bible. He is proven in the Resurrection. He is demonstrated in the lives of those who follow him wholly.

This God, who became incarnate in the person of Jesus Christ, had already done the most for me when he provided me with forgiveness. Yet he has done even more! I had to learn that he was holding me. Think of it! He was not a product of my own mind. He was greater than my mind, greater than my body. When I could no longer hold on to him, I learned the most glorious truth—he was holding on to me. When I could no longer hold on to my own life, he was still holding on to me.

Kathleen was forty-nine when she discovered she had cancer. A growth in her right thigh first felt like a "charley-horse" and gradually worsened. The diagnosis was frightening, the worst strain of cancer—rate of cure less than 5 percent.

At first she diverted fear by remaining occupied with efforts to help herself. Kathleen learned that diet, lifestyle, and temperament played a major role in the advancement of carcinoma cells. She lost no time in beginning a program of nutrition and counseling to reverse such a process.

"As long as I felt I could *do something* to correct the problem, I was able to win my fight against anxiety," she states. However, two years later during a routine checkup, a new patch of cancer was discovered. She read the doctor's chart—metastasized sarcoma. Horror engulfed her.

"I could see in my mind Jesus standing off in the woods, arms outstretched, beckoning me. I believe it was my wish to die. I had fought the best I knew how and wished to struggle no more."

Kathleen had used all of her own resources. She could no longer hold on. No wonder she longed to die. Kathleen did not die. Why? Because ultimately God was holding Kathleen. When Kathleen came to the end of her rope, she could see that God's resources were fathomless, his strength unlimited. Today, Kathleen Santucci lives in Moraga, California, serving the God who healed her.

The sense of being overpowered by fear is probably the worse threat for many of the sick. One woman writes concerning the challenge of facing fear: " 'Fear is lack of faith,' I told myself. 'It dishonors God.' But then I discovered that I could not handle fear any more than I could mastermind any other strong emotion."[6]

When education, effort, diversion, or honesty no longer prevents the ultimate spread of fear; when a sense of control, which the medical profession seeks to give the sick, and which Kathleen eventually lost, is gone, how does one deal with fear? Several experiences in my life serve to illustrate the answer.

Before I discovered many of my health problems I lived with a type of inner shaking that would not budge. At nighttime when symptoms were often exaggerated, I would lie in my bed in dreaded anticipation. The more tired I became, the less success I found at putting to rest vague and unrelenting fears and trepidation. I often thought I was going to lose my mind. Fear of total insanity tracked me as a lion does its prey.

During a very severe period, when no treatment effectively touched any corner of my illness, I sat alone in a rocking chair pondering my futile circumstances. I laid out my case before the Lord.

"There's no control," I said. "No wonder I live with terror. Everything is out of control."

The Lord responded with a clear idea within my mind. "Linda, if you could be in control of every facet of your life, or if I could be in control of every facet of your life, which would you choose?"

Such a question provoked serious thought. I mulled over the query for weeks. Even though my greatest fear was losing control, I had to acknowledge that it was best that God was in control.

When my ability was not sufficient, I would confront fear by

reminding myself that God was in control. This was done by gar-
nering Bible principles of God's faithfulness and care. I found
many.

I concentrated on verses reminding me of God's presence:

- "Fear not, for I am with you. Do not be dismayed. I am
  your God. I will strengthen you; I will help you; I will
  uphold you with my victorious right hand."[7]
- "Be strong and of good courage, do not fear or be in
  dread . . . for it is the LORD your God who goes with you;
  he will not fail you or forsake you."[8]

Since nighttime was the most fearful part of the day, I recalled:

- "The steadfast love of the Lord never ceases, His mercies
  never come to an end; they are new every morning; great is
  thy faithfulness."[9]

When I feared losing my mind I would recall:

- "Thou wilt keep him in perfect peace, whose mind is
  stayed on thee: because he trusteth in thee. Trust ye in the
  LORD for ever: for in the LORD JEHOVAH is everlasting
  strength."[10]

When I feared fear itself I was reminded of:

- "I sought the Lord, and He answered me, and delivered
  me from all my fears."[11]

I continued to do my part in the fight against fear—saturating
myself in the Bible and rehearsing its truths. At times this meant
that my will took authority over my emotions, steadfastly refusing
to be intimidated by fear. God did his part in and amidst these
exercises as well by providing me with the power of the Holy Spirit
to stand firm.

Sacrifice of Praise

There was another discovery I made to help bridge the gap
between God's adequacy and my fears—something that would recall the greatness of God to my situation. The practice helps establish peace and victory over fear—the practice is praise.

For the blessed, praise is just an echo of the blessing, but for the oppressed, praise is a sacrifice. The Bible uses the phrase the "sacrifice of praise" to express what this discipline often involves. It needn't start out as heartfelt. Thankfully, that is not a requirement put upon us. For the Lord knows that if we simply begin to glorify and praise him, a deeper peace will come. Our emotions will be pulled more in line with God's ability to care for us. *A person who exercises his praise muscles will not be lost in deep fear for long.*

I learned this lesson most readily at points of greatest anxiety. Mechanically, like turning on a switch, I would begin, "Praise you, Lord. I thank you that you are in control of my situation. Praise you that you are with me and will help me in my circumstances. Praise you that I am not alone." Over and over I would repeat the words. Eventually the "empty" syllables became reality. The reaching out provided a continuity between my thoughts and God's. In fact, often after a period of praising, a sweetness came upon my soul which was so dear and holy that I forgot temporarily the pain, fear, isolation, and trials which accompany bodily affliction.

Psalm 77:6 says, "I call to remembrance my song in the night." For many praise is the only song they sing in the midst of tribulation—they can do nothing else—but oh what a glorious melody it can become.

The reason for the ministering and enlightening power of praise is relatively simple. The heart of life is relationship. It is neither Christian principle nor creed—these two only support the sense of relationship. When we are blocked from the face of the Lord, and from the reality of his goodness, many negatives can emerge threatening our peace, even inviting death. God does not desire this.

Understanding the nature of catastrophe, he has provided a wedge, a connector, a link to his love. So great is his care for us that if we will start the process of praise he will complete it—supernaturally lifting the veil, providing us glimpses of his greatness and love.

Exodus 20:21 records, "Moses drew near unto the thick darkness where God was." When we begin praising it is from out of our darkness. But plunging forth we may pass the gloom and move into the light.

For those too sick or desolate to even praise—do not fear, the love of God is still near! God is bigger than any fear.

However, for some, the ability to help oneself is highly limited. With those we must have patience and understanding.

Dr. Earl Radmacher wrote this following poignant account. It is included here to encourage those who love the sick and have experienced a similar ordeal.

*W*ith quivering lips, Dr. Paul Kaufman voiced his prayer request at our May 15th Western family prayer meeting: "One wonders how long one is expected to take it. It seems that 15½ years is enough."

Those words came from the heart of a man who had lovingly cared for his invalid wife, Freeda, the victim of a stroke as the result of surgery almost 16 years ago. For most of those years Freeda could take care of herself with some help, but Paul did all the cooking, baking, gardening, canning and housekeeping. In addition, he taught a full load of Greek grammar and a laymen's class of several doctors before breakfast every Thursday morning. More than a lecturer, Paul was constantly pastoring his students. They stayed in his home. They traveled with him to conferences. This was a true shepherd with his sheep.

Then Paul began to experience real trauma when it became necessary for him to transfer Freeda to a foster home. At that time he said, "We've been blessed to have each other for so long—after 42 years of married life, you become quite attached to someone." Actually Freeda did quite well in the foster home, but the emptiness created in the Kaufman home was very difficult for Paul to handle (apparently more difficult than anyone thought). Consequently, Paul took his own life at approximately midnight on Monday, May 20, 1985.

I was called out of class on Tuesday morning by Rich Hagenbaugh, Paul's pastor and dear friend, who had met with Paul every week for years to read the Greek New Testament. Called to Paul's house by a student friend, Pastor Rich found the following note taped to the front door.

May 20, 1985

Dear Pastor Rich:

My poor brain is hard to figure out. It is not sending me the messages one wants to hear. You know that deep depression has been my unwanted lot for a long time. It may be a Satanic attack, but it has seemingly not been possible for me to shake it. If something happens unforseen because of scrambled signals, please have the deacons and/ or deaconesses distribute to any needy all the food in the refrigerator, two freezers and fruit pantry at the back of the rumpus room. Thank you, dear brother in the Lord. Your message on Sunday was so excellent (II Timothy 2:2). Love to you and all my brothers and sisters in Christ—Paul.

When I arrived at the house, Pastor Rich, the police officers, the medical examiner and a friend were there. On the seat of Paul's easy chair was his Greek New Testament opened to the well-worn pages of Luke 10. Stacks of magazines and books were on both sides of the chair, but it was apparent that Paul was, as usual, in the Word before he took his life.

My heart cried out to God: "Lord, how do I put all of this together? How will I explain it to the stunned faculty, staff and student body?" God answered me even as He answered when David cried out in his distress (cf. Psalm 118), God reminded me that He does not see as we see. We see one event at a time, often focusing on the last thing. God sees all things simultaneously. He doesn't see anything more vividly than He sees other things; that is, He sees everything equally.

In the light of what God is like, we need to correct our seeing. We need to look at the whole of Paul Kaufman's life and recognize, for example, the tremendous teaching ministry that God allowed him to have over many, many years. Surely, that will be among the "gold, silver and precious stones" at the Judgment Seat of Christ.

On the other hand, we must not minimize the seriousness of sin. Taking one's life is the sin of murder,

and it was a tragedy for Paul to end his life in that way.
Yet, Christ paid for that sin, along with all others, on the
cross.

What may we learn from this experience? Here was a
situation where the immediate needs were not essentially
spiritual—such as time in the Word of God and fellowship
with the people of God. Paul was surrounded by both.
Paul never let the Word get away from him; he was always
in the Word of God. Furthermore, he was surrounded by
friends from the student body, the faculty, the church and
others. People knew the difficulties he was facing, and
they prayed for him regularly, reaching out to him. But in
those last weeks, Paul seemed to have difficulty processing
people's offers of love.

As I look at the situation now, I believe that this was
a time when Paul's mind was indeed "scrambled" and he
needed to have medical care from a psychiatrist. The
evidence suggests there may have been a physical or
chemical imbalance as a result of prolonged depression.
Perhaps someone should have insisted that he go see Dr.
Robert Buckler, a psychiatrist on our faculty. However, we
tend not to intrude into people's lives to that degree. But
here was an example where the need was undoubtedly
physical rather than spiritual.

The foregoing has been the dark side. The bright side
is that Paul Kaufman, because of Christ's gift at Calvary,
is now in the presence of our blessed Savior where there is
joy and rejoicing evermore. He will have no more
depression, sorrow or pain. There is also a very bright
side here at the seminary. We have seen God meet our
needs significantly and creatively in this time of testing.
Phone calls and letters continue to pour in as former
students and colleagues pay tribute to the impact Paul
Kaufman's teaching ministry had in their lives, and in
turn, in the lives of others. As the process of healing
continues, we remember that He does not allow us to
experience anything that has not first gone before His
review in the spirit of 1 Corinthians 10:13, and we are
comforted.

The Ultimate Release from Fear

Searching out the promises of God and practicing praise will rekindle a sense of peace. But is there more?

For years I had fought fear, maneuvered around it, fortified myself against it, educated myself to understand it, and prayed to be delivered of it. All efforts helped to some degree in my contest against mental tyranny.

Almost fourteen years into my battle with the quagmires of sickness and dread, I discovered for myself the best tool against fear. One night a new kind of peace was opened to me.

Previously I had cast my worries and fears upon a God I was learning to trust. As this conviction matured I was able to cast my total life and sanity at his feet, certain of his commitment to me. Before I had dealt with specifics. Now I would lay down my life in its entirety.

As my confidence in the Lord grew I added my new dimension.

"All right Lord," I would begin. "This is not my life. It is your life. If you want my body to settle down you must show me how to help it. But if not Lord, then I will not sleep. And if I do not sleep I may crack up. If I do not sleep I may die.

"So Lord, if I crack up—if they find me in the streets roaming around, not knowing who I am, I praise you for that. And if I die and can no longer serve you on earth—I praise you for that. If my body is so destroyed that I am in constant pain—I praise you for that. This is not *my* life. I have given it completely to you. You are responsible for me. And I know you will take care of me."

Psychologists tell us that the burdens of life are often culprits that weigh us down. How fitting that the Christian has a burden bearer.

"Cast your burden on the Lord, and he will sustain you."[12]

When I could let my body and my mind surrender completely to God's plan whatever it was, whatever it cost; when I could release the final burden of living into his hands, not my own; when I could relinquish my hold on my own person and stability, I found the arms of God bearing me up and bringing me peace. And fear lost its foothold.

This same truth exists for those who love the sick—who fight the fear of losing someone close to them. There is strength and freedom from fear as we are able to relinquish those we love. God cares far more about the sick than we care. Troubled souls can find peace in him.

Some may conceive that this fearlessness is a difficult place to achieve. The writer of the book of Hebrews states, "Let us labor, therefore, to enter his rest."[13] Could this be a hint that struggle precedes our entrance into quietness of soul? For me it resembled Indiana Jones forging through dense thicket, skillfully finessing his way through mines, perilously avoiding booby traps, teetering on the edge of sheer-faced cliffs, finally to arrive at the place of a rare jewel. Should I lose sight of that jewel then the presence of the Holy Spirit in my life and the sure-footedness of the Word of God—the Bible—will help me retrace my steps.

However, many people do not know where that jewel resides. To overcome fear, one must be pointed in the right direction. The psalmist wrote, "What time I am afraid, I will trust in [God]."[14] I claimed this promise years before I understood its release. But I was primed sufficiently and focused exclusively on the Giver of peace. It was only a matter of time before I would enjoy the fruit.

Points to Ponder

1. Are you aware of how the body, mind, and spirit affect one another? If not working properly, they can bring one another down. In the same way, if we build up each area, we can sustain that which is weaker. Seek to understand and build up your body, the vessel in which your person is housed. Understand that, when your mind is extremely negative, your body may need treating as well as your mental and spiritual resources. What are some of the things which physically contribute to depression? Mineral imbalance, low potassium, low lithium or trace minerals; toxicity (may need colon cleansing); allergic reactions to various foods; viruses; water retention; inadequate supply of oxygen; fatigue; improper balance (improper insulin supply), etc. May God lead you to those who are qualified to adequately treat these and other health problems.

2. We are a product of what we see and hear. Are your spiritual eyes and ears stronger than your physical ones? The sick individual will need these senses to compensate for the negative pull on his or her body. Christian music tapes, Christian television,

books, Scripture tapes, teaching tapes, can all help to build the mental and spiritual resources of the sick.

3. Can you avail yourself of God's many resources of diversion and refreshment? What things can you do that will lighten your burden? Would flowers, tasty food, a visit from a friend, a special treasure, an uplifting book, a friendly animal, or a time of reclining in the sunshine restore some of your joy?

4. Is your mind wandering to all the potential problems of tomorrows? Are you burdened for those you cannot help? You only have today and God is adequate.

5. The Bible has over seven thousand promises for the Christian to claim. What Bible promises can you find and stand on?

6. Have you praised God that in your difficulty he is adequate? Begin now. Have a time of praising him.

7. Have you understood that God is holding on to you? Yes we reach out to him and hold on to all that he is. But isn't it wonderful to know that underneath are the everlasting arms?

CHAPTER 11

HOW TO HELP THE SICK

I'd like to help the sick but what should I do?" There are several excellent sources to ask for ideas—God, the loved ones of the sick, the sick one. It is entirely appropriate to address the one who is ill by saying, "What is the best way I can help you? Would you just like a friend to sit with you? Would you like me to pray with you? Can I assist you in some way—reading? preparing food? running an errand? caring for your children?"

When it comes to helping the sick a church in my community sets a good example. When the husband died of cancer, he left his wife, Gloria, an eleven-year-old daughter, and an eight-year-old son. But when Gloria discovered she also had cancer, there were not adequate funds available to provide sufficient care. The women of Cedarpines Community Church put their heads together. Weren't there several nurses among them? Weren't others available to provide meals and transportation for the children? Individuals from the church cared for Gloria at home, made trips to doctors, helped the children, and shared in the arrangement of details after Gloria's death.

Sickness Is a Family Affair

Sickness isn't exclusive. It doesn't pick out one for testing and leave surrounding ones free.

"It is difficult to measure who suffers more," one mother told me, "the child, the parents, or the other siblings." She was stating the obvious—sickness is a family affair.

There are few families that are exempt from illness. If it does not strike the immediate family, one can always find a relative—an aunt, uncle, grandparent, niece, nephew, or cousin who is afflicted in some way. Often this requires that distant relatives contribute finances, housing, visitation, or prayer support. Since sickness is a family affair, how might a family best demonstrate care under the particular pressures illness brings?

Edith Schaeffer writes in *What Is a Family?*

> What is a family? A family is a well-regulated hospital, a nursing home, a shelter in time of physical need, a place where a sick person is greeted as a sick human being and not as a machine that has a loose bolt, or a mechanical doll that no longer works—to be shoved aside because it is no more fun, nor is it useful! A family should be a training place for growing human beings to know how to care for a great variety of sicknesses and for people who have just had accidents or operations, because each one has received both knowledgeable and loving care and has watched it being given to others . . . .
>
> When illness hits we should remember that this period of time is part of the whole of life. This is not just a non-time to be shoved aside, but a portion of time that counts. It is part of the well person's life, as well as part of the sick person's life . . . There is an importance attached to the use of the whole span of time which means that creativity, imagination, work, appropriate contribution, utilizing talents, and pitching in to do whatever needs to be done, applies to sickness as well as periods of health. . . ."[1]

Someone has said that great difficulties such as an illness or handicap will either make or break a family. I was privileged to be part of a family, while growing up, which banded together when the fourth and youngest child was born with cerebral palsy and deafness. Though nothing seemed special about it at the time, years later neighbors remarked how unusual, even exemplary our family was in dealing with Bill's sickness. My parents were not content to accept the doctor's verdict without a lot of effort to minimize the handicap.

My father, gifted as a carpenter, built special chairs and exercise equipment. We children were on hand to exercise Bill. My brother, Tom, would run round and round Bill's chair forcing Bill to use his neck as he strained to view Tom's antics. Specially built intense day Ron blurted out, "I'm just a little boy. What terrible thing could I have done to cause this to happen to me?"

Ron's mother sought in every way she could to alleviate her son's concern. Finally she called her pastor. "If you can handle seeing a child in such pain then come. But I'll understand if you choose not to come."

Ned Richardson, their pastor, bicycled to Ron's home. He entered Ron's room with a warm smile on his face. Talking with seven-year-old Ron as if with an adult, Ned chatted with him briefly then asked some basic questions.

"Ron, do you know Jesus? What happened to Jesus when he died on the cross for you?" Seven-year-old Ron knew the answers. Jesus had taken the punishment of the world upon himself. Jesus, bearing the sin of the world, made it possible for each person to be forgiven and restored to fellowship with his or her Creator.

Ned then responded, "Since Jesus was punished in our place, then there's no punishment left, is there?"

That explanation made a difference. Ron understood that God was not punishing him. His swollen body was a difficult challenge, but it did not come from an angry God. As Ron approached puberty, he left all trace of rheumatoid arthritis behind him.

When a child has questions and fears, it is important to create an atmosphere in which the child feels free to verbalize his concerns. A sensitive parent may need to draw this out of the child. Sometimes sitting and talking leisurely about other matters, without judgment, will assure the child that he can trust you with his deepest fears.

Allowing a child some decision-making power may give him or her a sense of participation. A child may not be able to decide on whether or not to have an operation, but could perhaps choose the date of such an operation. Perhaps their diet is limited but could they choose among several options? The sense of participation—whether decision-making or light family chores—folding clothes, polishing silver, etc., helps maintain self-worth and provides a sense of "contributing" as a family member.

Visits, cards, letters, games, and appropriate treats are usually appreciated by a sick child. One child received "fan" mail from a well-known baseball team. Another got a card from his favorite TV hero. A hospitalized young girl was delighted to re-

gymlike equipment became the scene of other exercises disguise
as games. We all took pride in Bill, watching him grow and de
velop.

Edith Schaeffer writes,

> For some people illness carries with it the memory of loving care
> cool hands stroking the forehead, sponge baths in bed, clean sheet
> under a hot chin, lovely flavored drinks, alcohol back rubs, medi
> cine given methodically by the clock, flowers near the bed, curtain
> drawn when fever is hurting the eyes, soft singing of a mother o
> father's voice during a sleepless night. Convalescence brings othe
> memories, but some people remember care of this sort during time
> when fever was high, and pain ripped through some part of the
> body, and the changing of perspiration-soaked pajamas for crisp
> dry ones brought an indescribable relief for a few moments, as did
> the crushed ice to suck, wrapped in a linen handkerchief or clean
> facecloth.²

For long-term illness, a cheery room can mean a great deal,
as well as special visits, opportunities to talk, special meals (as
allowed), and trips outdoors to sit in the sunshine. For those visiting the sick, be careful not to tire those you are seeking to refresh.
A call before a visit would be helpful, but not always necessary.

Helping Children

An area that requires sensitivity involves sick children. A
child focuses on the trauma, the pain, and discomfort of illness.
His or her world is small and self-oriented, with little experience
or patience built into their frame. It helps to keep a child's mind
diverted to happier things.

Keeping a child informed may help allay many fears. Ron
Clark was only four years old when rheumatoid arthritis turned
him into a semi-invalid. Painful swelling in his joints made movement impossible at times. Ordinarily a happy child, Ron would
become angry and cry ceaselessly when medication failed to halt
the pain. After two or three years with no turnabout, thoughtful
Ron wondered why other children could run and play but he could
not. Having attended Sunday school he knew that God loved him.
Yet what contradiction his suffering presented. On a particularly

ceive a phone call from her junior high classmates. Her teacher had organized the effort.

Tim and Joy Downs came up with a creative idea when their four-year-old daughter, Erin, developed leukemia. To offset long periods of difficult treatment this couple prepared a visual reminder of God's care for their daughter. They asked friends who were willing to pray for their daughter to send a family snapshot. These photos were placed in a special album and presented to Erin. Erin would rearrange her picture album—a reminder that people loved her and were praying for her.

If parents or loved ones know of special wishes, now might be the time to grant them. I remember, as a young child with measles, the day my dad returned my doll to me (it had been confiscated as discipline). Some cities provide "special wish" programs for children with serious disorders.

For entertaining a sick child, there is a marvelous display of children's and young people's books at Bible bookstores. Videos are also available. Picture puzzles and learning games can help pass the time. One mother, when her teenage son was particularly depressed, would pack a simple lunch, grab a blanket, and drive to a picnic spot. "If it was cold, we'd eat in the car. The brief diversion would cheer us both up."

Other suggestions? Keep the child on a schedule. Little things such as "routine" provide a sense of certainty, in the midst of uncertainty, for the child. As much as possible, keep the child involved in activities outside the home.

When a young girl was taken out of school due to health-related problems for an extended period, her mother watched as she slowly withdrew. Church was her solution. The mother says, "I made sure that Sandy was involved in Sunday school even though it meant extra effort to get her there." One Sunday the minister let Sandy and her mother pass out church bulletins.

In another instance sixteen-year-old Matt (struggling with paralysis) was asked to share with his church what he was experiencing. The church, in turn, had a time of prayer for him and kept him in prayer thereafter.

The more a child's life can be kept as normal as possible the more normal the child will feel. It also becomes easier to return to the world of the healthy. Adjustments into hospital life and reentry into school should be talked through with children. A difficult change can be eased by helping them visualize what to expect.

Books such as *An Exceptional View of Life,* help sick children identify with other such children. Here are some examples:

> It was a weird feeling when I first got sick. I couldn't do anything by myself. Everyone had to wait on me. I'd rather wait on somebody else. For a little while I couldn't talk because of the tracheotomy. When I was in a wheelchair, I couldn't walk. . . .
>
> My parents helped me accept myself. They wouldn't let me put myself down. They wouldn't let me say I was ugly. I knew I wasn't pretty but I was their daughter, and even in the condition I was in, I was pretty to them and that made me feel good inside.
>
> Now it's much better. I can walk again. It makes you feel real good to be able to walk. You have to build up your muscles. You've accomplished a task that has taken a lot of work and exercise. It makes you feel normal. You're all excited to tell your friends that you can walk again.
>
> "Now I know why it happened. God wanted it to. It made me appreciate life more.[3]

> When I have a seizure and somebody sees it, they get scared and wonder what's up. Once when we went on a field trip, the bus left me off and a friend was walking me home. I had a seizure and had to lay down in the driveway. The lady was real scared. She jumped out of her car. She didn't know what to do. I didn't want them to get worried, but there's no way I can stop them from worrying.
>
> I'm happy that people care when they see me and try to help me. I love everybody that cares for me—my parents, my teacher, my doctor who is trying so hard to help me get well.[4]

> When I have to go into the hospital, that really makes me sad. I've gone in twenty-four times for operations. I go to the doctor's every two or three months. That makes me all nervous. My first operation was three days after I was born. The reason I don't like it is being away from friends. You can't sleep in the hospital. I don't like immobility in the hospital. That makes me the saddest when I go to the hospital. . . .
>
> There's not a whole lot you can do. I like to go outside, for the air. You don't realize how much you miss being in the fresh air, the sun, the cool, the flowers, the trees, everything. I was always active before I fell. I never knew I appreciated being outside, kind of free.
>
> It hasn't changed my mental status. I'm gonna walk, right out of here. That's what's keeping me going.[5]

Creative hands with scissors and glue may fashion clever learning material within the sick room. One mother had her sick daughter look through a magazine and make a collage of what she would like to be doing. Collages can be made on different themes: "What is God's love like?" "How am I feeling today?" "What do I have to look forward to?" Even, "What is heaven like?"

Discipline must be maintained with a sick child, not only for the sake of the sick one but for the well-being of the entire family. Nine-year-old Karen suffered twice in three years with a hip persis which required surgery. Karen was in a cast from her armpits to her ankles. One afternoon a neighbor brought over a chocolate eclair. Instead of responding kindly Karen pouted and withdrew. Her mother, patient at first, finally picked Karen up, put her in her room and closed the door, firmly reprimanding her for her attitude.

Discipline is essential during a child's formative years. Though special exceptions must be made from time to time, depending on the problem, the ill child needs the security of being no different from any other member of the family. Discipline is also important with the sick child so that other siblings don't feel that the sick child, who is already getting additional attention, is overly favored.

Surprisingly one of the best ways to help sick children is to encourage them to think of others. For the family to concentrate unnecessarily on their own plight may actually burden the child further. But for the family to be mindful of others could be a curative exercise for all. Giving to others is learned largely by example. Ideas include: writing letters or postcards to other sick children; placing pictures of friends in their room to write to; making tape recordings; drawing pictures for friends to place on their refrigerators; saving pennies to sponsor a needy child.

As the Parent Is, So Is the Child

A general rule is: the child will take his or her cues from the parents or those in attendance. If the parents are trusting God, the sick child will pick up that response. If the parent is frantic, the child will most likely sense the anxiety.

Perhaps the best advice for helping children is that the parents seek Jesus fully and rest their young one with him. Concerning his disciples Jesus prayed, "And for their sakes I sanctify [set apart] Myself, that they themselves might be sanctified in truth."[6] Help your child by making sure you understand this wonderful God of the Bible.

A good suggestion for both parent and child is to pray together. "When I pray I don't feel alone. I feel safe," one sick child expressed. For the parent and child to talk with God aloud about fears, anxiety, treatments, and healing can make a big difference. The key is honesty coupled with asking. One young boy accustomed to praying (from the heart) with his dad was taken to Sunday school after a long absence. At the end of the time, Kevin asked, "When are we going to pray?"

"But Kevin, we already prayed," the man answered, referring to the customary asking of God's blessing on the start of the meeting.

"I mean, when are we going to just talk with God?" The teacher was taken aback.

One of Jesus' followers wrote: "Don't worry about anything; instead pray about everything; tell God your needs and don't forget to thank him for his answers. If you do this you will experience God's peace, which is far more wonderful than the human mind can understand. His peace will keep your thoughts and your hearts quiet and at rest as you trust in Christ Jesus."[7]

Family Caring

Jay and Sandy Davis are one couple who have met the challenges of family sickness largely because they have understood who Jesus is. Married in their mid-twenties, they were told that having children was out of the question. How blessed they felt when at age thirty-three (Jay) and age thirty-one (Sandy) learned that a baby was on its way. Three lovely daughters followed. Then tragedy; a brain aneurism threatened Sandy's life. Told she had less than a 5 percent chance, Sandy nonetheless made it through ten hours on the operating table. Dubbed a "miracle" Sandy emerged with a new lease on life.

Ten years passed during which time a boy was born. Six-year-old Jonathan had not been feeling well. The diagnosis of leukemia came as a shock. Jay reflects, "My first feelings were of disappointment, feeling that my only son may not have the opportunity to grow up and serve the Lord as I had hoped." Sandy reacted differently. "I felt as if I were choking. Tears rolled involuntarily down my face."

By evening the other children wanted to know what the doctor had said about their brother. Jay and Sandy caught one another's eye. Now was the time.

"I was surprised at how well we were able to share with the children," says Sandy. "The Lord was sustaining us. We explained that Jonathan was very sick, but that he was in the Lord's hands." After that, the children saw both Jay and Sandy in periods of frustration, tears, and especially feelings of helplessness, but they also observed that time and time again their mother and father took the matter back to the Lord.

"The spiritual part of me knew God was faithful," shares Sandy, "but sometimes the mother part of me experienced ups and downs. We have now settled the matter of who Jonathan really belongs to. He is God's property; only ours on loan. Therefore, peace would return as I looked to him; his loving, wise ways were trustworthy."

As a result this home has experienced stability amidst long-term hospitalization—at one point Sandy spent five weeks living at the hospital—painful therapy, and uncertainty.

How have the children responded to such an atmosphere?

The oldest teenage daughter could not talk at first about Jonathan. A discerning mother, Sandy prayed for the right time to sit and talk with Cynthia, asking her to share her feelings. Gradually she opened up. Another daughter required more time. She was one to retreat. Watchful love encouraged and supported this second daughter.

On another occasion still another daughter became very agitated over little things, something not normal for the members of this family. Jay and Sandy perceived the problem. "Are you feeling left out? Do you think that Jonathan is getting too much of our time?" Sandy then explained what Jonathan was going through— the shots, bone marrow testing, fatigue, and weakness. "It helped," says Sandy.

This family's stability has spoken to many people of the love of God spilling over. "We have always shared the Lord Jesus Christ with others because we know him to be the only real answer to peace," says Sandy. "In the hospital several came to realize that Christ can make a difference. Others we were able to encourage and pray with. I am convinced that the genuine inner joy we have exhibited in the hospital has opened doors to speak of the goodness of the Lord in a manner that nothing else could."

That peace is especially exhibited as Jonathan has the painful bone marrow test. Sandy prays aloud as Jonathan receives the treatment. The louder he screams the greater volume in her praying. After some time Sandy taught Jonathan to apply natural child birth breathing, which reduced Jonathan's pain, kept him still, and helped him not to scream.

Jay continues, "We have learned that God is not a magician. We do not rub a lamp and get our bidding, nor do we seek to maneuver God. God is great and above all. He has the right to do whatever he chooses. Since he is good and loving, he will do what's best for us."

"We get through," Jay concludes, "because God is with us."

Encouraging the Sick

What other practical things can be done in times of illness?

It is immensely important that the sick individual be seen as a person of worth. Look past present limitations. Focus on the individual's personal character and value. Verbalize the person's worth. Recall past contributions. Applaud current efforts of the sick individual to maintain a good attitude, follow doctors orders, and persevere.

Encouragement is in order. Let the sick one know you're standing with him or her and that you're available to help. Though your help may not be needed, a pledge of help, should the occasion arise, may alleviate fears of the sick person. Be sincere in this offer. Follow through.

It may be important to talk with an individual about practical matters—diet, treatment, handling stress, avoiding wrong attitudes, discipline, and so forth. Millard Erickson writes:

> Man is to be treated as a unity. His spiritual condition cannot be dealt with independently of his physical and psychological condition and vice versa . . . any attempt to deal with man's spiritual condition apart from his physical condition and mental and emotional state will be less than completely successful.[8]

Those who wish to help the sick should be mindful of the totality of health and well-being, that they might care for the sick most effectively.

Be a good listener. Encourage the sick one to share what's on his or her mind. Resist the temptation to offer suggestions unless you know the situation. Of course the sick may occasionally need a loving "kick in the pants." An incident in the life of Jesus illustrates this point.

> And a certain man . . . had been thirty-eight years in his sickness. When Jesus saw him lying there, and knew that he had already been a long time in that condition, He said to him, "Do you wish to get well?"
>
> The sick man answered Him, "Sir, I have no man to put me into the pool when the water is stirred up, but while I am coming, another steps down before me."
>
> Jesus said to him, "Arise, take up your pallet and walk."
>
> And immediately the man took up his pallet and began to walk.[9]

Jesus' question to the lame man, "Do you wish to get well?" has provoked much thought. It is speculated that the lame man didn't really want health or that he feared having health.

Fear of Health

I think different sick ones might fall under both categories. It may be true that some:

- don't want the responsibility of health
- prefer the attention they receive as an invalid
- fear the unknown
- don't wish to put out the needed effort to improve

It may further be true that those attending the sick may:

- like being a martyr
- feel useful as long as they can attend the sick
- fear the sick person would achieve a life apart from themselves.

The complexity of responses in individuals suggests that we may have many motivations, not just one, and they may vary.

As desperately as I sought health there were times when I wondered if I were instantly healed, whether I could cope with the abrupt change—new responsibilities, adjustments, and the increasing expectations of those around me. But in defense of myself and others who have had long-term illnesses, the level of mental fatigue coupled with mental patterns set over a long period can make it very difficult to visualize a better time, a better way. Although truly desiring health, the sick individual may lack the energy to fight. Resignation sets in all too quickly, causing many to settle for sickness while health is an option. God's unmistakable message to me and one those who attend the ill may need to employ was that he would be with me in health as he was with me in sickness. Life would not overwhelm me when I became well. I needn't fear change for the better.

Along these lines the ill may need help in areas of choices, encouragement, perseverance, motivation, and faith. I talked with Tom about his health problem. He had a degenerative disease—but one with a "cure." ("Cure" is in quotes because effort and perseverance would be necessary to make the clinical treatment work.) Tom explained to me that he had tried various treatments, even diets, and had come to the conclusion there was no answer to his health problem. His doctor agreed.

"I have sent five people to this clinic," I informed him. "Four of them stuck with the treatment with tremendous results."

Tom's face looked tired and defeated. Even so I marveled at his answer. "I think that God has spoken and I am to be sick."

"Not as long as there is treatment available," I replied. "If you were out of work and a job was available, could you sit home and say God wants you poor? If education was available could you sit here and say God wants you ignorant? Tom, you're making God say 'no' without seeking all that is available."

Given the defeated mentality of many of the sick, it behooves those who love the sick to provide and encourage opportunities of healing. Some individuals need persistent encouragement before finally enlisting in a treatment. Acquaintances of mine are either improved or well today as a result of repeated urging. I needed to hear about certain treatments a number of times before it sunk in that they were for me. What if no one had cared?

Money may be needed in order for the sick to afford life-changing treatment. Helping pay for various treatments may be one of the best gifts you could make to the sick. In short, the sick may need the resources, help, and motivation of the well.

Prayer for the Sick

"Help the weak"[10] is a simple and clear command from the Bible. "Pray for the sick"[11] couldn't be said any plainer. One pastor, challenged that his prayers had not always resulted in healings, countered with, "My job isn't to concern myself with results. Those are in God's hands. My job is to pray. I'm commanded to pray for the sick. And as long as they are sick, I'm going to keep on praying."

In regards to prayer, it is always a good idea to seek the Lord diligently on behalf of the one you pray for. It is appropriate to ask the sick how they would like you to pray on their behalf. When Gloria, mentioned earlier in this chapter, was near death I felt deep concern for her. Though her health had progressively gone downhill she emphatically did not want to die. She worried about what would become of her two children, not wanting to leave them without a father and a mother. Round-the-clock nurses said they had rarely seen anyone put up such a battle against death.

After visiting her at home one day, I left, explaining I did not know what was best for her. God did. His idea for her was far better than mine, I assured her. Nevertheless, if she wished to live, I would stand with her. I then prayed thoroughly for every possible part of her body. Near the end of the prayer I asked that she could rest in God's love and that God would fill her with his peace.

That evening Gloria was tranquil. She shared with the night nurse, "I finally realize that God knows what is best for me and the children." Hours later she went peacefully home to be with the Lord. The Lord provided adequate care for her two children.

One frustration I experience is having an abundance of insight—medical, spiritual, and practical—obtained through many years in the school of sickness—wanting to offer it to the ill who are not always ready for it. We need to carefully seek God in these matters. Sometimes, instead of doing something, God directs us to simply keep praying on behalf of a loved one who is ill.

He is at work in an individual; we can leave the sick one to his care.

On one occasion I sensed the Lord instructing me concerning a relative: "I am allowing sickness in this man's life in order to help him see his need of me."

This word came so clearly and unmistakably that it has succored me at times when this individual has faltered on the edge of death. But I am observing God break down pride and self-sufficiency in that person, creating an openness to hear about our wonderful Savior.

On other occasions God may direct us to "pray in faith" for healing.

Dorothy Clark, head of Congregational Awareness, tells the story of her struggle with the Lord over an assignment he had given her. In her community there was a man considered by doctors to be terminally ill.

"In prayer, I sensed God's leading to go to this man and invite him to a healing service in our area. I was not accustomed to such matters and it took some prodding by the Holy Spirit to get me to go."

"I asked this man if he would go with me to the healing service but he said, and it was agreed, that he was too ill. 'You don't have to go,' I suddenly found myself saying. 'I can go for you.'"

Dorothy and the man's wife went on his behalf. He immediately improved. Later, God again began to impress upon Dorothy that he wanted her to go and pray for the man herself. All of the normal fears that accompany such a request assailed Dorothy. "What if he isn't healed?" "What will I pray?" "What if the man resents my being there?" However, Dorothy knew that God was asking this of her.

Again Dorothy visited the man. "I entered Kaiser Hospital in Walnut Creek, California. I stood on one side of his bed. His wife stood on the other. As tactfully as I could I asked the man if I could pray for him. He consented." Dorothy laid hands on the man not knowing what would come out of her mouth, "Lord, you've asked me to be here. All I can do is to ask in the name of Jesus that you heal this man of cancer." To Dorothy's amazement and relief the patient was completely cured of the cancer—so much so that for many coffee breaks thereafter nurses and doctors discussed the cancer healing of this "terminally ill" man.

How many healings may occur if followers of Jesus, even in their inexperience and hesitancy, stand in faith on behalf of others?

It is always necessary to instill hope in those we care about. Unfortunately discouraging remarks, lack of support, and other hindrances are sometimes placed in the path of those who seek healing. Carolyn developed a brain tumor which was accompanied by daily seizures, disorientation, and falls. The situation progressed. With every effort made, including prayer, with no positive results, it looked as if death was imminent. The doctors saw no hope. Neither did Carolyn's friends. Privately they made remarks to one another about Carolyn's inability to accept the obvious reality. Though Carolyn was not inclined to accept the "inevitable," the added stress that her friends were not continuing to stand with her in the greatest fight of her life increased Carolyn's tension and her seizures.

"Linda," she said to me one day, "you are the only friend who is believing with me." Carolyn's last days were occupied with a sense of aloneness and feeling forsaken.

No human being should be guilty of taking away someone's most basic hope. After all do we really know what God might do? He can and has reversed chronic health situations at the last minute. Do we know for sure what might have happened if friends, instead of resigning themselves to the situation, would have continued to stand together in faith?

Such was the case of a woman whose story appeared in *Guideposts* magazine. She was critically ill and not expected to live. But prayer for this sick woman was unrelenting. It did not stop with blood relatives. Family members enlisted neighbors and friends. Requests for her healing were included on prayer chains throughout the country. Small groups met together continuously approaching God with a multitude of requests on her behalf.

She shares that one night Jesus gloriously stood at her bedside. She remembered him saying, "I have come because of an overwhelming number of prayers for you." The woman was completely healed.

Others have reported complete turnarounds in their health at their most critical hour—reversing the humanly irreversible. The admonition "the *effective, fervent* prayer of a righteous man avails much," is given in the book of James as an example for those who would pray for the sick.[12] Do we know what God might do if the friends of the sick and loved ones of the sick beseech him earnestly?

What if God intends to take an individual off this earth to stand before him no matter what human effort is made? Does not God have the last word on his creation? Does he not ultimately know what is right and fair? I am suggesting that the thing to do in a critical situation (such as Carolyn's) is to keep on hoping and believing with the individual. Let that encouragement be vocal. Pray with them for healing. If it seems possible that God's intention may be to take the sick out of this world make sure they're ready to go. Ask God to work his will into their hearts. But don't let the sick feel forsaken at their most needy hour.

Attitudes that Hinder

One of Jesus' experiences illustrates another need of the sick.

> And as He (Jesus) was going out from Jericho with His disciples and a great multitude, a blind beggar named Bartimaeus, the son of Timaeus, was sitting by the road. And when he heard that it was Jesus the Nazarene, he began to cry out . . .
> Jesus said, *"What do you want Me to do for you?"*
> And the blind man said to Him, "Rabboni, I want to regain my sight!"
> And Jesus said to him, "Go your way; your faith has made you well." And immediately he received his sight and began following Him on the road.[13] (italics mine)

Wouldn't it seem obvious what Bartimaeus wanted? Did Jesus sense that Bartimaeus' needs extended past the healing of his eyesight? One of Jesus' followers, accustomed to watching the Master provide for others, wrote, "[He] is able to do exceedingly abundantly above all that we ask or think."[14]

Parallel to believing *big* is believing *strategically*. Getting well is not our most important need. Nor is it an end in itself. Health is a means to an end—being all that God designed us to be for our own fulfillment and his ultimate purposes. The idea that God has much more; and that healing is for his purposes, not our selfish desires—needs to be constantly kept in mind. The reality—

God's will, not my own—is a catalyst to good health. It frees our body to heal. It unleashes God's power on our behalf.

Help the Helpers

Prayer and assistance need to be given to those who must care for the sick as well. Have you considered giving them a day off while you watch over their sick one? praying with them on behalf of their loved one? providing financial assistance? calling with encouragement? taking them out for lunch? buying them a special treat? providing a special need? listening and understanding? visiting with a surprise? going with them to doctors, hospitals, clinics? providing a "getaway"?

Whether we are helping the sick or those who care for the sick, we should follow Jesus' example, "To the extent that you did it to one of these brothers [and sisters] of Mine, even the least of them, you did it to me."[15]

Points to Ponder

1. What attitudes might we want to consider as we approach those who are sick? Have we asked the Lord, those who know the sick one, or the sick individual what we can do to assist?

2. Have we considered how to help those who care for the sick?

3. It might be a good exercise to think about the needs of those who are sick or caring for the sick. This is probably an area many have given little thought to. You could make a difference. Even a small gesture would be appreciated.

GETTING WELL

The following material has been compiled for the purpose of helping the sick evaluate their own part in health care and available treatments.

Appendix A discusses treatments that have helped (and not helped) me in my efforts to obtain health.

Appendix B is an article by Monte Kline, Ph.D., to help the reader discern the pros and cons of alternative treatments. Dr. Kline received his Ph.D. in Nutrition from Columbia Pacific University and a Master of Bible Theology from the International Bible Institute and Seminary. He is a professional member of the American Association of Nutritional Consultants. He is a nationally known lecturer and seminar teacher and the author of four books. His book, *The Junk Food Withdrawal Manual*, has sold 275,000 copies. Dr. Kline currently practices clinical nutrition in Bellevue, Washington. His newsletter, "Christian Health Counselor," is available by writing: Total Living, P.O. Box 3581, Bellevue, Wash., 98009.

In evaluating treatments it is important to note that material discussing treatments is presented to offer health care options for the sick. It is in no way meant to question the integrity of those who choose otherwise.

GOD'S PROVISION: TREATMENTS THAT MADE A DIFFERENCE

Provision Number One

I walked hesitantly into the doctor's office less than five blocks from my apartment in Houston, Texas. The year was 1966.

I filled out tedious forms as I waited in the Richmond Avenue office. The friendly nurses answered questions as I tried to be accurate about my previous ills: eye infections, colds, fatigue.

When I was finally ushered into the doctor's private office, a handsome, gray-haired man in his forties greeted me. He was not gruff but one might wrongly construe him to be that way. His speech was filled with precision and authority.

Dr. Ralph Ford commenced tests immediately which in a week gave evidence that hypothyroidism and low blood sugar were factors in my bouts with ill health. It was an accurate diagnosis. I was put on a small dose of thyroid medicine which was increased until I reached four and a half grains a day, a dosage I have maintained based on frequent testing. The diet instructions were designed to eliminate junk food and sugar from my diet. Dr. Ford succeeded in convincing me that sugar really is difficult for many, if not most, people to handle. It affects the immune system, the nerves, and the general well-being of the body. Dr. Ford never told me to cut down on my quantity of sweets. Instead he looked at me with a final word on the subject, "Don't ever touch sugar again." Jogging and walking were thereupon prescribed—a regimen I began and maintained until mononucleosis so debilitated me that exercise weakened rather than strengthened me.

Many people who do not feel well notice remarkable changes for the better simply by eliminating sugar and junk food from their diet and adding exercise. A thyroid check and pituitary check may benefit the sick as well.

Note: In this appendix I share the health treatments that have worked for me. I am not a doctor. I do not diagnose. Nor can I guarantee what may or may not work for you. I merely want to explain what has worked for me.

Provision Number Two

After I contracted mononucleosis God providentially moved me to a new location in order to make contact with a second diagnosis and treatment. One afternoon, in 1969, sometime after illness seriously began to affect my mind as well as my body, I attended a small tea party at the Arrowhead Springs Hotel in San Bernardino, California. A friendly and portly man with gentle and keen eyes engaged me in conversation. Dr. Howard Blandau, of Philadelphia, was a practicing psychologist with a great deal of knowledge on how the circulatory system, when damaged, can affect the mind as well as the body. He had felt led by God to talk with me.

"There is a clinic you need to go to, Linda, which will help you deal with many of your mental and physical problems." Dr. Blandau informed me the Frederick Erdman Association, in Havertown, Pennsylvania, treated arterial tone with a simple and inexpensive method. Living in California as a self-supporting single woman with little income or energy, it seemed a great effort to follow up on this advice. But, I also made the mistake that many sick individuals make—I failed to see the importance of pursuing reasonable information. It would be years before I would get to this clinic; years in which I became much worse, hence requiring far more time to heal.

In 1975 I finally went for a week's stay at the Frederick Erdman Clinic, located at that time in the lovely area of Germantown, Pennsylvania. A large, stately, four-story home, which looked as if it could have housed ten German families at once, was the facility for the clinic. Dr. William Erdman, the director, was a renowned doctor who for years had held the position of Medical Director of the University of Pennsylvania Hospital. He also had more memberships, honors, awards, certifications, appointments, degrees, and prestigious positions than one could count.

At the clinic I was educated in the role that the arterial system plays in the human body. The Bible states, "The life of the flesh is in the blood."[1] The blood carries nutrition and oxygen—both vital for survival and proper biological functioning—to every part of the human body. It also carries toxic substances from the cells to be deposited by the organism outside the body, via lungs, skin, urine, and feces. A breakdown in this arterial system could easily result in a breakdown in one's health.

Evidences of a faulty circulation system would normally include cold hands and feet—the tone of the arteries being impaired in such a way that a proper blood supply could not be adequately pushed to the extremities—and an intolerance for heat. I began to understand the reason why my mind was in trouble. My brain, the organ which houses the mind, was not getting proper blood supply.

There was an excellent treatment for the condition available at Erdman's clinic, one which over the years greatly aided my recovery. Those with mental problems, multiple sclerosis, diabetes, heart disease, insomnia, stroke and related problems, or those who may be experiencing difficulties in the extremities of their bodies—head (ear, nose, and eye), arms and legs—may be greatly helped by investigating this clinic.²

Provision Number Three

In 1973 I first learned the benefits of chiropractic care. For years this form of spinal manipulation was questioned and often condemned by the American Medical Association, yet millions swore by the difference such treatment brought—slipped discs were repositioned without the aid of surgery; on-the-job injuries, which kept both men and women curtailed from work, were sometimes set right overnight; colds, flus, and related illness ran a quicker course when spinal realignment increased blood and nerve supply to weakened areas. Chiropractic care has played its role in my life, certainly not as a final answer, but as another tool to enable my body to respond better.

It was from chiropractors that I learned other important principles of healing: sleeping posture should be on the sides or back, allowing muscles not to tighten and pull unnecessarily during sleep, thus keeping body tone in line; warming techniques to tense muscles can be beneficial; proper posture contributes to good health.

I am grateful to this branch of healing which, in 1988, won a Supreme Court decision against the American Medical Association for unnecessary harassment. This branch of health care, finally vindicated, stands solidly on its own merits.

Provision Number Four

Another important tool of healing I employed was colon care. Not much attention is given this vital organ by most doctors or patients. After all, the large intestine just moves the leftover material out of our bodies. What many fail to see is that if this organ does not carry out the "leftovers" properly, the leftovers stay in the colon and ferment. A toxic build-up can be the source of many diseases. Some contend that "death starts in the colon." I have seen how quickly my body has turned around at points when this area of colon care was addressed.

Provision Number Five

In 1977 my friend Sybil Stanton received help from an eye doctor in Scottsdale, Arizona. Twice I had been to eye doctors convinced that something was wrong with my eyes. After all, why would my head, neck, shoulders, and stomach become unbearably tight if I tried to read for more than five minutes? Often, in the sunshine or the snow, I had to keep my eyes closed to ward off dizziness and nausea. Headaches seemed connected with eye strain. "I need that doctor," I informed Sybil.

Dr. Veatch specialized in treating a disorder called hyperopthalmia (vertical imbalance). Simply put, it meant that my eyes were unbalanced. In the process of trying to focus my eyes (involuntarily), great stress was placed on my system.

The post office was within walking distance of my house. The day my glasses were due to arrive I had planned to stop at the church, adjacent to the post office, and play the piano. At the church I tried with difficulty to read the hymnbook. The strain was causing my whole body to tense. Halfway through the music I thought of the glasses securely wrapped at my side. I opened the package and put them on. I glanced back at the music. What had happened? My head had noticeably relaxed. My shoulders and stomach calmed.

Basically an individual who has vertical imbalance has the same problems that stress induces except more so. Normal efforts to relieve the stress do not help. Additional symptoms of this eye problem can include: neck problems; migraine headaches, which may be increasing in frequency and duration, and are especially connected with reading, computer watching, truck driving—anything requiring long hours of eye use; stomach tension, ulcers; colitis; and reading problems (frequently losing one's place, constantly rereading lines, poor comprehension which worsens as the person fatigues).[3]

Not God's Provision

It was in 1979 that my father offered to pay for a thorough testing and examination at a prestigious medical research center. This west coast clinic seemed to have the best personnel, methods, and research facilities in the medical field. Surely they could diagnose and cure some of my problems. I stayed with my parents. Daily my mother drove me to the institute where for two long weeks every conceivable part of me went through some sort of test.

The beautiful facilities of the research center were highlighted by the surroundings—torrey pines, palm trees and the ocean, suggesting a sense of peace. Inside the institute, peace was not the order of the day. All about me were individuals many of whom had chosen the expensive diagnostic and research facilities as their last hope in a long line of medical pursuits. Individuals in wheelchairs, young and old alike, sat throughout the stately building, heads bowed from lack of stamina, and others maybe in prayer.

My contact doctor, a likeable and intelligent young man, assigned me to all the various departments and physicians. After receiving extensive reports, he kept shaking his head and sending me to someone else to have a look. One day, after another embarrassing examination, I overheard him say to another doctor, "Hey, you ought to take a look at this one." The young male doctor, my contact doctor's crony, seemed to take an extra long time examining my naked body. I wasn't naive. I was dealing with a lust-filled man who had the advantage in the situation. I felt so helpless! And too sick and intimidated to do anything about the situation.

There was another incident which is worth mentioning simply for the sake of preparing others. As part of the routine checkup I was assigned a visit with the staff psychiatrist. No tests were given. The entire procedure consisted of a forty-minute talk with the psychiatrist—a sort of question and answer time. I had answered her initial questions simply by stating that my mind gave me a lot of trouble—sorting details was difficult as was concentrating. Midway through the conversation she learned that I was Christian. The direction of the questions turned abruptly at that point. "Why had I sought out a religious crutch?" "Did I expect it to shield me from life's problems?" "What personal problems were behind my need for religion?" I was a bit amused until the report came back from her office indicating that I was suffering from delusions.

Fortunately my contact doctor dismissed her findings as foolish. However, he had no answers for me. After a strenuous twelve days at the institute he handed me my final report. It read something like: "I am aware that the patient is suffering from chronic fatigue; however I cannot determine its cause or cure. There is an experimental drug Linda could try but I would not recommend it."

Obviously, this acclaimed medical center, with many fine doctors and a multi-million dollar research budget, was not God's provision for me. I had gone to please my family. It had seemed a normal route to follow since it was world renowned. But it was another lesson that God's ways are not always what we humans think they might be. We are not to assume, but seek him for the direction we take. We are to divorce ourselves from the idea that doctors or practitioners, however skilled, are the healers. God is the healer.

The Bible gives a small illustration to remind us of this fact.

> In the thirty-ninth year of his reign, Asa became seriously diseased in his feet but he didn't go to the Lord with the problem, but to the doctors. So he died in the forty-first year of his reign, and was buried in his own vault that he had hewn out for himself in Jerusalem. He was laid on a bed perfumed with sweet spices and ointments, and his people made a very great burning of incense for him at his funeral.[4]

The results of Asa's trust in his physicians resulted in his death. God may use physicians, or he may choose not to, but *he* does the healing. Make sure you are not trusting in a medical system, but in the Lord and seeking him on the treatment you pursue.

Provision Number Six

I first heard of Corinne Adams (not her real name) in 1984 from a friend who boasted about this woman's amazing ability to assist the body to health. Corinne, a Christian counselor, had become very ill while counseling others. For four years she searched out ways of healing and finally became well. She believed the Lord was leading her to make her new knowledge about natural healing methods available to others who were sick.

The year was 1984. I went to Corinne because I kept flu continuously. Actually it had seemed too much of an effort to make the hour and a half trips to see her. (I wish I had gone years earlier.) But one day, when I could not stand the flus any longer, I got in my car and drove the California freeways, stopping continuously to keep fever and fatigue from overcoming me, and finally falling onto Corinne's couch, sure I'd never move again.

Corinne's procedures were new to me. One of the first things she did was to instruct me in homeopathy. This science of healing came to fruition in the 1800s. Unfortunately when antibiotics made their entrance in the 1900s, homeopathy became relegated to the background. Superior to any drug or antibiotic treatments, homeopathic remedies do their task of healing not by countering a disease, as might a drug, but by stimulating the body to rally its own defense. Homeopathy is used by medical doctors worldwide.

Corinne's efforts initially centered in helping my body build its own defense so that it had the ability to remove dormant but vicious viruses. I didn't know that could be done. In fact I didn't know bacteria and viruses could store or hide themselves in one's body. But I came to accept this definition as each homeopathic remedy for viruses, strep, Epstein-Barr, mononucleosis, insecticides, metals, chemicals, radiation, parasites, worms, and other invaders left me stronger and stronger.

Since that time I have come to appreciate this mode of healing—removing the bad, building the good—as being consistent with the manner in which God heals in other areas of our lives. To experience God's love and plan more fully, certain attitudes must be eliminated from our lives—pride, critical spirit, resentment, unforgiveness, fear, etc. Spiritual progress is in proportion to this work of grace and the effort on our part to thwart and eradicate the mental attitude of sin. Simultaneously we should strengthen ourselves in biblical perspectives.

Likewise, for physical healing to come about one should seek the same mode—remove the bad; build up the good. Whatever is taxing the body should be disposed of. The toxic effects of chemicals, pollutants, drugs, dormant viruses, bacteria, and so forth must be released from the system so that health can be rebuilt. Vitamins, minerals, and herbal additions can then make a remarkable difference in rebuilding one's health.

Giving assistance to the entire body makes more sense than only treating the area that has gone wrong. I sat in a friend's home and sought to explain this perspective—treating the entire body—to the parents of a young boy with leukemia. I drew a picture to explain in a simple way the difference between isolated treatment and universal treatments.

First I sketched a body. I pointed to blood cells that I haphazardly drew inside the body frame. "When you treat with drugs such as chemotherapy or radiation you are seeking to destroy the disease by centering on the specific problem, in this case leukemia, and trying to wipe out the wrong type of blood cell. In doing so, much else in the body is being destroyed. Now," I continued, "if that is the only way to treat the problem then we must. However, what natural forms of medicine—supplements, herbs, homeopathy, etc.—seek to do is to balance the body and return the body's chemistry, functions, and energy level to normal, because true healing comes from the body's own defense and immune system."

Regardless of the manner of treatment, it always makes sense to get additional support (vitamin, mineral, herbal, homeopathy, etc.) in order to save a life. One of the most distressing situations I know of concerned my friend Paula. Twice cancer was found in Paula and twice she underwent chemotherapy and radiation treatment. Amazingly optimistic, she believed that soon the cancer would be totally eradicated. She had complete trust in her doctor.

When I learned that Paula could not return to work because of a third recurrence ("Just five more treatments and I'll be good as new," she wrote), I called her. As tactfully and kindly as I knew how I urged her to please get extra vitamin and mineral treatment (Vitamin C is a strong immune builder, one of the systems chemotherapy and radiation tear down) and told of a nutritionist in the area who could supply support for her body while she went through chemotherapy. Paula assured me that she was in good hands. My suggestion was not remotely considered.

Four months later after completing five more rounds of chemotherapy Paula, at the age of forty-six, died in her sleep of toxic poisoning caused by chemotherapy and radiation. There was not a shred of cancer left in her body when she died. The cure had killed her. Some say that we will look back on this period of medical history and marvel at how much the medical profession experimented in poisoning (drugs, chemotherapy, and radiation) and excessive surgery. I say this realizing that there are many sincere doctors who want more than anything to heal their patients. But many will not even investigate how measures outside the realm of traditional medicine might help their patients.

Though many facets of traditional medicine provide needed help, is traditional medicine practiced in the twentieth century the only answer to sickness? Would God have waited thousands of years since Creation to finally give individuals a method of healing? Or has he built into our bodies and nature many wonderful techniques and provisions of healing? Special thanks should be given those doctors who use progressive natural measures in conjunction with other treatment and who are seeking to reinstate the practice of healing the "whole" person.

Some people ask, "If sugar, pollutants, and dormant viruses are so bad, why isn't everyone sick? After all most people are exposed." A parallel between the design of the soul and the body illustrates. If a person has a strong self-image, he or she may receive criticism . . . but . . . "throw it off." It may do little damage. However, if a person has a poor self-image criticism may be absorbed by the person and cause much suffering. Likewise, one who is initially very healthy may endure junk food, smog, pesticides, and so forth—the body "throwing it off" so to speak. But the one who is sick does not have the proper defenses to dismiss incoming pollutants, viruses, and junk food. They are absorbed usually making the intolerant person sicker.

Even a healthy body cannot tolerate pollutants, junk food, drugs, and so forth, for long. Eventually the body will break down. Marvella Bayh, the former wife of Birch Bayh, democratic candidate for president in the 1976 election, writes in her book *Marvella,* that years on the farm where she received pesticide poisoning contributed to her struggle with cancer. She died long before her three score and ten.

The amount of pesticides in our food, the toxic chemicals we use in our homes (cleaners, polishers, waxes, sprays), the radiation poisoning that affects many areas, paint fumes, perfumes, smog, excessive exposure to electromagnetic fields, and toxic substances used by many companies, are seriously affecting the health of many people around the world. Worldwide government has been remiss in allowing many toxic substances to be labeled "nontoxic" or used indiscriminately when, in fact, they play havoc on the human body. We need more people to rise up and fight a system that is more responsive to lobbyist interest groups than to concerned citizens; a system that sanctions toxic substances and engages in irresponsible monitoring of potential health threats rather than in protecting the health of world inhabitants.

Since I had been sick seventeen years at the time of my first visit to Corinne Adams and had tried the help from two well-known medical facilities with no progress reported, I did not need to be knocked in the head to notice that real changes were taking place in my energy when I applied measures of homeopathy, herbs, nutrition, and so forth. (The addition of potassium, lithium, and trace minerals, if needed, can make a difference in mental outlook. Protein, B vitamins, and iron, if needed, can lift fatigue.)

Questionable Provision

I first met Stephanie (not her real name) in 1985. A specialist in the area of physical therapy, she felt she could teach me how to work with my body in order to alleviate TMJ and the constant neck pain resulting from whiplash. The method she employed was excellent. However a few of the fringe benefits I came to question.

I observed Stephanie's selection of books displayed in the bookcase in her office. She obviously read widely on Eastern religions, scientology, consciousness raising, est, meditation, and the like. As I got to know Stephanie I found her to be very caring. She wanted more out of life than her contemporaries. Expanding her horizons had given Stephanie a sense of more control over her life especially in the area of stress reduction.

Some of us need to have our minds altered and our consciousness raised, but it should be in the direction of becoming more God oriented—the real key to stress reduction. Unfortunately prevailing popular philosophies tend to focus more and more on the universe within ourselves and our own power and potential. Surely there is more to understand about ourselves. Many fail to appeciate much that God has built into our minds and bodies. But that is a far cry from the overrated, ultimate "emphasis" on self.

After reading a top-selling book by contemporary New Age thinkers, which Stephanie recommended, I was amazed to observe the contradictions which fed into the conscious attempts to make humans unified in thought and being. This book, much of it well-written, contained articles on marriage, psychology, health, family, sex, and religion. Various articles came at issues from vastly different viewpoints, often with worldviews in open contradiction of each other. But all were viewed as truth. Such thinking I came to understand broke down logic and critical thinking needed to evaluate truth. When logic goes the mind is open to *anything*.

"New Age" thinking is throughout much of the healing profession. Many health centers major on such mental reprogramming in connection with innovative healing procedures. As in Stephanie's case, there are plenty of legitimate treatments supervised by New Age (sometimes occult) thinkers. One must consider seriously whether he or she wishes to become involved.

When Stephanie suggested I meditate on nothing in order to relax my muscles, I informed her that I never let my mind go blank. "There are forces other than God, which have access to our minds. I don't leave myself open for them. I use active meditation to direct my thinking to God, his purposes and goodness, his beauty, creation, provision, and so forth. This is the emphasis of Scripture."

In a discussion with her about Christ, Stephanie assured me that she held great respect for Jesus. But she held high respect for Buddha as well as other gurus and leaders, "all of whom had much to offer us."

"Jesus," I explained to Stephanie, "would never put himself in the same category with other religious leaders. He said he was God, the true God, the Savior of the world. Most importantly, only Jesus dealt with the problem of sin." I urged her to read the gospel of John in the New Testament to investigate such matters.

One day Stephanie suggested I see a psychic healer. I informed her that I would prefer ill health to healing by sources other than the true God. God was sufficient to provide for me. "There's a price to pay for that kind of involvement," I said. She responded positively, assuring me that she respected—even believed—all points of view (even though they were greatly at odds with one another).

One day, while Stephanie was doing physical therapy with me, I mentioned that my adrenals weren't functioning well. Stephanie laid her hand on the area of my adrenals. Suddenly a wave of fear and panic swept over me.

"What did you do, Stephanie?" I asked.

"I just healed your adrenals."

"How?" I inquired. "I just felt as if I left this world and visited hell."

"I just loved your adrenals," she informed me.

When I returned home I commanded forces of darkness that had come upon me to get off me in the name of Jesus. Curious to see if any change had come about in my adrenals, I had them tested. None had. Trips to Stephanie ceased.

It is difficult to discern many things in today's health care. It may even be more difficult to discern the mindset of the one treating us and their impact on us. There are forces other than God in this world. Satan can heal. And does heal. Satan's healings may even seem wonderful at first. But as the saying goes, "There may be the devil to pay!" (Read *The Beautiful Side of Evil*, Johanna Michaelson.)

How shall we judge the impact of a treatment? God's healings bring one closer to him and to biblical truth. You must know the Bible to know if you are being led in line with it or away from it. I use this principle as a standard.

I love Stephanie. The treatment, in spite of confusing overtones, helped me. I commend her for her desire to gather knowledge so she can help others. I understand the many forms one employs to divert stress when power from God isn't available; the uncertainty within an individual that causes one to want people to think in unity, and why certain irresponsibility, fostered by some in the movement, is appealing. I also appreciate the problem of sin and guilt and why philosophies are purported to deny it or define it away. Christ alone can answer it. But I weep over the knowledge that is leading Stephanie and others like her away from ultimate answers, answers that don't have to be bent or watered down in order to accommodate an illogical system. Only by encountering the biblical Jesus, can she ever know the difference.

I urge the sick, who are especially vulnerable in their sickness, to avoid those who practice philosophies opposed to biblical truth. You may get better . . . but then you may open yourself to philosophies and spirits that will hurt you worse than any sickness.

Provision Number Seven

Besides learning to avoid (literally and emphatically) the many pollutants in the air—pesticides, chemicals, perfumes, etc. I also try to stay away from tap water which in many parts of the world has reached high levels of toxicity. Even Ralph Nader says so. I know of at least one person who by switching from tap water to distilled put to rest years of health problems.

One has several options in this regard—drink bottled mineral water, distilled water (many distill their own inexpensively), or get a water purifier featuring reverse osmosis with carbon.[5]

One has to wonder why ordinary precautions can't be taken to insure better drinking water—stricter requirements and punishment for those companies who dump pollutants into fresh streams and rivers, a call to the public not to dump toxic substances down toilets and sinks, better means of disposing chemicals and pollutants worldwide. The public is going to insist that this problem be solved.

Provision Number Eight

Premenstrual Syndrome (PMS) took a beating for many years. Women who went to their doctors complaining of erratic behavior the week before their periods were told, "Take a tranquilizer. You'll feel better." Yet they didn't feel better. Corinne told me that she had never seen a worse case of hormone imbalance than mine. She recommended several remedies which helped greatly. One was that, for a brief period, I took natural progesterone suppositories each day for two weeks out of the month. I obtained these by prescription through a physician. I also learned that protein, Vitamin B, calcium, Vitamin E, manganese, lecithin, primrose oil, and plenty of drinking water were very beneficial in lifting PMS. I now take a light dose of "Female—herbal" tablets (the name of a Life Force product, Brea, California), which aids any hormonal flareups. Sugar is deadly for PMS'ers.

Provision Number Nine

One of the many toxic substances I got out of my body may suprise you. I received a call from Joyce Hopping. She had been learning through the dental profession about a dentist named Harold Huggins in Colorado Springs, Colorado. He was arguing that in the 1800s when the dental profession was young and experimental someone decided to add mercury to the silver fillings that are placed in cavity-ridden teeth. Of course most people know that mercury, even in minute quantities, can be fatal to the human body. But some dentists argue that the metal in fillings is inactive and unable to affect the human body. The Dental Association actually split over this issue in the mid-1800s. Today many dentists continue to use up to 50 percent mercury in each silver filling.

After World War II with the advancement of technology, reliable testing became possible to determine the effects of silver-mercury fillings on the state of the health of an individual. Dr. Harold Huggins pioneered this work. He not only sought medical evidence but investigated thousands of case histories and determined that effects of mercury poisoning as the result of silver-mercury fillings could lead to arthritis, mental disorders, and other ills.

Since I had no less than seventeen fillings in my mouth, I was going to investigate. What I learned, and what is available from research from Dr. Huggins, was alarming. My fillings were removed and replaced with an excellent grade of porcelain which is four percent stronger than teeth. I then took homeopathy to remove mercury that had accumulated in my system. *Never, in all my years, had such dramatic healing taken place from a single treatment.* I felt as if a veil had been lifted from my eyes. Life seemed worth living again in a way that I had not felt since I was ten years old.

Sometime later I went back to two different dentists (at different times) for cleaning. I told them my story. One said, "Boy, are you gullible." The other said, "There is no basis for your assertion." Neither had read the material from Dr. Huggins. They had believed the negative report on his findings published by the American Dental Association. As I reflected on this I realized that for the average dentist to believe this report would be an admission that his treatment had possibly hurt thousands of patients. This would be a difficult admission. However, for dentists not to investigate Huggins' claim may cause an unsuspecting public to risk serious health problems. Twenty thousand dentists no longer use silver-mercury fillings because they believe Huggins' findings.

The specific problems that Higgins has pinpointed as being directly connected to mercury poisoning include: neurological problems—depression, irritability, anxiety as well as neural effects—facial twitch, muscle spasm, epilepsy and multiple sclerosis; Collagen diseases—arthritis, scleroderma, bursitis, lupus; Cardiovascular—rapid heart rate, unidentified chest pain; Immunological—lowered immune system resulting in frequent flus and colds; Allergies.[6] If you decide to have mercury fillings replaced please work directly with Dr. Huggins on the procedure. The manner in which the fillings are removed is as important as that they be removed.

One Final Tip

I had to learn one thing about treatments: just because a doctor or practitioner is an expert in one area of healing doesn't make that individual proficient in other areas of healing. I learned this the hard way. I tried asking my circulation doctor for nutrition tips. He could get no further than the importance of protein and B-1 in the treatment of dilated arteries. When I asked my nutritionist about my circulation treatment, she wondered if it was worthwhile. The allergist thought that his treatment would clear up *all* of my problems. "No reason to waste time and money on anyone else," he said. When I had the fillings removed from my teeth some of my other practitioners thought I was crazy. (They no longer do.) Make sure your source is experienced in the area you are asking about.

HEALING ALTERNATIVES

by Monte Kline, Ph.D.

Unless you've been on another planet for the past several years, you know that the "New Age Movement" is one of the hottest topics in today's media. Tied into the attacks on the New Age Movement are exposes on the holistic health movement. When this storm first started brewing several years ago, I received a letter with an overdose of New Age paranoia. An individual wrote:

> I have been taking a hard look at the subject of applied kinesiology and have decided to avoid it and any other related therapy that involves manipulation of invisible energies and depends upon needles, hand passes, touch, arm pulling, etc. To me applied kinesiology lacks reliable, observable, testable evidence which is expected of true science. These forms of manipulative therapy are all apparently related to Taoism which brings them under the umbrella of psychic forces and healing and occult phenomena.

With such reasoning, I, and other practitioners dealing with innovative methods, have been found guilty by association.

Let me make very clear that I am not a defender of the New Age Movement. There is much spiritual error in the New Age Movement that needs to be exposed and confronted with the truth of Jesus Christ and the Word of God. However, there's also a lot of truth in "holistic health," wrongfully labeled "New Age," which the average individual is literally dying for the lack of.

One of the originators of the term "holistic," as related to health, was Dr. H. Ray Evers, a committed Christian pioneer in metabolic therapy for degenerative diseases. A holistic therapy is simply one that pursues health building by dealing with the "whole" person—body, mind, and spirit. Historically this has been the approach of all true healers. However, with the advent of platonic philosophy into our culture in the late nineteenth century, along with evolution and secular humanism, man's body came to be regarded as separate from the rest of his total self. Thus, "orthodox" medicine today deals with external symptoms of the body, largely ignoring the role of the mind and spirit. But there is absolutely no doubt in Scripture that God created a person's body, mind, and spirit and that each interrelates with the other. The biblical concept of a human being is "holistic."

There is tremendous opportunity to proclaim ways of health which are distinct from the New Age approach and distinct from humanistic, orthodox medicine. A balance must and can be achieved between being drawn into false thinking and being paranoid over areas from which all may benefit.

New Age Thought

We should begin with some definition of what the New Age Movement believes. Doug Groothuis, in one of the more balanced books on the subject, *Unmasking the New Age,* lists six fundamentals of New Age thinking which have been adapted here:

1. everything is one,
2. everything is God,
3. mankind is God,
4. consciousness can evolve,
5. all religions are one in essence,
6. we are evolving for the better.[1]

Obviously, these basic "doctrines" of the New Age (except for no. 4) definitely run counter to the Scriptures. However, a lot of people and practices are being labeled "New Age" that in no way embrace the above errors. This is particularly true in holistic health.

The critics of the New Age Movement see most holistic concepts of health as offshoots of that movement. For example, Reisser, Reisser, and Weldon in their book, *The Holistic Healers,* use the subtitle, "A Christian Perspective on New-Age Health Care." They provide a fairly accurate definition of what typical holistic health stands for in their "Ten Articles of Faith in the New Medicine." Their ten articles are adapted below with this writer's comments under each one.

1. ***The whole is greater than all its parts.*** The author agrees with this premise, recognizing that God has made us body, mind, and spirit. Therefore the total person must be treated. Traditional medicine still largely denies this scriptural model.
2. ***Health is more than the absence of sickness.*** The lack of clinical symptoms of disease does not make one healthy. Health is a matter of wholeness of the total person, of operating at our optimum in all areas.
3. ***Individuals are ultimately responsible for their own health or sickness.*** With a few possible exceptions this is true, contrary

to the dictates of the traditional medical model which has accidental microbes randomly choosing their victims, who then are required to put themselves in the doctor's hands to take responsibility for healing. Holistic practitioners deal with participants rather than (as well as) patients, and become teachers more so than therapists.

4. *Natural forms of healing are better than drugs and surgery.* Drugs and surgery generally compete with the body's natural healing mechanism, though there are times when they are necessary. A natural approach which stimulates the body's own healing mechanism is preferable.

5. *Any method of promoting health or preventing disease has the potential for being holistic, but some methods are more clearly holistic than others.* Acupuncture, acupressure, biofeedback, chiropractic, kinesiology, osteopathy, homeopathy, iridology, massage, and nutritional therapies are some of the more "innately holistic" and accepted methods.

6. *Health implies change.* The more typical New Age person sees the healthy individual evolving toward a higher plateau of existence, as well as humanity at large being on the verge of a quantum leap into an "Age of Aquarius." Suffice it to say that, at this point, the holistic health movement, as described by Reisser, Reisser, and Weldon, departs from biblical truth.

7. *To understand health and sickness, we need an alternative model, one that is based primarily on energy rather than matter.* It's not hard, based upon quantum physics to come to this conclusion. Indeed, various frequencies of electromagnetic energy are the common denominator of all things. I acknowledge this as a fact of God's creation. The New Age pantheist, however, sees energy as part of the "all is One" system that postulates a nonpersonal God.

8. *Death is the last stage of growth.* Between the idea of reincarnation and the popularization of near-death experiences by Dr. Raymond Moody and Dr. Elisabeth Kübler-Ross, New Age holistic health people hold to a nonbiblical concept of death, devoid of eternal judgment. This is a serious spiritual error.

9. *The thinking and practices of many ancient civilizations are a rich storehouse of knowledge for healthy lives.* Though this can be a reasonable assertion, without the discernment provided by God's Word and Spirit, a lot of ancient garbage can get mingled with that which is of value.

10. *Holistic health practices must be integrated into the main-*

stream of life and health care through influencing public opinion. Understandably holistic practitioners of all sorts are tired of sitting in the back of the bus, desiring a more equal footing with the orthodox medical monopoly. You don't have to be a New Ager to agree with that.[2]

These ten points are a pretty good summary of the New Age view of holistic health. Many of these, as I've pointed out, are biblically sound and relevant, while some are not. With the Bible, wisdom and discernment, we are to separate the "carrots from the tops."

"Flat Earth" Christianity

Many individuals, for the most part, tend toward paranoia with anything outside their realm of knowledge, including certain aspects of holistic health care. We may not reject certain scientific observations because they conflict with the Bible so much as because they conflict with our existing knowledge—our traditions. Regrettably the church as a religious system, the political hierarchy and many leaders in the scientific area have historically rejected new truth in favor of old traditions. This is unnecessary. (The church as I refer to it here does not necessarily include all or true followers of Jesus.)

For centuries, with the full support of these institutions, the world was considered flat. Those suggesting the world was round were considered heretics. Though some may have cited literalistic interpretations of biblical passages referring to the "four corners of the earth" as contradictory with anything other than a flat earth, for most people a round earth was offensive to their long-held traditions. It may seem silly to us now, but it was a serious question in the fifteenth century.

Are we any different? What natural laws that explain various holistic health practices are yet to be elucidated? Dare we assume that we know all there is to be known about Creation?

Copernicus and Galileo were regarded as heretics for suggesting that the earth was not the center of the solar system. Though their scientific teaching was in no way contradicted within the Bible (which was silent on the subject), nevertheless it was a new and therefore unacceptable idea.

If a scientific discovery is not in conflict with God's revealed truth (the Bible), it should be presumed to be part of God's creation.

Therefore, to say that invisible energy forces are the common denominator of all creation is not scripturally heretical; it's only offensive to our traditionally accepted view. We're all involved everyday with invisible energy forces through television, radio, and household electricity.

All Truth Is God's Truth

Those on the extreme of New Age paranoia take exception to the premise that "all truth is God's truth." Doug Groothuis in *Unmasking the New Age* avoids this paranoia:

> A world-view analysis of wholistic health is indispensable, but specific considerations must also enter the picture. Should Christians shun wholistic health because some of its practices are based on a non-biblical world view? This is not a simple issue. Non-Christian cultures have produced great works of art, science and literature that can be appreciated by Christians. The maxim, All truth is God's truth, should be taken seriously. Although all practices that smack of spiritism, mediumship or psychic manipulation should be avoided because of demonic involvement, not all practices somehow associated with wholistic health should be shunned.

Many consider various health procedures guilty by association. I won't disagree for a moment that the acupuncture meridians and points used in kinesiology were discovered in the Orient and were incorporated into the religious systems of that area. Aren't most discoveries of the natural world usually incorporated into the larger belief system of a culture? Astronomy, for example, started with discoveries in the natural world about the stars, the planets and their movements. But for the one not knowing the true God a false religion of astrology was built around that scientific fact. Is astronomy invalid and occult because an occult religion (astrology) is built around it?

Truth needs no vindication. If something is true, it's true: if it's false, it's false, *No matter who believes it or doesn't believe it.* The truths of God's creation are true in and of themselves, regardless of who believes and practices them—a Taoist, a Hindu, a Buddhist, or a Christian.

Likewise, are there occult health practices and nonoccult health practices? Or are there just occult practitioners and nonoccult practitioners? Anything can be used in an occult way, depending on the spiritual condition of its practitioner. Can kinesiology be used in an occult way? Of course. Can acupuncture be used in an occult way? Yes. Can nutrition be used in an occult way? You bet. Can surgery be used in an occult way? Yes. In fact traditional medical methods are employed to perform abortion, one of Satan's greatest coups.

God created many ways to help and treat the body. Satan has perverted many of those truths by building religious systems around them. Will we deny God's creation just because Satan has gotten in and perverted it for his own use? What good, true thing has God created that Satan has not perverted in some way—nutrition, education, money, sex, health care?

Lessons From Romans 1

Paul wrote to the church in Rome concerning the practice of some:
For they "exchanged the truth of God for a lie, and worshiped and served the creature rather than the Creator, who is blessed forever."[3]

This simple statement can explain a lot of the problem between the New Age wholistic health, traditional non-wholistic health, and true comprehensive Christianity. It brings to mind four basic possibilities in how we relate to creation and the Creator.

1. Worship the creation; deny the Creator. This is basically the standard New Age pantheistic view. Denying a personal God, the creation itself becomes God. Actually this is a form of basic paganism as exposed in Romans 1, though the current New Age paganism comes in a more sophisticated wrapper than that of a primitive tribe. C. S. Lewis put it this way:

> Pantheism is a creed not so much false as hopelessly behind the times. Once, before creation, it would have been true to say that everything was God. But God created. He caused things to be other than Himself.

2. Acknowledge the creation; deny the Creator. This version would be that of secular humanism, rather than New Age. The typical secular humanist scientist is involved in the study and usage of the natural laws of the creation, though he denies a personal God behind those laws. Unlike the New Age thinker, the humanist does not project a supernatural pantheism into all the natural realm.

3. Deny the creation; worship the Creator. This tends to be the position of those promoting paranoia over holistic healing. Their worship of and devotion to the Creator is unquestioned. However, their assumption is that anything outside their knowledge of creation is supernatural in the demonic sense and therefore to be denied. Thus, anything unknown to them could not possibly be just another part of God's creation.

4. Acknowledge the creation; worship the Creator. I believe this is the correct approach. Worship belongs to the personal God alone, who is distinct from his creation. Yet we are called to exercise dominion over his creation[4] and how can we do that without exploration and discovery? True science is merely the process of discovering, quantifying, and applying what God has built into his creation. A right view of the wonders of the natural realm of creation should drive us to worship the Creator.

> When I consider the heavens, the work of Your fingers, the moon and the stars, which You have ordained; what is man, that You take thought of him? And the son of man, that You care for him?[5]

Discoveries of new laws or forces in God's creation should be no threat to us. The more we uncover about how God has made his universe, the greater our opportunity to praise his unsearchable greatness.

Arrogance of Partial Knowledge

> For we know in part, and we prophesy in part; but when the perfect comes, the partial will be done away . . . For now we see in a mirror dimly, but then face to face; now I know in part, but then I shall know fully just as I also have been fully known.[6]

Frankly one of the greatest difficulties with the critics of holistic health practices is the unstated, though unmistakable view that: "My knowledge defines the boundaries of the natural realm. Therefore, any phenomenon going on outside the realm of my knowledge must be in error."

That attitude has persecuted truth-seeking people throughout history. It punished Galileo and Copernicus and Columbus and a host of others eager to discover new aspects of what God has built into his creation.

I often wonder how pushers of the current holistic health paranoia would react if they lived one hundred years ago and were shown a television set. Surely such a transference of images through the air would have been regarded as magic, as witchcraft, as sorcery because their *partial* knowledge of God's creation could lead to such a conclusion.

After I became involved in teaching principles of health, I was amazed at how similar that process was to my former evangelistic campus ministry. Confrontation with the truth, whether the truth about salvation in Christ or the truth about health or the truth about anything else, always elicits the same responses: openness, conviction, and acceptance; or resistance, arrogance, and rejection.

As a staff member with Campus Crusade for Christ, I discovered that when I would tell a college student that there was a personal God incarnated in Jesus Christ who loved him and wanted to have a relationship with him, he might say, "I don't believe there's a God because. . . ." Borrowing a line from a Christian apologist, Dr. J. Edwin Orr, I would reply:

"Of all the knowledge that exists in the universe, what percentage do you suppose you might have? Is it safe to assume that you probably possess less than 10 percent of all the possible knowledge there is? (He agrees). Then do you suppose that the God you deny might possibly exist in that other 90 percent of knowledge you don't possess?" (He is forced to agree.)

I receive similar reactions when I talk about principles of diet and nutrition. People resist the truth. I would tell people that white sugar, white flour, pork, or whatever was harmful to their health. They would deny it. They would say, "I don't believe that."

Why? Because it wasn't true? Because there was no evidence? No! Because they didn't want to believe it—because they didn't want to change their lifestyles. *Embracing truth, no matter in what area, is not always so much a problem of evidence as a problem of openness.*

Testing Occult Activity

A balance must be struck between openness to unknown aspects of God's creation and true discernment of the demonic realm. The Bible gives us three basic tests for any suspect activity.

1. Direct Scriptural Reference. The Scripture speaks directly about a number of occult practices forbidden to believers. Moses, for example, lists witchcraft, divining, child sacrifice, sorcery, casting spells, and the like as occult activities.[7] Let there be no doubt on the avoidance of occult practices the Scripture clearly defines. However, I don't find acupuncture, acupressure, applied kinesiology, iridology, reflexology, biofeedback, nutritional therapy, homeopathy, or most other common "holistic health" practices on that list. When Scripture speaks clearly, let us stand firmly. But where Scripture does not speak definitively, let us not presume and hastily judge. Instead let's go to the second test.

2. The Fruit. A biblical test of particular practice is the fruit it bears. Jesus said:

> You will know them [prophets; Deuteronomy 13, 18] by their fruits. Grapes are not gathered from thorn bushes, nor figs from thistles, are they? Even so, every good tree bears good fruit; but the rotten tree bears bad fruit. A good tree cannot produce bad fruit, nor can a rotten tree produce good fruit.[8]

Along the same lines Jesus was once confronted by the Pharisees and accused of using satanic power to cast out demons—basically the same argument used against health practitioners, including some Christians. Jesus replied:

> Any kingdom divided against itself is laid waste; and any city or house divided against itself shall not stand. And if Satan casts out Satan, he is divided against himself; how then shall his kingdom stand? . . . Therefore I say to you, any sin and blasphemy shall be forgiven men; but blasphemy against the Spirit shall not be forgiven . . . either make the tree good, and its fruit good; or make the tree rotten, and its fruit rotten; for the tree is known by its fruit.[9]

Over a period of time the fruit in people's lives associated with a given holistic health practice will become obvious. Does it turn them toward greater wholeness in Christ or away from his Lordship?

3. *The Gift of Discernment.* One of the gifts of the Holy Spirit is discernment.[10] I believe God is still giving this gift; but is the church developing and using it? This gift must likewise be checked in the gifted individual over a period of time for its validity. True discernment from the Holy Spirit must not be confused with human biases in the supposedly gifted person.

True vs. Counterfeit

There is a true holistic health and a counterfeit one. There is an approach to health, centered in God's revelation in Scripture and in his creation, that deals with the nature of man and his health problems in body, mind, and spirit. It can use a wide variety of natural and supernatural methods. It doesn't conflict with the Bible and it produces good fruit.

There's also a counterfeit holistic health centered in a monistic and pantheistic worldview. It does not correctly define man's problem or God's solution, though it often uses effective methods that are part of God's creation. People may achieve limited benefits, but they may also be drawn into the false spiritual ideology of the practitioner.

Finally we must not focus so much on the holistic health practice, as on the holistic health practitioner. A practice such as nutrition, homeopathy, acupuncture, or applied kinesiology is based upon principles of God's creation. Nevertheless, any method, including traditional medicine (AMA), can have an occult contamination from a practitioner not in a relationship with the true God and Savior. Seek committed Christian practitioners who are sensitive to both the truths of God's natural and supernatural realms. Be open, but also be discerning.

NOTES

Chapter 2. Who Will Heal You?

1. Mark 14:61–64; John 1:12; 10:30; 14:9.
2. Flavius Josephus, *Antiquities,* XVIII, III (Grand Rapids: Kregel Publishers, 1960), 379.
3. Mark 2:5–10.
4. Bill Bright, *Ten Basic Steps Teacher's Manual* (Arrowhead Springs, Calif.: Campus Crusade, 1983), 34.
5. Mark 6:53–56.
6. Matthew 4:23 KJV.
7. Matthew 9:35.
8. John 5:1–9.
9. Luke 13:10–17.
10. Mark 5:25–34.
11. John 9.
12. Matthew 14:13–14.
13. Matthew 20:34.
14. Mark 1:41–42.
15. Luke 7:13–15.
16. Matthew 28:18 KJV.
17. Luke 5:15.
18. Mark 6:1–6.
19. *Mission Frontiers* (U.S. Center for World Missions, July 1987), 11.
20. Matthew 8:16–17.
21. Isaiah 53:4.

Chapter 3. Does Anyone Care?

1. James 1:17 NKJV.
2. Psalm 102:1–7 TLB.
3. Lamentations 3:22 TLB.
4. Psalm 103:14.
5. Psalm 139:15.
6. Psalm 139:1–18 TLB.
7. Vincent Bozzi, "A Healthy Dose of Religion," *Psychology Today,* November 1988, 14–15.
8. Ian Gunn-Russell, M.D., "Everything Possible?" *Guideposts,* July 1989, 38.
9. Pamela Rosewell, *Five Silent Years of Corrie Ten Boom* (Grand Rapids: Zondervan, 1986), 173–174.
10. Romans 12:1–2 TLB.

Chapter 4. Why Am I Sick?

1. C. S. Lewis, *Mere Christianity.*
2. Henry Van Dyke.
3. Proverbs 17:22 KJV.
4. S. I. McMillen, *None of These Diseases,* revised edition (Old Tappan, N.J.: Revell, 1984), 125.
5. Romans 12:10.
6. Ephesians 4:32 NKJV.

7. Philippians 2:2-3.
8. 1 Corinthians 13:4-8 TLB.
9. Matthew 22:37 NKJV.
10. Eleanor Doan, *The New Speaker's Sourcebook* (Grand Rapids: Zondervan, 1968), 215.
11. See Appendix A.
12. See Appendix A, note 2.
13. Ecclesiastes 3:2.
14. McMillen, *None of These Diseases*, 64.
15. Deuteronomy 7:9.
16. Deuteronomy 7:15.

Chapter 5. God Has the Last Word

1. Glaphre Gilliland, *When the Pieces Don't Fit God Makes the Difference* (Grand Rapids: Zondervan, 1984).
2. C. S. Lewis, *Mere Christianity*.
3. Psalm 8:1; 10:16.
4. Psalm 9:8; 25:8; 119:137.
5. Deuteronomy 32:4.
6. Matthew 7:11; 1 John 4:8.
7. Deuteronomy 33:27.
8. 2 Chronicles 16:9; Matthew 10:29-30.
9. Psalm 139:7-10.
10. Job 42:2.
11. Psalm 5:6; 31:6.
12. Malachi 3:6.
13. Job 40:2 RSV.
14. Luke 7:11-15.
15. Daniel 5:18-21 TLB.
16. Luke 1:17-20.
17. 2 Kings 5:27.
18. 2 Chronicles 26:16-21.
19. Acts 5:1-5.
20. 2 Chronicles 21:12-15 RSV.
21. Numbers 12.
22. Numbers 21:6.
23. 1 Corinthians 11:27-32.
24. 2 Chronicles 16:12 RSV.
25. Deuteronomy 7:15.
26. See also Leviticus 26; Exodus 10:26; 23:25; Deuteronomy 7:14-15; 20:20.
27. Hebrews 12:5-7.
28. Jeanette Clift George, *Travel Tips from a Reluctant Traveler* (Nashville: Nelson, 1987), 114.
29. Luke 13:11-13.
30. Matthew 9:33, 17:18; Mark 5:18, 7:29; Luke 4:33, 10:20, 11:14.
31. See Job 1.
32. Luke 22:31.
33. 2 Corinthians 12:7.
34. See 1 Samuel 16:14-15.
35. 1 John 3:8.
36. Catherine Marshall, *Something More* (New York: Avon, 1976), 14.
37. Amy Carmichael, *Rose from Brier* (Ft. Washington, Penn.: Christian Lit., 1972), 190.

38. Sharon Chrisafulli, "The Dream," *Guideposts*, July 1989, 42–44.
39. Romans 6:23.
40. John 3:16.
41. Romans 3:23.
42. Romans 6:23.
43. 2 Corinthians 5:21; 1 Peter 2:24.
44. 1 John 5:10–13.
45. 2 Timothy 2:19.
46. Isaiah 41:10.
47. Romans 8:32.
48. John 14:6.
49. Hebrews 13:8.
50. C. S. Lewis.
51. John 1:12.
52. Hebrews 13:5.
53. Matthew 28:20.
54. 1 John 5:11–13.

Chapter 6. What Faith Can Do

1. Luke 5:18–20; James 5:15.
2. George A. Buttrick, *Prayer* (Nashville: Abingdon Press, 1942), 107.
3. Ibid., 107.
4. George, *Travel Tips*, 21.
5. Josh McDowell, *Evidence That Demands a Verdict* (Colorado Springs: Campus Crusade, 1981).
6. Psalm 91:16 RSV.
7. Matthew 21:22.
8. 1 Peter 4:12.
9. 2 Corinthians 4:16.
10. Luke 7:2–10.
11. 1 John 5:14–15.
12. Matthew 6:9.
13. Isaiah 55:8–9.
14. John Edmund Haggai, *My Son Johnny* 50, 158, 198.
15. James 3:1–12.
16. Some would say that Enoch and Elijah also qualified.
17. Luke 5:17.
18. John 5:19.
19. Acts 3:16; 5:16; 28:5.
20. Acts 3:1–8.
21. 1 Corinthians 12:9–10.
22. Matthew 10:1; Mark 3:18; 6:7; Luke 9:1.
23. James 5:16–18.
24. Matthew 9:35–38.
25. Matthew 9:35–38.
26. Matthew 8:16; 12:15.
27. Luke 5:19.
28. Luke 7:11.
29. John 5:2–4.
30. John 5:14.
31. Hebrews 13:8.
32. James 5:14.
33. James 5:10–11.

34. James 5:15.
35. James 5:16.
36. John 16:13-14; Acts 1:8; Galatians 5:22-23; Ephesians 6:18.
37. Romans 8:27.
38. Ephesians 5:18.
39. Ephesians 4:30.
40. 1 Thessalonians 5:19.
41. Luke 8:41-42, 49-56.
42. John 11.
43. Matthew 17:14-20.
44. Rosalind Goforth, *Goforth in China* (Minneapolis: Dimension Books), 169-170.
45. John 9:5-7.
46. James 5:14.
47. Mark 6:13.
48. Luke 10:34.
49. Catherine Marshall, *To Live Again* (New York: Avon, 1976).
50. 2 Corinthians 4:14-16.
51. 1 Corinthians 15:35-58.

Chapter 7. Prayer and Healing

1. Romans 8:14.
2. Luke 2:25; Acts 8:29; 20:23.
3. Norman P. Grubb, *Rees Howells: Intercessor* (Ft. Washington, Penn.: Christian Lit., 1952), 161.
4. Psalm 31:15 KJV.
5. Ecclesiastes 3:11.
6. Psalm 37:7 NKJV.
7. Romans 8:28 TLB.
8. Mrs. Charles E. Cowan, *Streams in the Desert* (Grand Rapids: Zondervan, 1986).
9. Simpson.
10. Jowett.
11. Ruthe White, *Touch Me Again, Lord* (San Bernardino, Calif.: Here's Life, 1983), 59-61.
12. Romans 4:20-21 RSV.
13. Exodus 15:26.
14. Luke 8:50.
15. John Pollack, *Billy Graham* (Minneapolis: Worldwide Publishers), 287.
16. Isaiah 38:1-5 TLB.
17. Luke 10:19 TLB.
18. Luke 9:1.
19. Viv Grigg, *Companion to the Poor* 140-141.
20. Corrie Ten Boom, *Defeated Enemies* (Ft. Washington, Penn.: Christian Lit., 1962).
21. Rosewell, *Five Silent Years of Corrie Ten Boom*, 139-140.
22. Matthew 12:29 KJV.
23. John 15:10.
24. Proverbs 3:5-6.
25. Luke 17:12-14.
26. 2 Kings 5:1-14 TLB.
27. Pollack, *Billy Graham*, 157.
28. 2 Corinthians 15:54-57; Revelation 21:4.
29. Revelation 20:14.
30. 2 Corinthians 5:10-11.

31. *Streams in the Desert*, Gordon.
32. *Gospel of China* 111–112.

Chapter 8. Can There Be a Reason?

1. 2 Corinthians 12:9–10.
2. Oswald Chambers, *My Utmost for His Highest* (Westwood, N.J.: Barbour Books, 1987), 215.
3. Matthew 5:1–12.
4. Exodus 4:11.
5. John 9:3.
6. 2 Corinthians 9:15.
7. Gilliland, *When the Pieces Don't Fit*, 199–222.
8. 2 Corinthians 1:8–9.
9. Carmichael, *Rose from Brier*, 34–35.
10. Exodus 1:7.
11. 1 Samuel 1.
12. James 1:2–3 TLB.
13. James 1:3–4 TLB.
14. Greg Anderson, "Beating the Odds," *Guideposts*, August 1989, 20–22.
15. Isaiah 53:4; Matthew 8:17.
16. Romans.
17. Isaiah 53:5.
18. Author unknown.
19. Romans 8:18; James 1:12.
20. Earl Radmacher.
21. Galatians 5:22.
22. 2 Corinthians 1:3–6.
23. 1 Corinthians 12:26.
24. Galatians 6:2.
25. Psalm 119:71.
26. 1 Peter 4:1–2.
27. Romans 8:18–39.

Chapter 9. Will You Take Responsibility?

1. Bernie S. Siegel, "The Medicine Was Love," *Redbook*, December 1987.
2. Psalm 139:14 NIV.
3. 1 Corinthians 6:19 NIV.
4. 1 Corinthians 9:27 TLB.
5. 1 Kings 1:1–4.
6. 1 Kings 19:1–8.
7. 1 Timothy 4:8.
8. Mark 5:25–34.
9. Matthew 7:7–8 TLB.
10. Mark 8:22–25.
11. Psalm 34:19 RSV.
12. Jeremiah 31:3 RSV.
13. Deuteronomy 31:3 TLB.
14. Proverbs 3:5–6.
15. Philippians 2:13.
16. Isaiah 58:11 RSV.
17. Ephesians 3:20 NKJV.
18. Isaiah 59:1.

19. Philippians 4:13.
20. Isaiah 41:10 TLB.
21. Psalm 69:6.
22. Isaiah 43:2 RSV.
23. Psalm 37:24.
24. John 14:3.
25. Psalm 55:22.

Chapter 10. Overcoming Fear

1. Catherine Marshall, *A Closer Walk*, (Old Tappan, N.J.: Revell, 1986), 173.
2. Matthew 6:34 KJV.
3. See James 4:13–17.
4. Deuteronomy 33:25.
5. 2 Corinthians 4:8–11.
6. Marshall, *A Closer Walk*, 158.
7. Isaiah 41:10 TLB.
8. Deuteronomy 31:6 RSV.
9. Lamentations 3:22–23 RSV.
10. Isaiah 26:3–4 KJV.
11. Psalm 34:4 RSV.
12. Psalm 55:22 RSV.
13. Hebrews 4:11 KJV.
14. Psalm 56:3 KJV.

Chapter 11. How to Help the Sick

1. Edith Schaeffer, *What Is a Family?* (Old Tappan, N. J.: Revell, 1982), 95–96.
2. Ibid, 94.
3. Edward J. Grath, Jr., *An Exceptional View of Life* (Norfolk Island, Australia: Island Heritage Ltd.), 25.
4. Ibid, 26.
5. Ibid, 19.
6. John 17:19.
7. Philippians 4:6–7 TLB.
8. Millard J. Erickson, *Christian Theology* (Grand Rapids: Baker, 1986), 539.
9. John 5:5–9.
10. 1 Thessalonians 5:14.
11. James 5:15.
12. James 5:16 NKJV.
13. Mark 10:46–52.
14. Ephesians 3:20 NKJV.
15. Matthew 25:36.

Appendix A

1. Leviticus 17:11.
2. Frederick Erdman Association, 2050 Westchester Pike, Havertown, Penn. (215) 853-2445.
3. Robert Maynard, 114 West Camelback Road, Phoenix, Ariz. 85013 (602) 264-4104.
4. 2 Chronicles 16:12–14 TLB.
5. Glacier Springs of Georgia, Atlanta, Ga. (404) 636-9621.
6. Harold Huggins, D.D.S., P.O. Box 2589, Colorado Springs, Colo. 80901, (1-800) 331-2303.

Appendix B

1. Doug Groothuis, *Unmasking the New Age* (Downers Grove, Ill.: InterVarsity).
2. Reisser, Reisser, and Weldon, *The Holistic Healers* (Downers Grove, Ill.: Inter-Varsity).
3. Romans 1:25 NKJV.
4. Genesis 1:28.
5. Psalm 8:3-4.
6. 1 Corinthians 13:9-10, 12.
7. Deuteronomy 18:9-14.
8. Matthew 7:16-18.
9. Matthew 12:25-26, 31, 33.
10. 1 Corinthians 12:10.